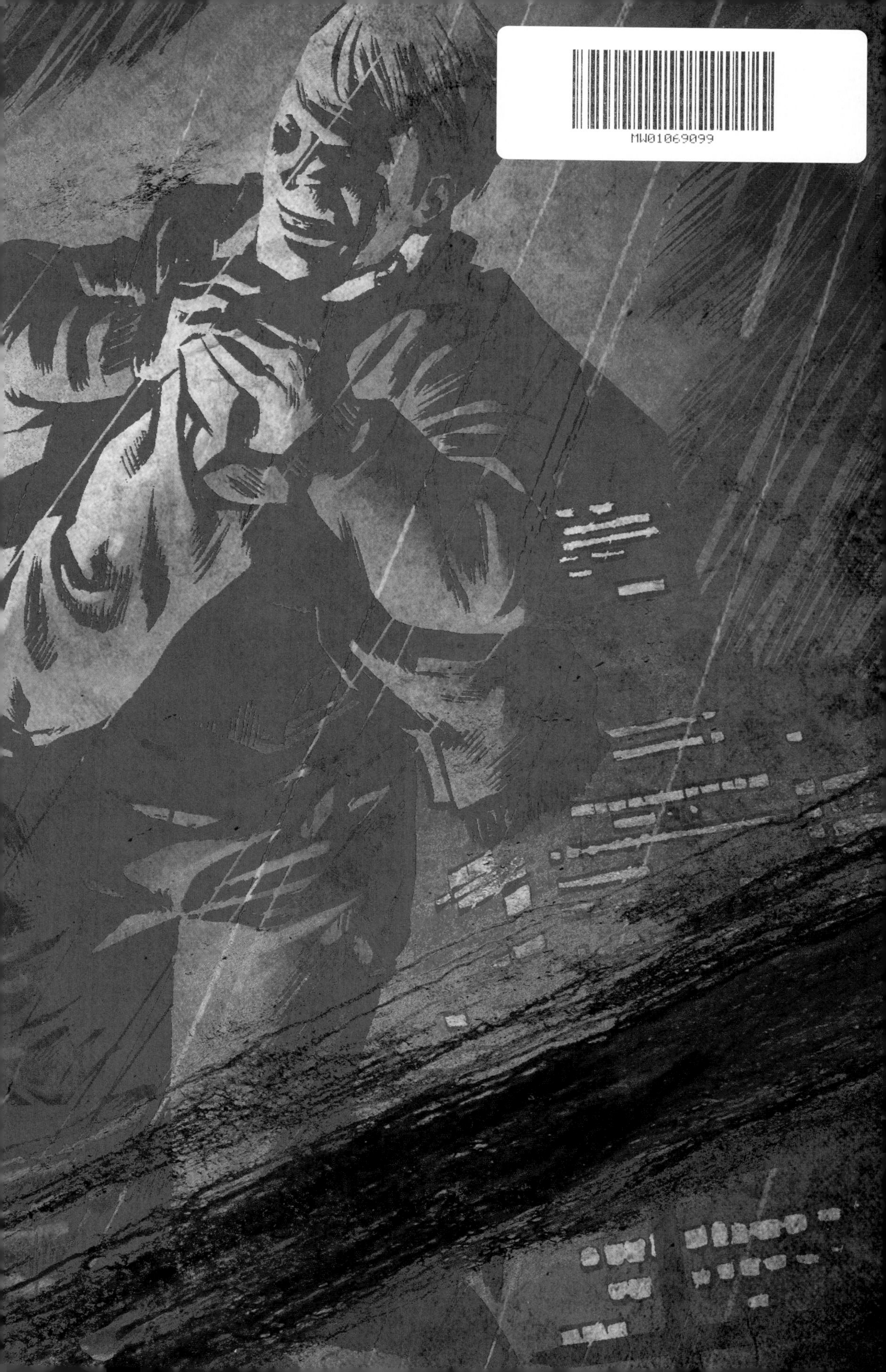

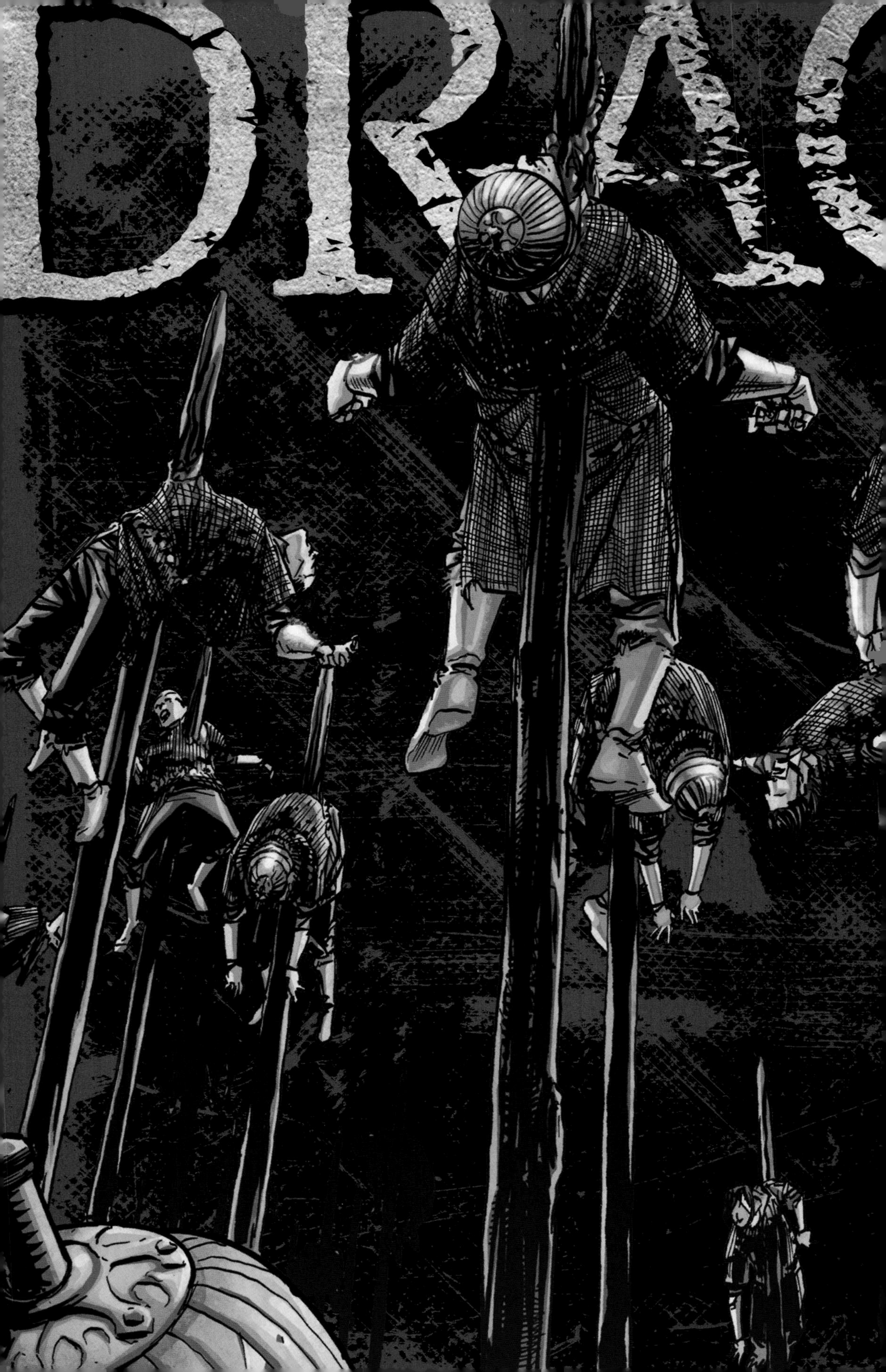
DRA

DRACULA

The Company of Monsters

Ross Richie - Chief Executive Officer
Matt Gagnon - Editor-in-Chief
Adam Fortier - VP-New Business
Wes Harris - VP-Publishing
Lance Kreiter - VP-Licensing & Merchandising
Chip Mosher - Marketing Director
Bryce Carlson - Managing Editor

Ian Brill - Editor
Dafna Pleban - Editor
Christopher Burns - Editor
Christopher Meyer - Editor
Shannon Watters - Assistant Editor
Eric Harburn - Assistant Editor
Adam Staffaroni - Assistant Editor

Neil Loughrie - Publishing Coordinator
Brian Latimer - Lead Graphic Designer
Stephanie Gonzaga - Graphic Designer
Travis Beaty - Traffic Coordinator
Ivan Salazar - Marketing Assistant
Brett Grinnell - Executive Assistant

DRACULA: THE COMPANY OF MONSTERS Volume One — January 2011. Published by BOOM! Studios, a division of Boom Entertainment, Inc.
Dracula: The Company of Monsters is Copyright © 2011 Kurt Busiek and Boom Entertainment, Inc. Originally published in single magazine form as
DRACULA: THE COMPANY OF MONSTERS 1-4. Copyright © 2010 Kurt Busiek and Boom Entertainment, Inc. All rights reserved. BOOM! Studios™
and the BOOM! Studios logo are trademarks of Boom Entertainment, Inc., registered in various countries and categories. All characters, events, and
institutions depicted herein are fictional. Any similarity between any of the names, characters, persons, events, and/or institutions in this publication to
actual names, characters, and persons, whether living or dead, events, and/or institutions is unintended and purely coincidental. BOOM! Studios does
not read or accept unsolicited submissions of ideas, stories, or artwork.

For information regarding the CPSIA on this printed material, call: (203) 595-3636 and provide reference #EAST – 99999. A catalog record of this book
is available from OCLC and from the BOOM! Studios website, www.boom-studios.com, on the Librarians Page.

BOOM! Studios, 6310 San Vicente Boulevard, Suite 107, Los Angeles, CA 90048-5457. Printed in Canada. First Printing. ISBN: 978-1-60886-044-9

'ULA

The Company of Monsters

Created and Story by:

Kurt Busiek

Written by:

Daryl Gregory

Art by:

Scott Godlewski (Chapters 1, 2, 4)
Damian Couceiro (Chapter 3)

Colors: Stephen Downer
Letters: Johnny Lowe

Cover: Ron Salas
colors: Nick Filardi

Editor: Daina Pleban
Trade Designer: Stephanie Gonzaga

CHAPTER 1

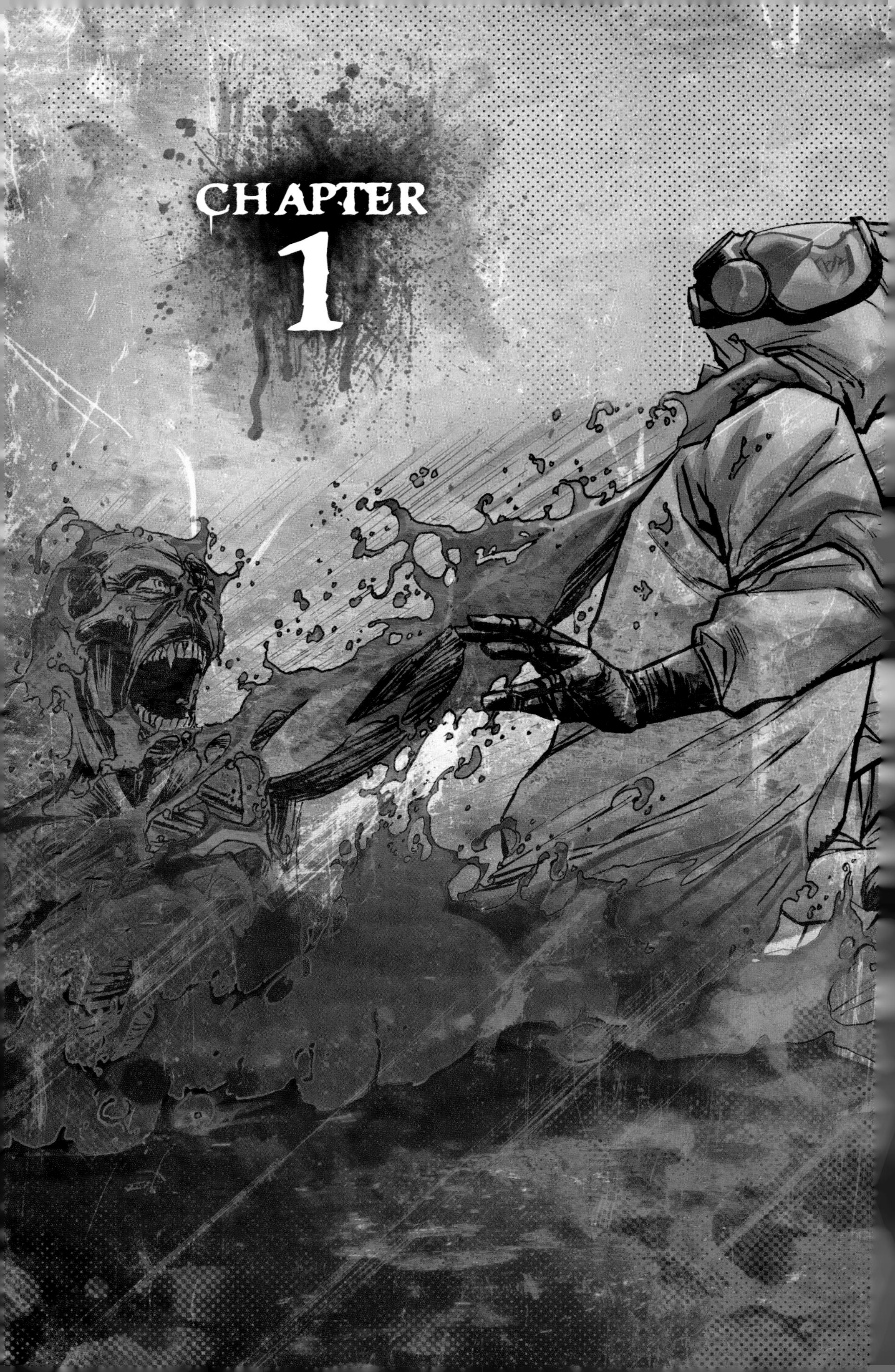

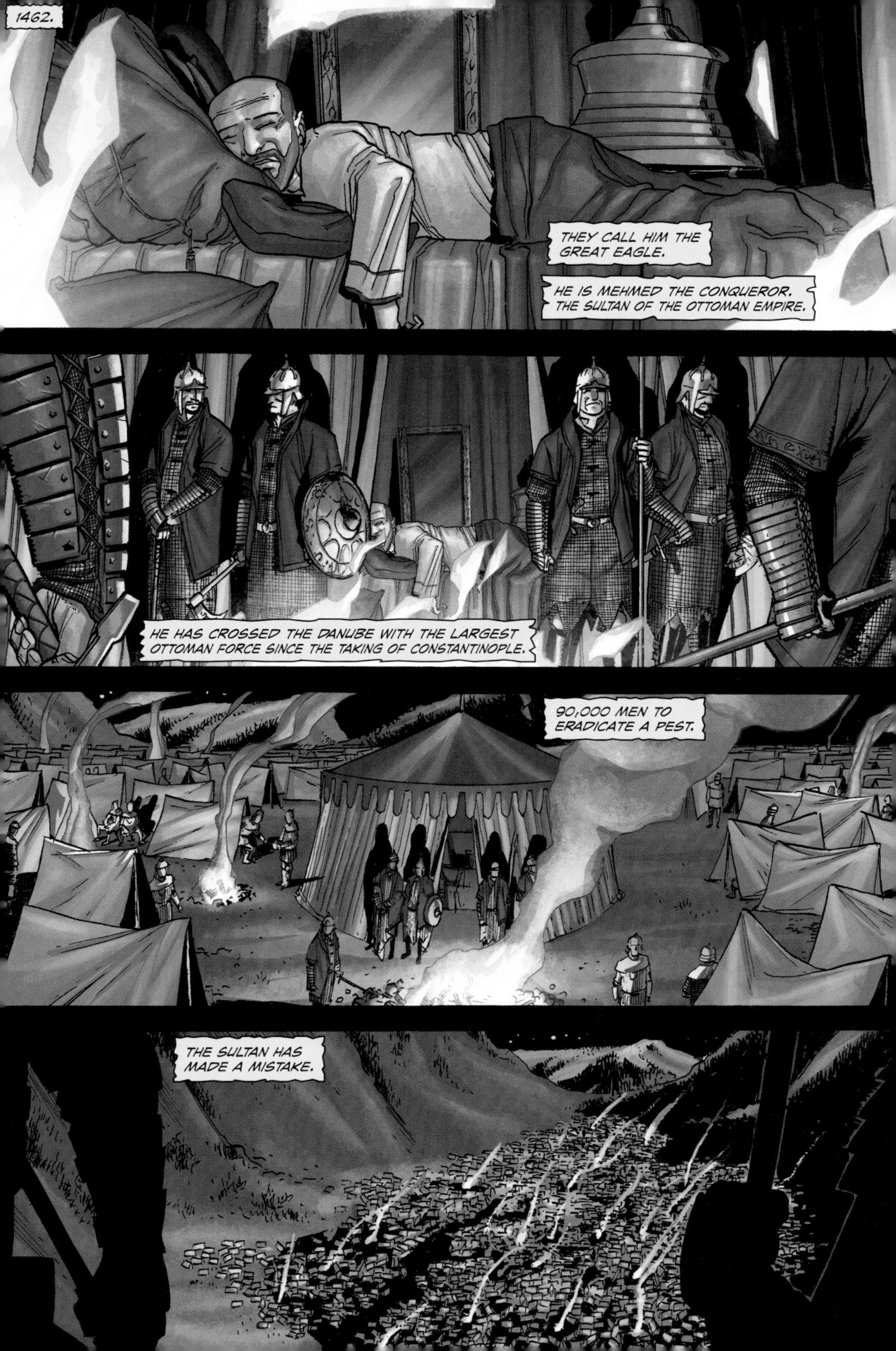
1462.
THEY CALL HIM THE GREAT EAGLE.
HE IS MEHMED THE CONQUEROR. THE SULTAN OF THE OTTOMAN EMPIRE.
HE HAS CROSSED THE DANUBE WITH THE LARGEST OTTOMAN FORCE SINCE THE TAKING OF CONSTANTINOPLE.
90,000 MEN TO ERADICATE A PEST.
THE SULTAN HAS MADE A MISTAKE.

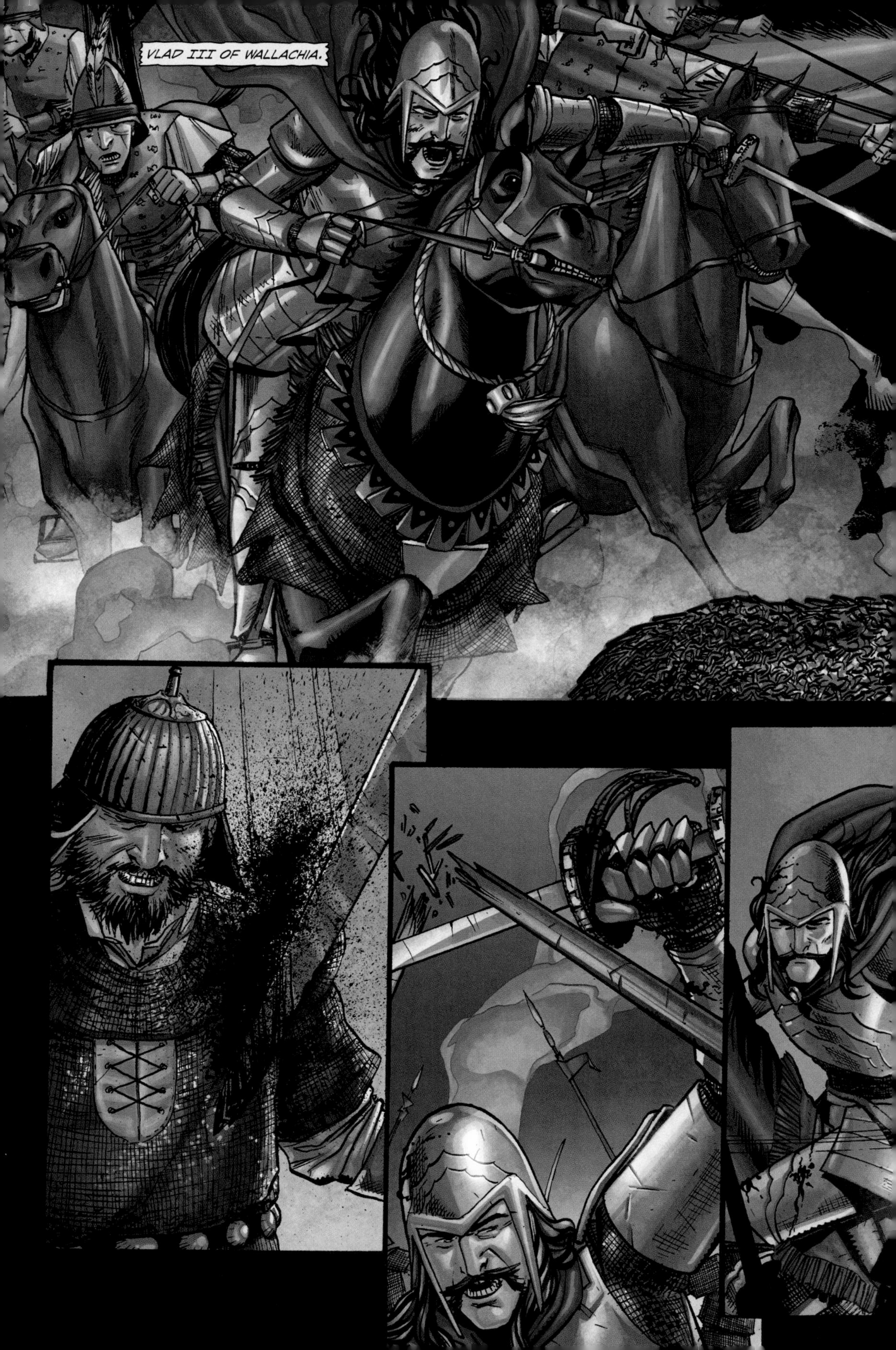
VLAD III OF WALLACHIA.

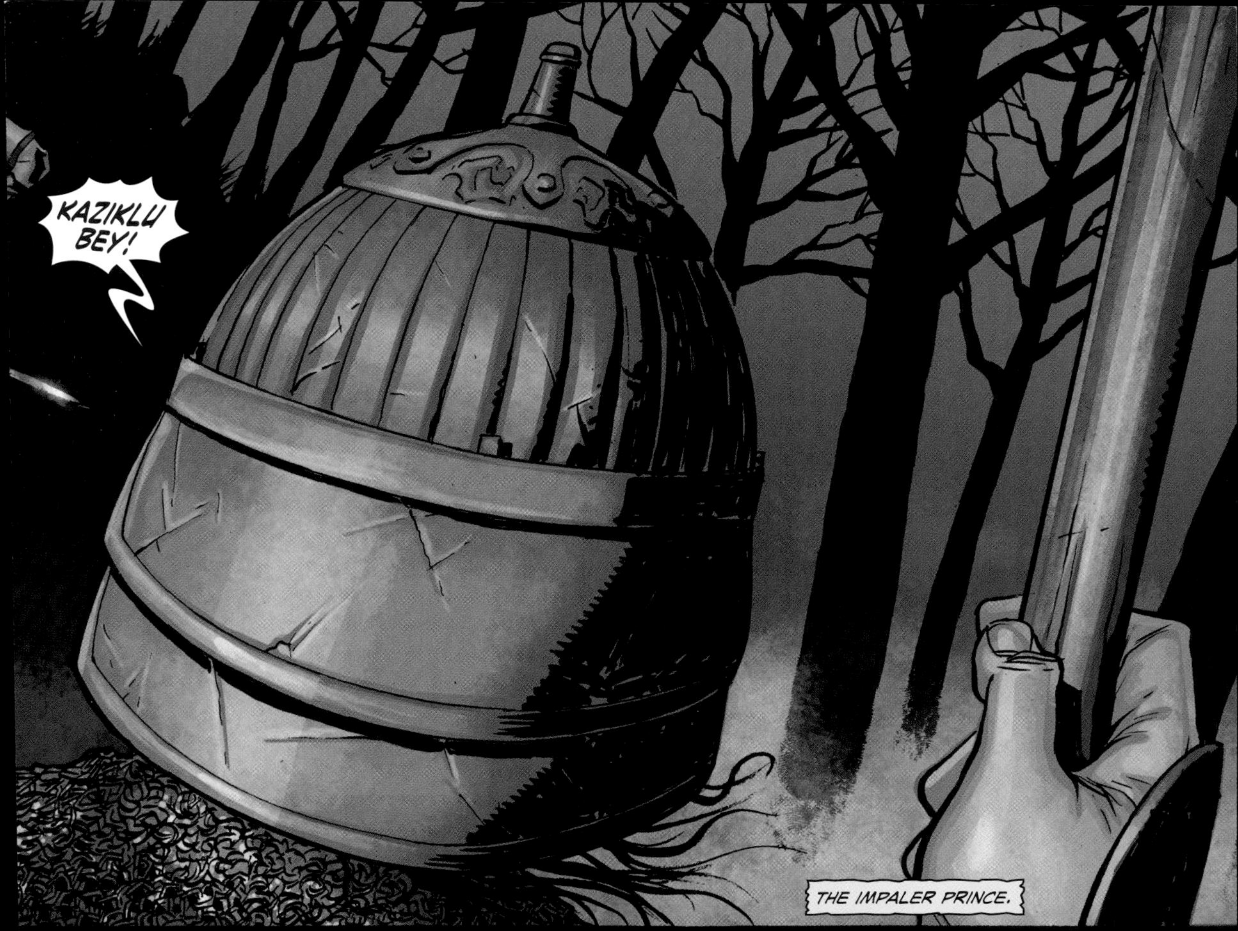
KAZIKLU BEY!
THE IMPALER PRINCE.

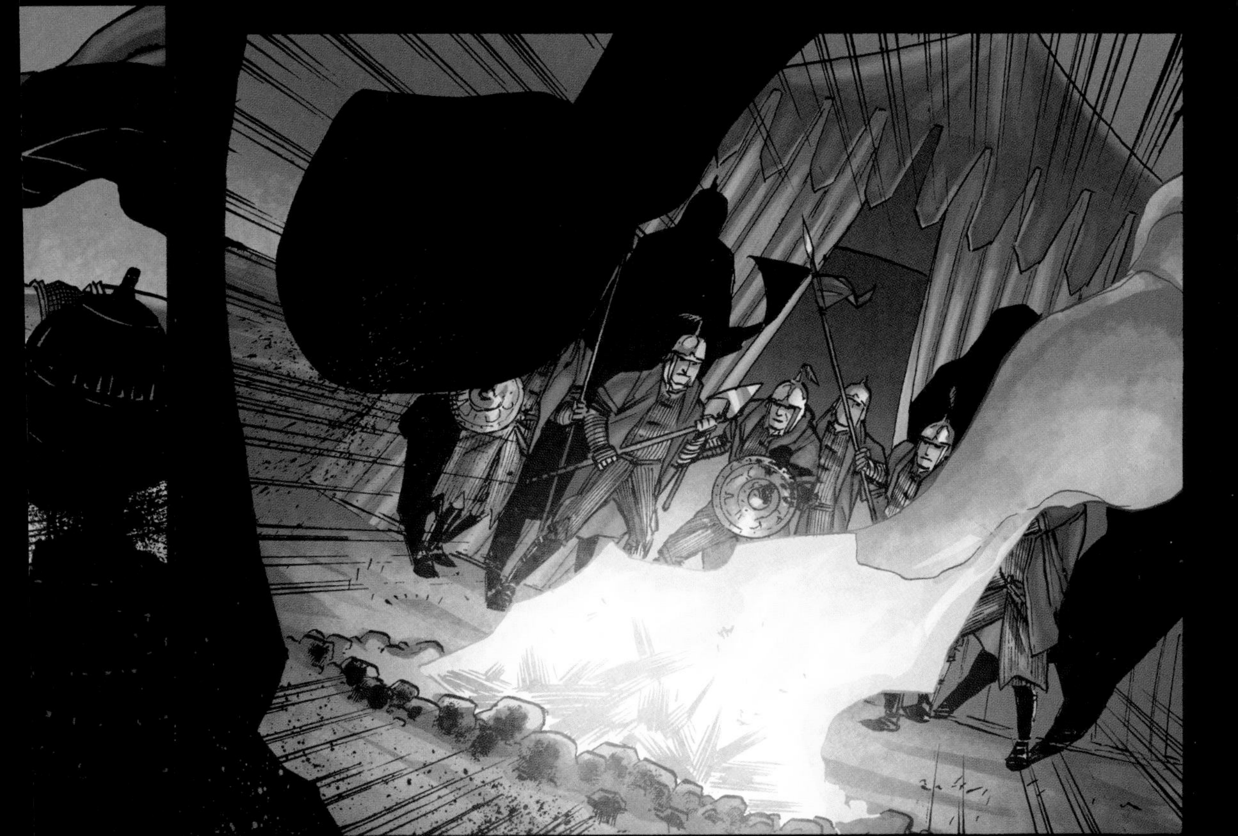

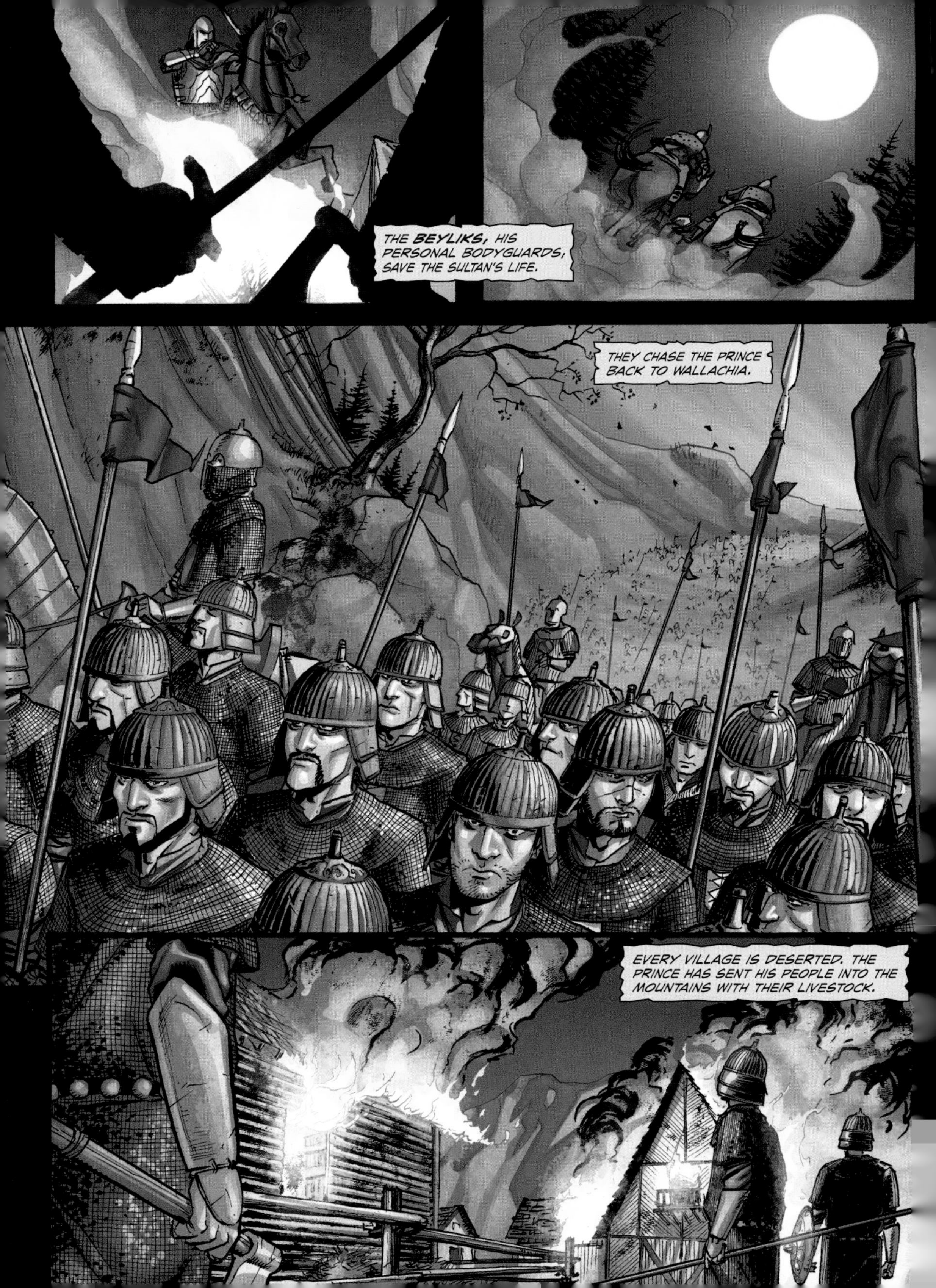

THE **BEYLIKS**, HIS PERSONAL BODYGUARDS, SAVE THE SULTAN'S LIFE.
THEY CHASE THE PRINCE BACK TO WALLACHIA.
EVERY VILLAGE IS DESERTED. THE PRINCE HAS SENT HIS PEOPLE INTO THE MOUNTAINS WITH THEIR LIVESTOCK.

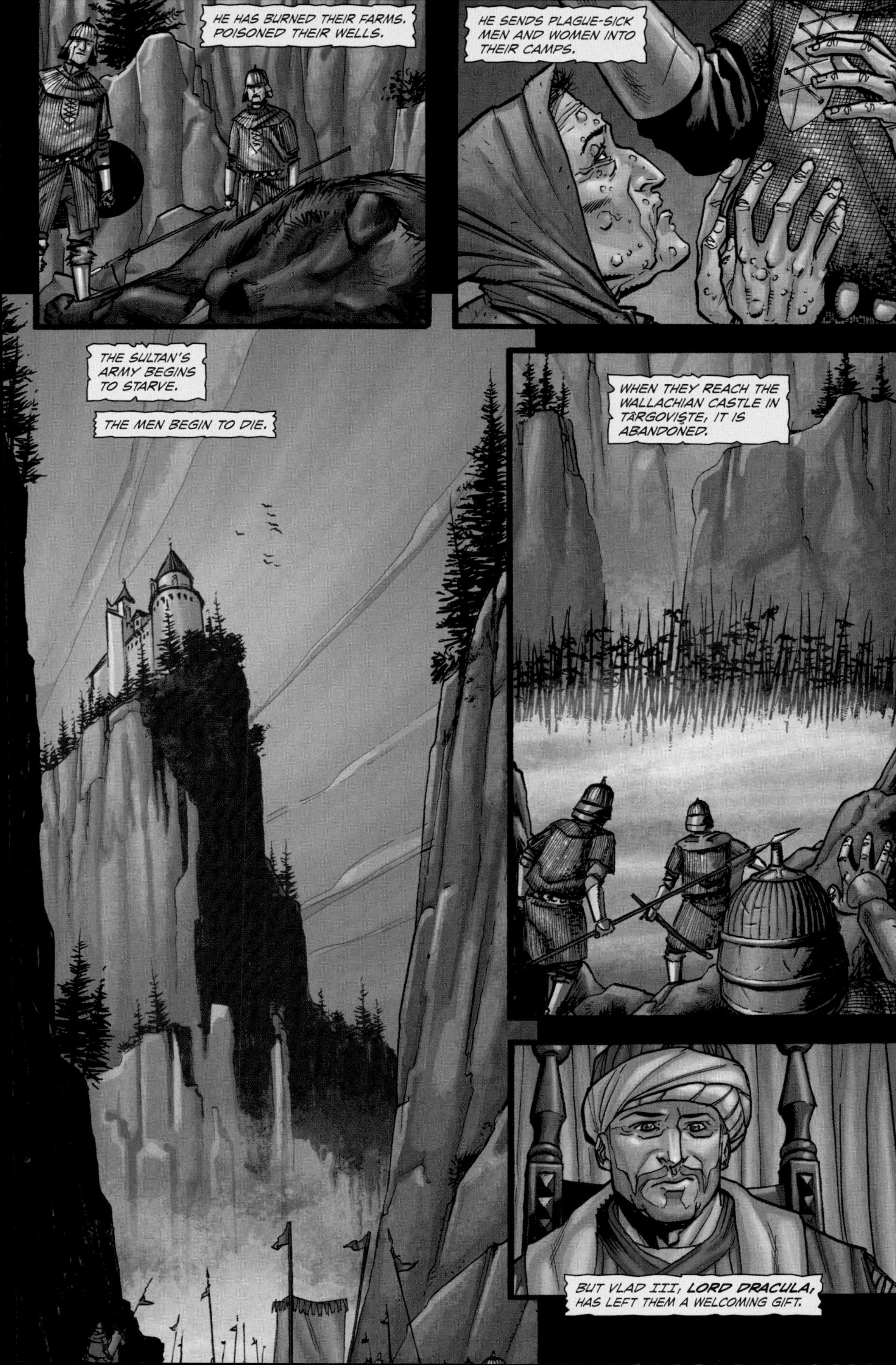
HE HAS BURNED THEIR FARMS. POISONED THEIR WELLS.
HE SENDS PLAGUE-SICK MEN AND WOMEN INTO THEIR CAMPS.
THE SULTAN'S ARMY BEGINS TO STARVE.
THE MEN BEGIN TO DIE.
WHEN THEY REACH THE WALLACHIAN CASTLE IN TÂRGOVIŞTE, IT IS ABANDONED.
BUT VLAD III, LORD DRACULA, HAS LEFT THEM A WELCOMING GIFT.

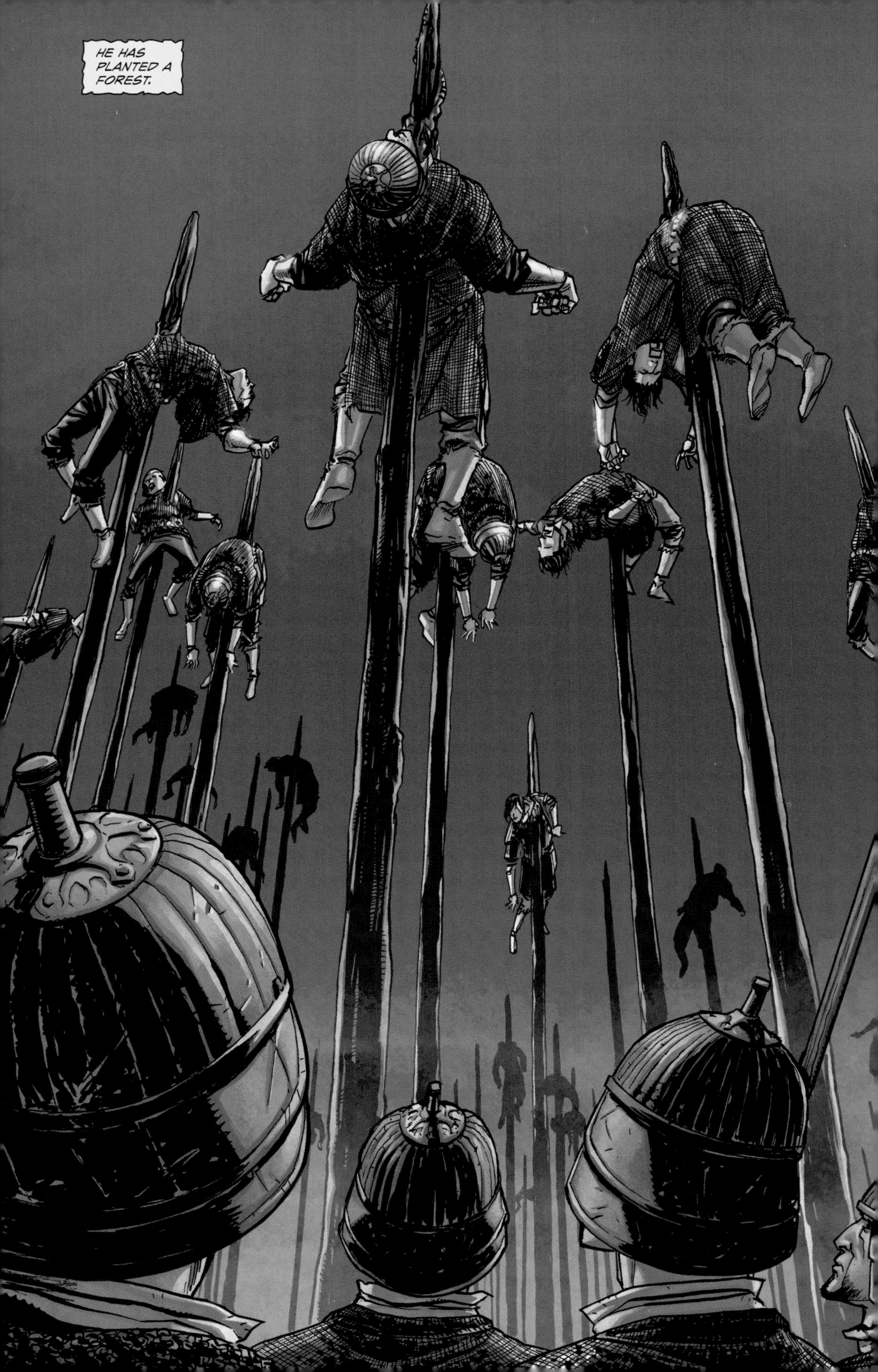
HE HAS PLANTED A FOREST.

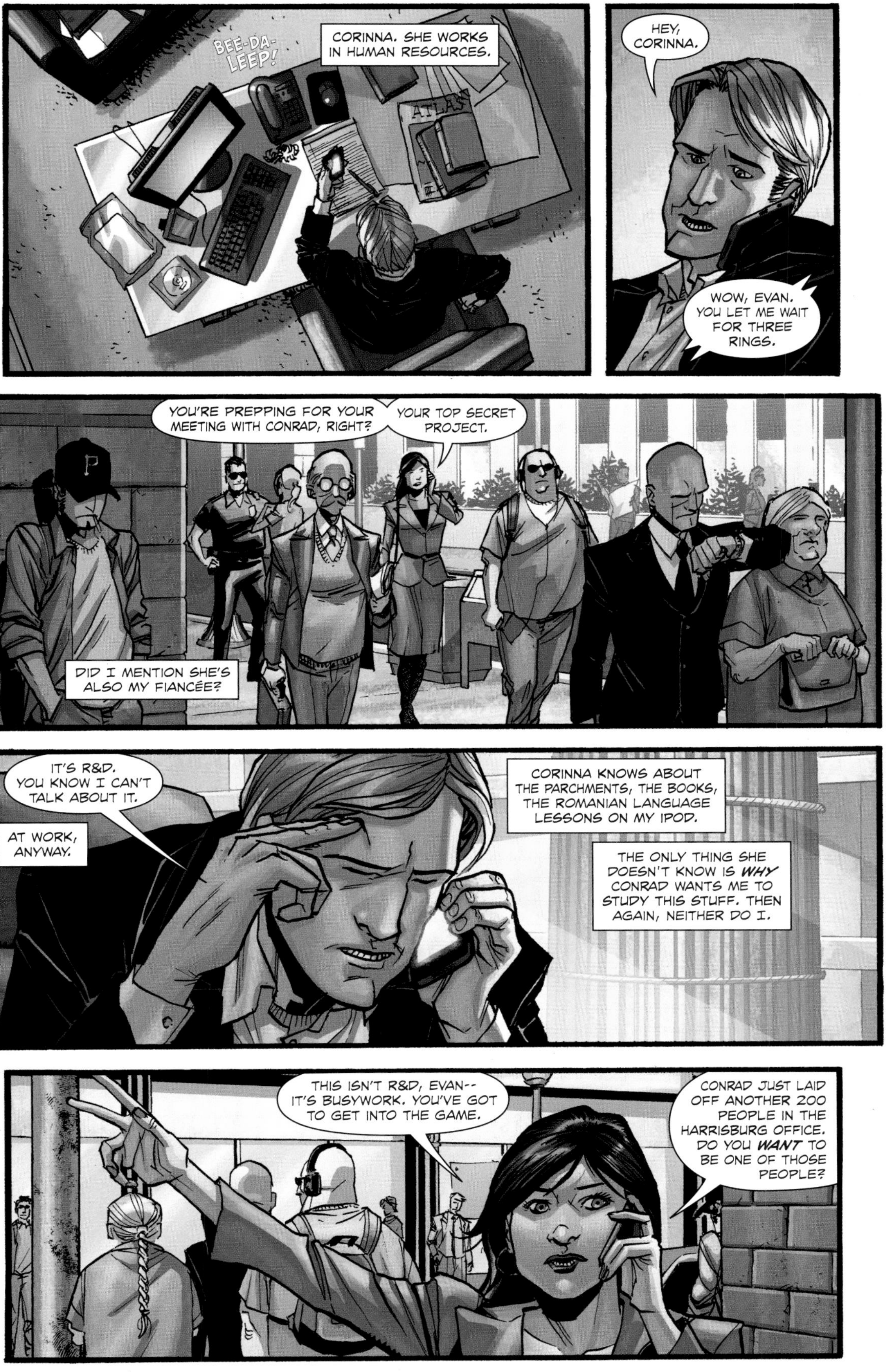
BEE-DA-LEEP!
CORINNA. SHE WORKS IN HUMAN RESOURCES.
ATLAS
HEY, CORINNA.
WOW, EVAN. YOU LET ME WAIT FOR THREE RINGS.
YOU'RE PREPPING FOR YOUR MEETING WITH CONRAD, RIGHT?
YOUR TOP SECRET PROJECT.
DID I MENTION SHE'S ALSO MY FIANCÉE?
IT'S R&D. YOU KNOW I CAN'T TALK ABOUT IT.
AT WORK, ANYWAY.
CORINNA KNOWS ABOUT THE PARCHMENTS, THE BOOKS, THE ROMANIAN LANGUAGE LESSONS ON MY IPOD.
THE ONLY THING SHE DOESN'T KNOW IS ***WHY*** CONRAD WANTS ME TO STUDY THIS STUFF. THEN AGAIN, NEITHER DO I.
THIS ISN'T R&D, EVAN-- IT'S BUSYWORK. YOU'VE GOT TO GET INTO THE GAME.
CONRAD JUST LAID OFF ANOTHER 200 PEOPLE IN THE HARRISBURG OFFICE. DO YOU ***WANT*** TO BE ONE OF THOSE PEOPLE?

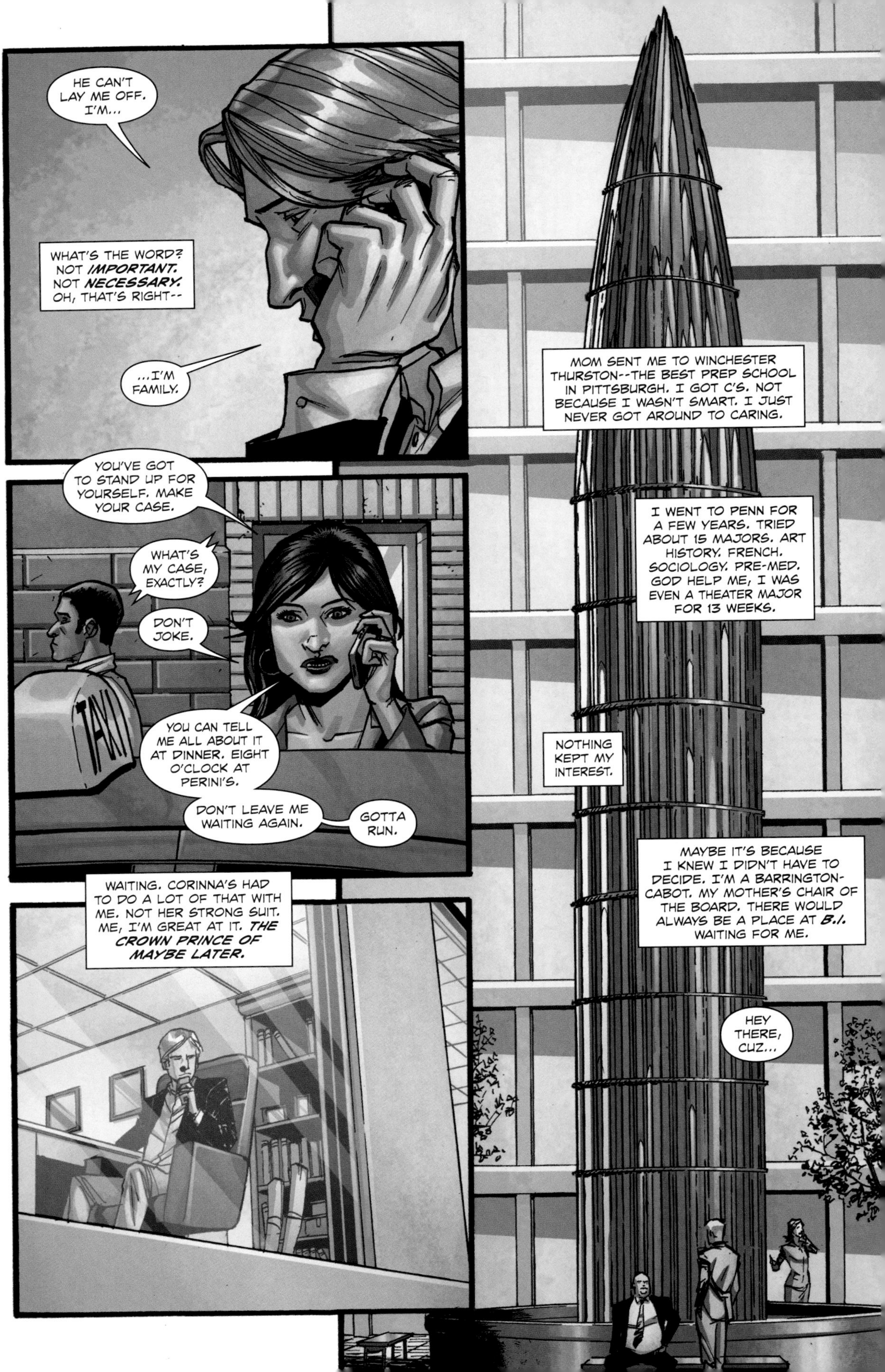
HE CAN'T LAY ME OFF. I'M...
WHAT'S THE WORD? NOT *IMPORTANT.* NOT *NECESSARY.* OH, THAT'S RIGHT--
...I'M FAMILY.
MOM SENT ME TO WINCHESTER THURSTON--THE BEST PREP SCHOOL IN PITTSBURGH. I GOT C'S. NOT BECAUSE I WASN'T SMART. I JUST NEVER GOT AROUND TO CARING.
YOU'VE GOT TO STAND UP FOR YOURSELF. MAKE YOUR CASE.
WHAT'S MY CASE, EXACTLY?
DON'T JOKE.
YOU CAN TELL ME ALL ABOUT IT AT DINNER. EIGHT O'CLOCK AT PERINI'S.
DON'T LEAVE ME WAITING AGAIN.
GOTTA RUN.
TAXI
I WENT TO PENN FOR A FEW YEARS. TRIED ABOUT 15 MAJORS. ART HISTORY. FRENCH. SOCIOLOGY. PRE-MED. GOD HELP ME, I WAS EVEN A THEATER MAJOR FOR 13 WEEKS.
NOTHING KEPT MY INTEREST.
WAITING. CORINNA'S HAD TO DO A LOT OF THAT WITH ME. NOT HER STRONG SUIT. ME, I'M GREAT AT IT. *THE CROWN PRINCE OF MAYBE LATER.*
MAYBE IT'S BECAUSE I KNEW I DIDN'T HAVE TO DECIDE. I'M A BARRINGTON-CABOT. MY MOTHER'S CHAIR OF THE BOARD. THERE WOULD ALWAYS BE A PLACE AT *B.I.* WAITING FOR ME.
HEY THERE, CUZ...

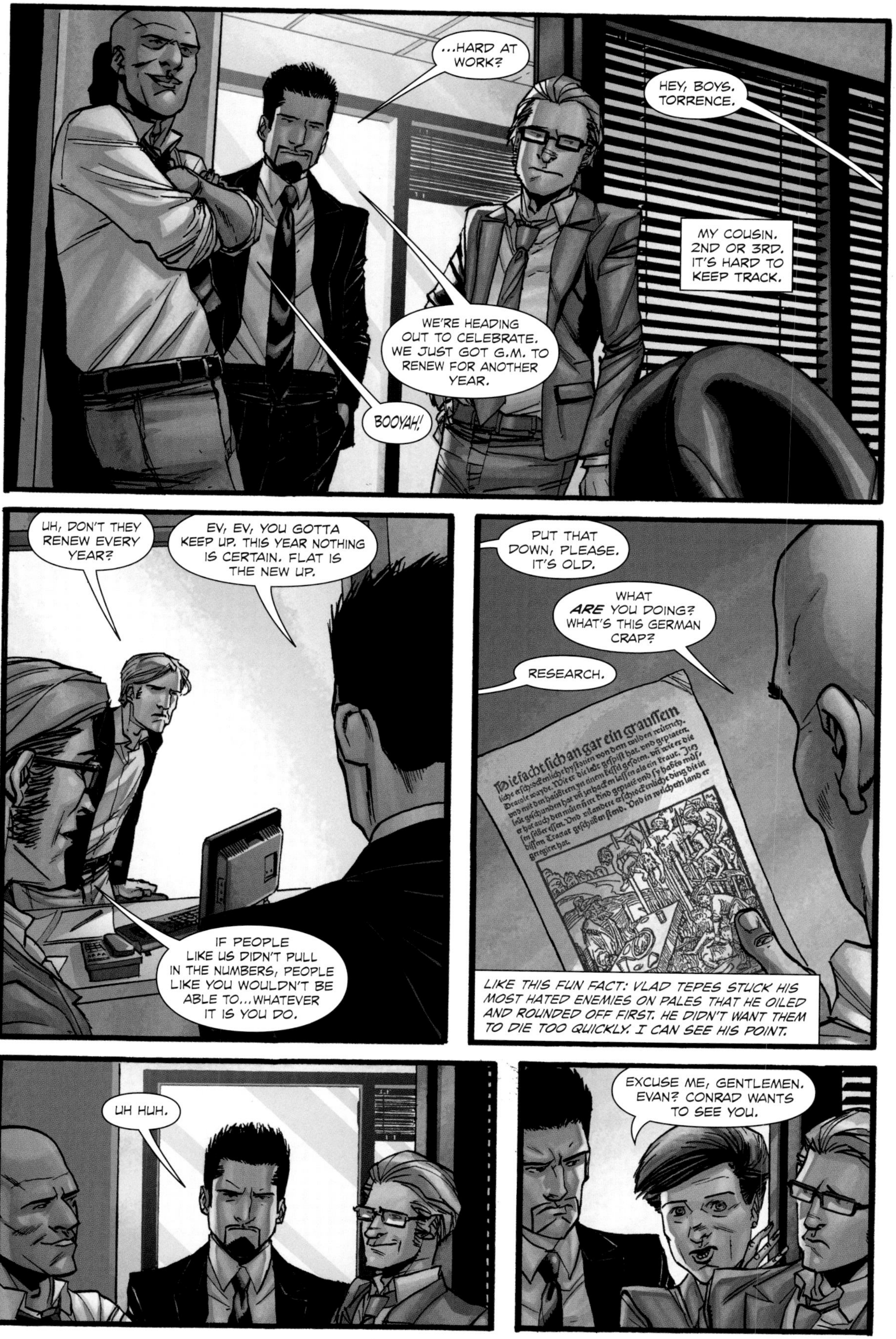

...HARD AT WORK?
HEY, BOYS. TORRENCE.
MY COUSIN. 2ND OR 3RD. IT'S HARD TO KEEP TRACK.
WE'RE HEADING OUT TO CELEBRATE. WE JUST GOT G.M. TO RENEW FOR ANOTHER YEAR.
BOOYAH!
UH, DON'T THEY RENEW EVERY YEAR?
EV, EV, YOU GOTTA KEEP UP. THIS YEAR NOTHING IS CERTAIN. FLAT IS THE NEW UP.
IF PEOPLE LIKE US DIDN'T PULL IN THE NUMBERS, PEOPLE LIKE YOU WOULDN'T BE ABLE TO...WHATEVER IT IS YOU DO.
PUT THAT DOWN, PLEASE. IT'S OLD.
WHAT *ARE* YOU DOING? WHAT'S THIS GERMAN CRAP?
RESEARCH.
LIKE THIS FUN FACT: VLAD TEPES STUCK HIS MOST HATED ENEMIES ON PALES THAT HE OILED AND ROUNDED OFF FIRST. HE DIDN'T WANT THEM TO DIE TOO QUICKLY. I CAN SEE HIS POINT.
UH HUH.
EXCUSE ME, GENTLEMEN. EVAN? CONRAD WANTS TO SEE YOU.

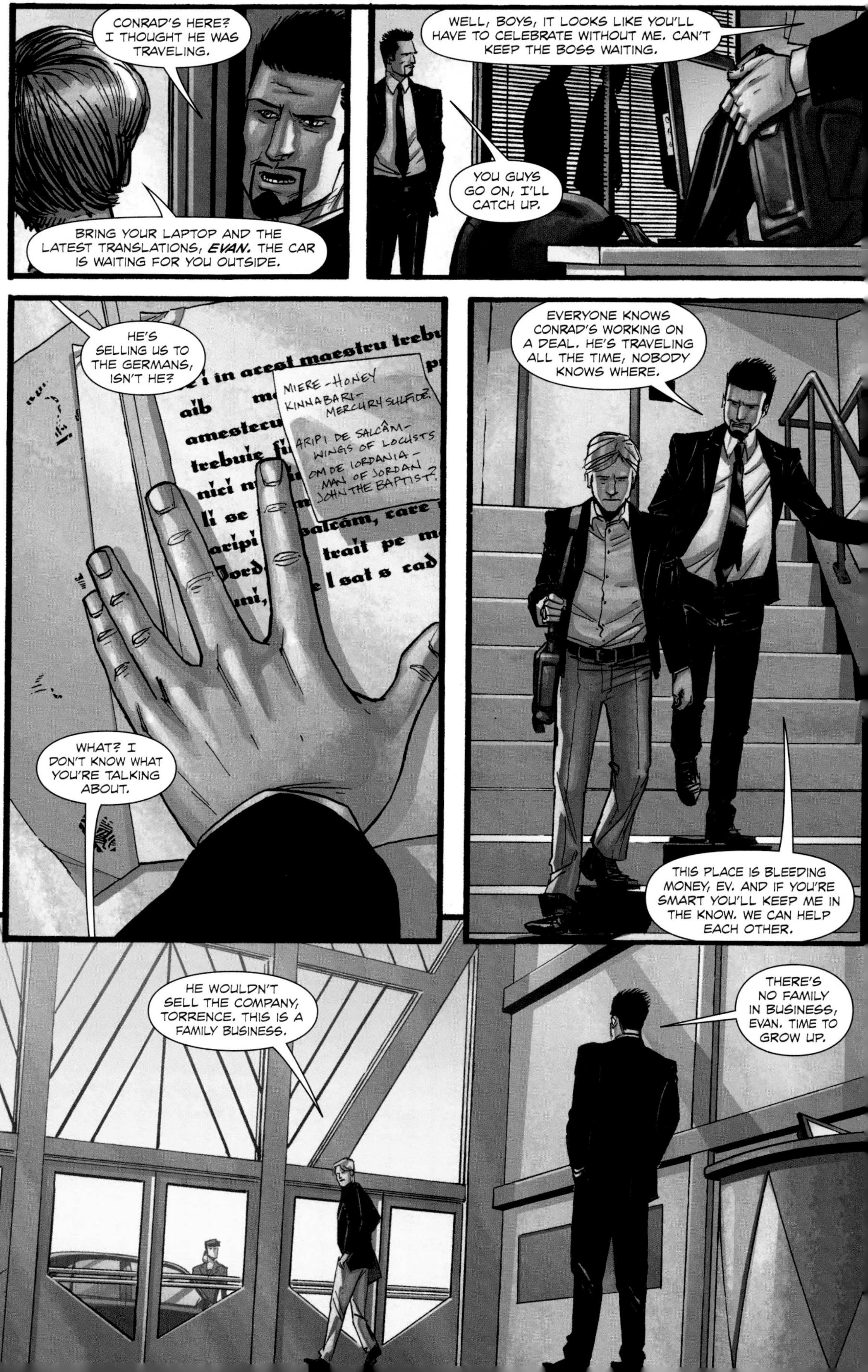
CONRAD'S HERE? I THOUGHT HE WAS TRAVELING.
BRING YOUR LAPTOP AND THE LATEST TRANSLATIONS, *EVAN.* THE CAR IS WAITING FOR YOU OUTSIDE.
WELL, BOYS, IT LOOKS LIKE YOU'LL HAVE TO CELEBRATE WITHOUT ME. CAN'T KEEP THE BOSS WAITING.
YOU GUYS GO ON, I'LL CATCH UP.
HE'S SELLING US TO THE GERMANS, ISN'T HE?
MIERE - HONEY
KINNABARI - MERCURY SULFIDE?
ARIPI DE SALCÂM - WINGS OF LOCUSTS
OM DE IORDANIA - MAN OF JORDAN
JOHN THE BAPTIST?
WHAT? I DON'T KNOW WHAT YOU'RE TALKING ABOUT.
EVERYONE KNOWS CONRAD'S WORKING ON A DEAL. HE'S TRAVELING ALL THE TIME, NOBODY KNOWS WHERE.
THIS PLACE IS BLEEDING MONEY, EV. AND IF YOU'RE SMART YOU'LL KEEP ME IN THE KNOW. WE CAN HELP EACH OTHER.
HE WOULDN'T SELL THE COMPANY, TORRENCE. THIS IS A FAMILY BUSINESS.
THERE'S NO FAMILY IN BUSINESS, EVAN. TIME TO GROW UP.

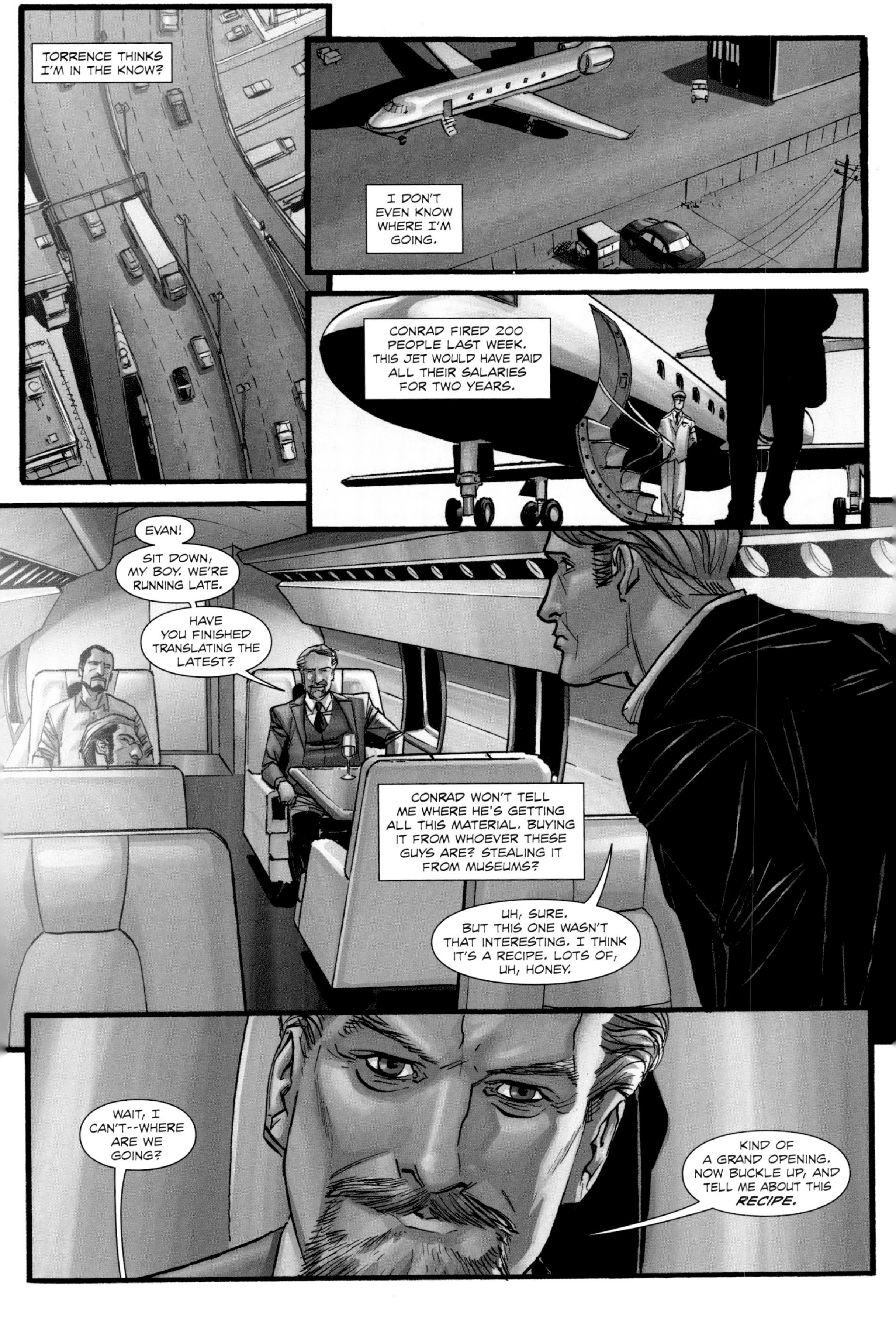
TORRENCE THINKS I'M IN THE KNOW?
I DON'T EVEN KNOW WHERE I'M GOING.
CONRAD FIRED 200 PEOPLE LAST WEEK. THIS JET WOULD HAVE PAID ALL THEIR SALARIES FOR TWO YEARS.
EVAN!
SIT DOWN, MY BOY. WE'RE RUNNING LATE.
HAVE YOU FINISHED TRANSLATING THE LATEST?
CONRAD WON'T TELL ME WHERE HE'S GETTING ALL THIS MATERIAL. BUYING IT FROM WHOEVER THESE GUYS ARE? STEALING IT FROM MUSEUMS?
UH, SURE. BUT THIS ONE WASN'T THAT INTERESTING. I THINK IT'S A RECIPE. LOTS OF, UH, HONEY.
WAIT, I CAN'T--WHERE ARE WE GOING?
KIND OF A GRAND OPENING. NOW BUCKLE UP, AND TELL ME ABOUT THIS *RECIPE.*

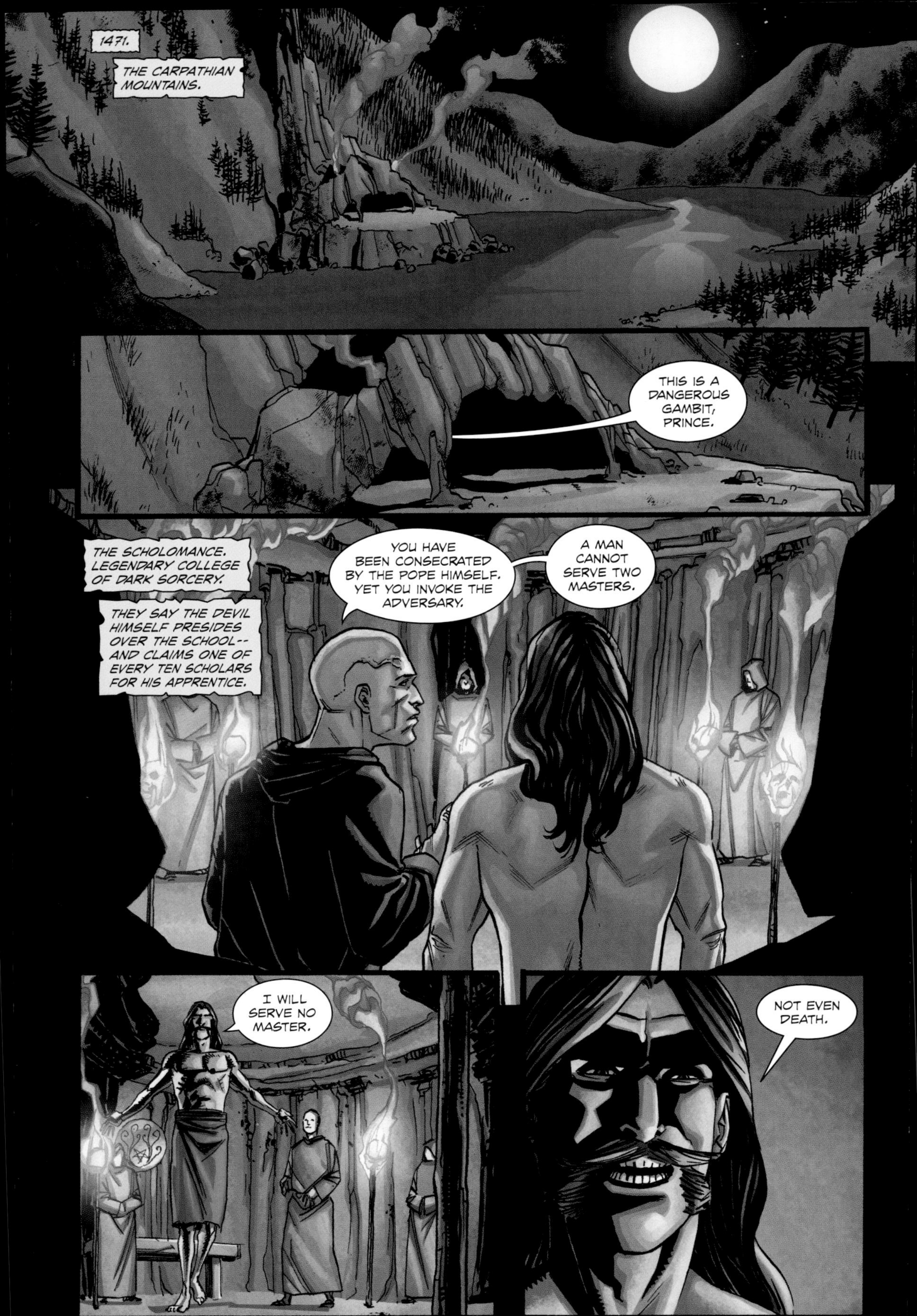
1471.
THE CARPATHIAN MOUNTAINS.
THIS IS A DANGEROUS GAMBIT, PRINCE.
THE SCHOLOMANCE. LEGENDARY COLLEGE OF DARK SORCERY.
THEY SAY THE DEVIL HIMSELF PRESIDES OVER THE SCHOOL-- AND CLAIMS ONE OF EVERY TEN SCHOLARS FOR HIS APPRENTICE.
YOU HAVE BEEN CONSECRATED BY THE POPE HIMSELF. YET YOU INVOKE THE ADVERSARY.
A MAN CANNOT SERVE TWO MASTERS.
I WILL SERVE NO MASTER.
NOT EVEN DEATH.

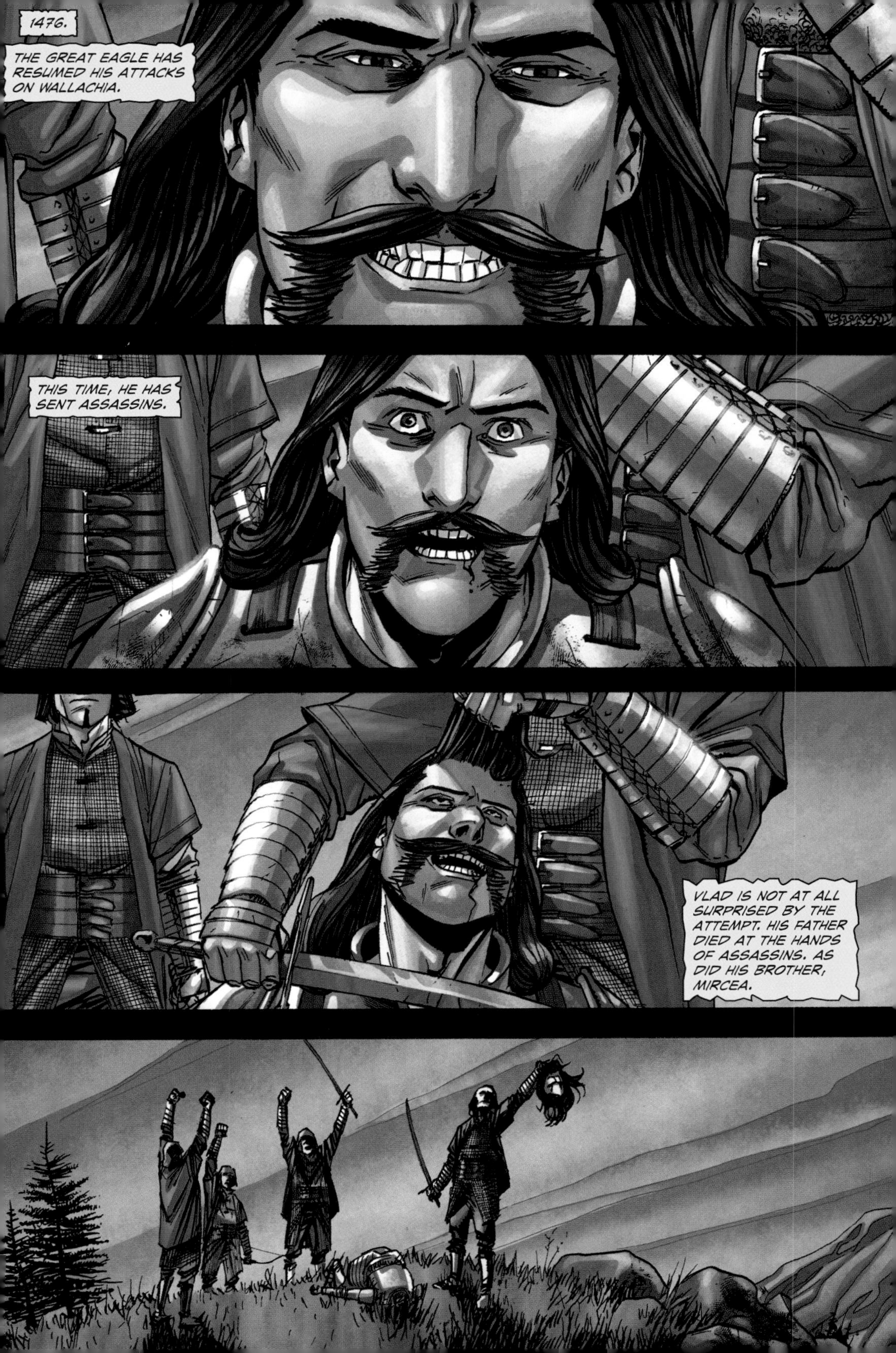
1476.
THE GREAT EAGLE HAS RESUMED HIS ATTACKS ON WALLACHIA.
THIS TIME, HE HAS SENT ASSASSINS.
VLAD IS NOT AT ALL SURPRISED BY THE ATTEMPT. HIS FATHER DIED AT THE HANDS OF ASSASSINS. AS DID HIS BROTHER, MIRCEA.

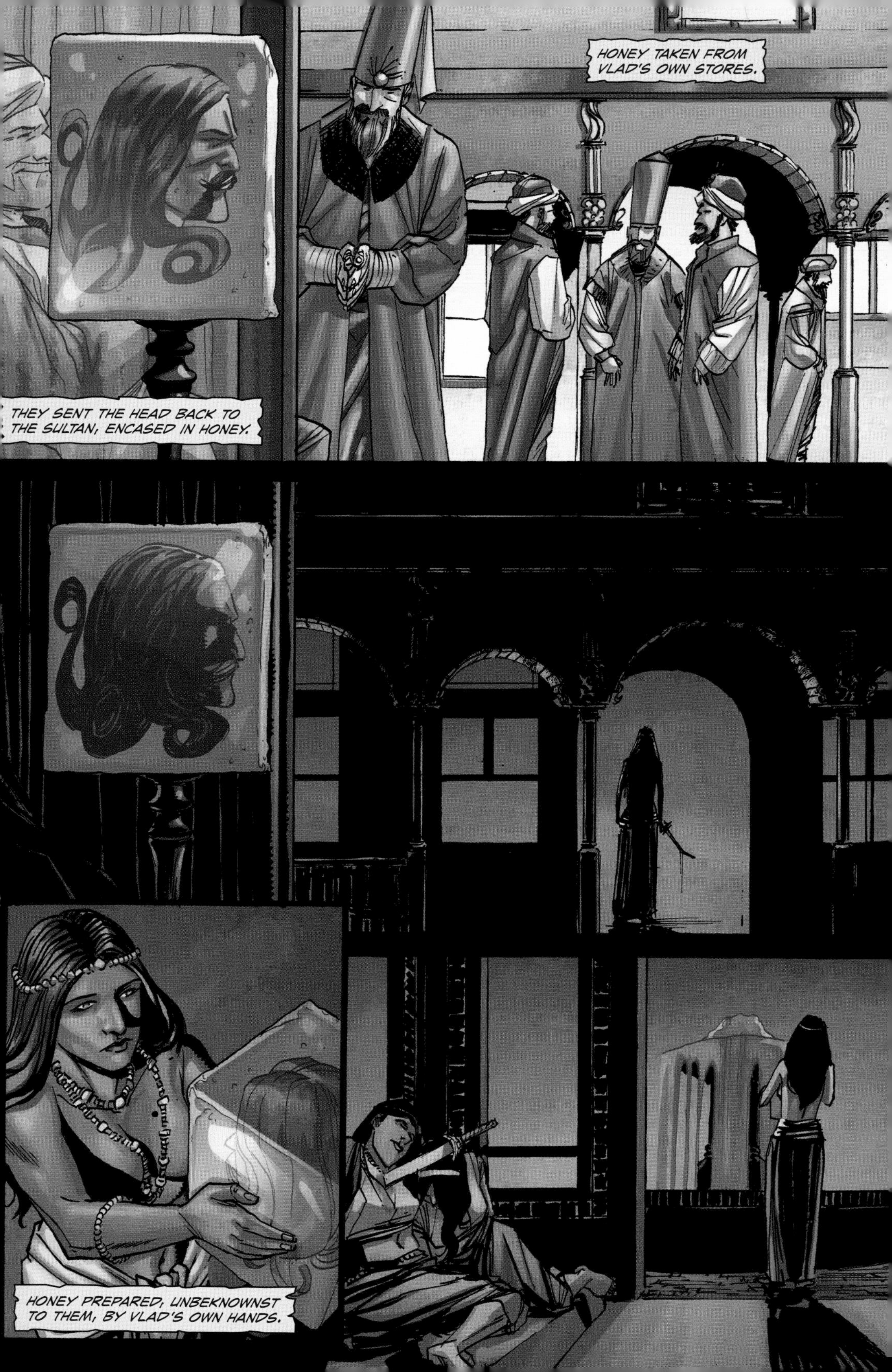
HONEY TAKEN FROM VLAD'S OWN STORES.
THEY SENT THE HEAD BACK TO THE SULTAN, ENCASED IN HONEY.
HONEY PREPARED, UNBEKNOWNST TO THEM, BY VLAD'S OWN HANDS.

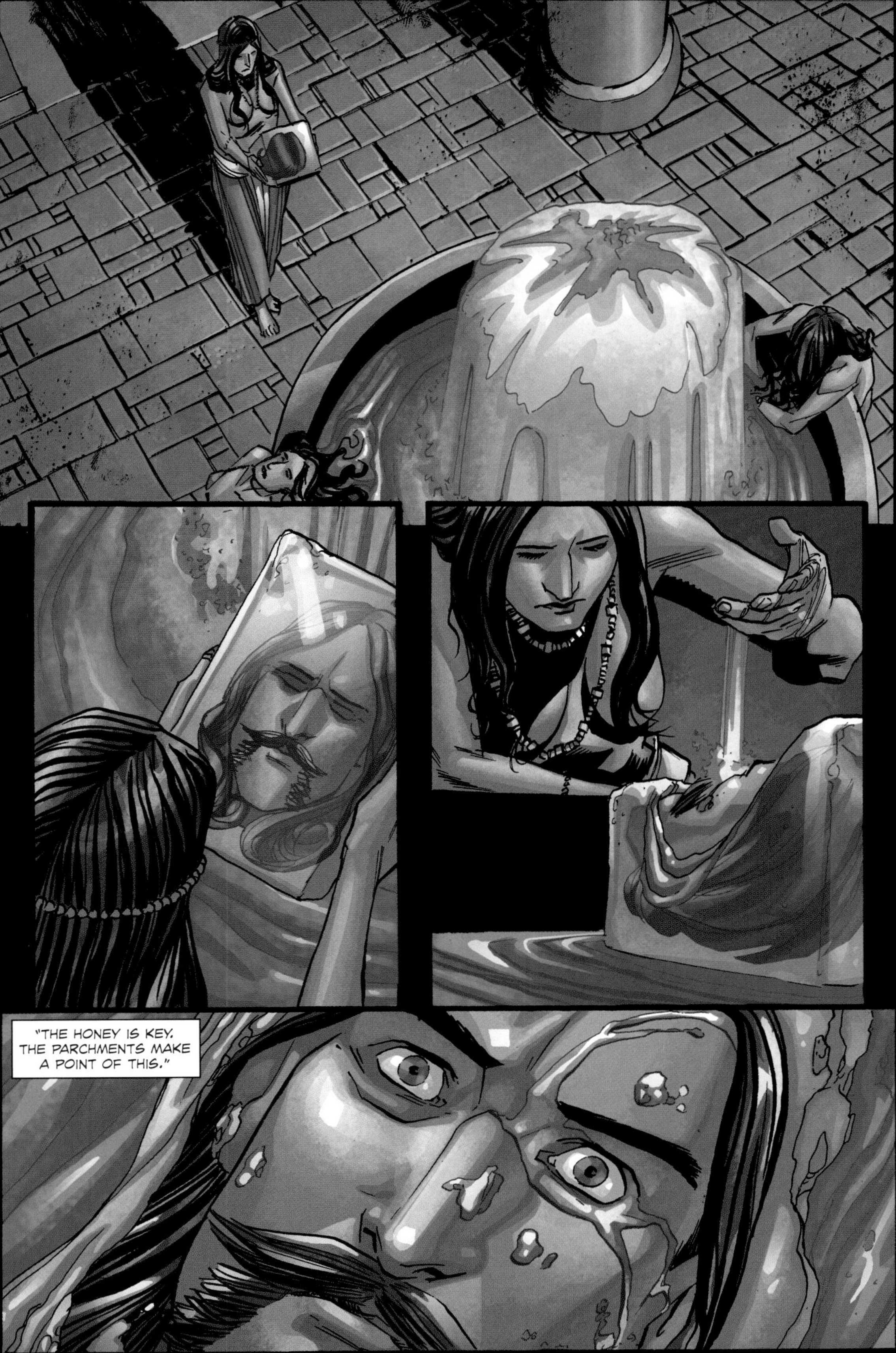
"THE HONEY IS KEY.
THE PARCHMENTS MAKE
A POINT OF THIS."

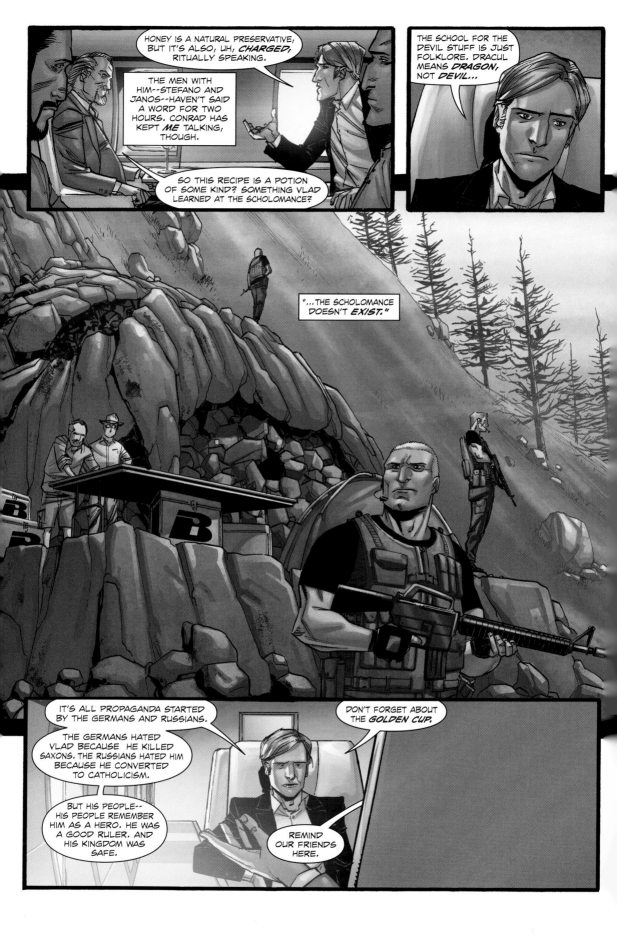

HONEY IS A NATURAL PRESERVATIVE, BUT IT'S ALSO, UH, *CHARGED*, RITUALLY SPEAKING.

THE MEN WITH HIM--STEFANO AND JANOS--HAVEN'T SAID A WORD FOR TWO HOURS. CONRAD HAS KEPT *ME* TALKING, THOUGH.

SO THIS RECIPE IS A POTION OF SOME KIND? SOMETHING VLAD LEARNED AT THE SCHOLOMANCE?

THE SCHOOL FOR THE DEVIL STUFF IS JUST FOLKLORE. DRACUL MEANS *DRAGON*, NOT *DEVIL*...

"...THE SCHOLOMANCE DOESN'T *EXIST*."

IT'S ALL PROPAGANDA STARTED BY THE GERMANS AND RUSSIANS.

THE GERMANS HATED VLAD BECAUSE HE KILLED SAXONS. THE RUSSIANS HATED HIM BECAUSE HE CONVERTED TO CATHOLICISM.

BUT HIS PEOPLE-- HIS PEOPLE REMEMBER HIM AS A HERO. HE WAS A GOOD RULER. AND HIS KINGDOM WAS SAFE.

DON'T FORGET ABOUT THE *GOLDEN CUP.*

REMIND OUR FRIENDS HERE.

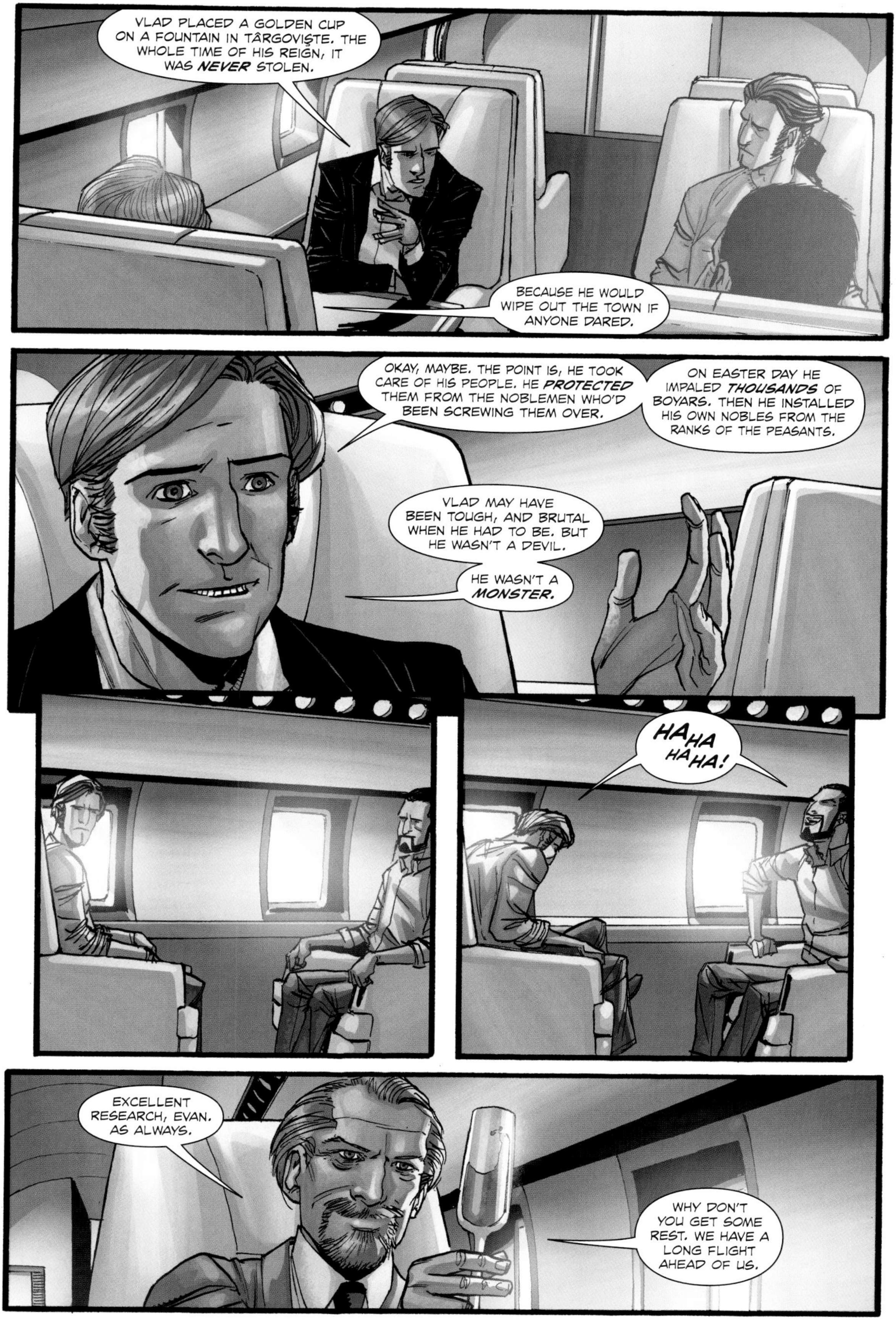

VLAD PLACED A GOLDEN CUP ON A FOUNTAIN IN TÂRGOVIŞTE. THE WHOLE TIME OF HIS REIGN, IT WAS *NEVER* STOLEN.
BECAUSE HE WOULD WIPE OUT THE TOWN IF ANYONE DARED.
OKAY, MAYBE. THE POINT IS, HE TOOK CARE OF HIS PEOPLE. HE *PROTECTED* THEM FROM THE NOBLEMEN WHO'D BEEN SCREWING THEM OVER.
ON EASTER DAY HE IMPALED *THOUSANDS* OF BOYARS. THEN HE INSTALLED HIS OWN NOBLES FROM THE RANKS OF THE PEASANTS.
VLAD MAY HAVE BEEN TOUGH, AND BRUTAL WHEN HE HAD TO BE. BUT HE WASN'T A DEVIL.
HE WASN'T A *MONSTER.*
HAHA HAHA!
EXCELLENT RESEARCH, EVAN. AS ALWAYS.
WHY DON'T YOU GET SOME REST. WE HAVE A LONG FLIGHT AHEAD OF US.

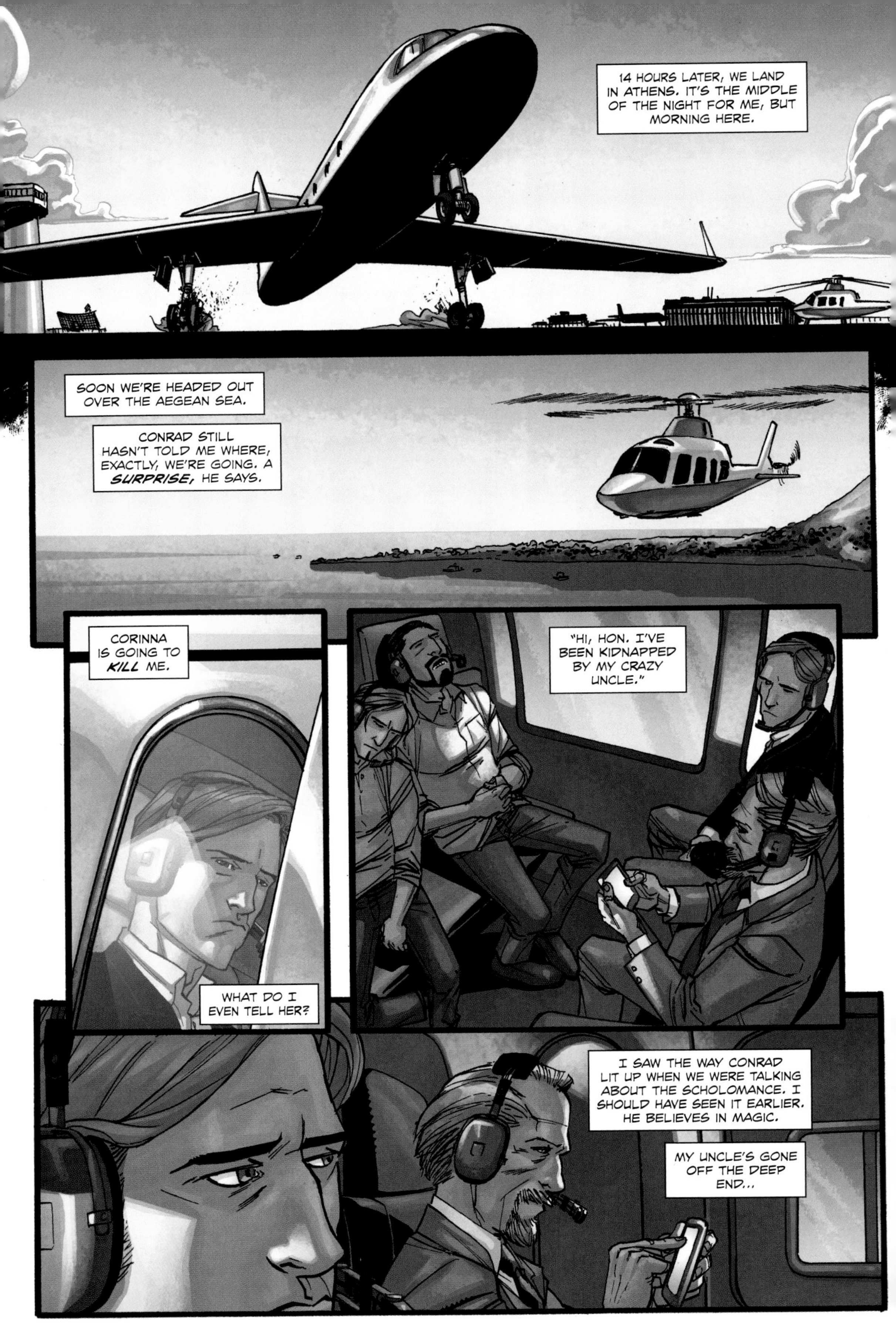
14 HOURS LATER, WE LAND IN ATHENS. IT'S THE MIDDLE OF THE NIGHT FOR ME, BUT MORNING HERE.
SOON WE'RE HEADED OUT OVER THE AEGEAN SEA.
CONRAD STILL HASN'T TOLD ME WHERE, EXACTLY, WE'RE GOING. A SURPRISE, HE SAYS.
CORINNA IS GOING TO KILL ME.
WHAT DO I EVEN TELL HER?
"HI, HON. I'VE BEEN KIDNAPPED BY MY CRAZY UNCLE."
I SAW THE WAY CONRAD LIT UP WHEN WE WERE TALKING ABOUT THE SCHOLOMANCE. I SHOULD HAVE SEEN IT EARLIER. HE BELIEVES IN MAGIC.
MY UNCLE'S GONE OFF THE DEEP END...

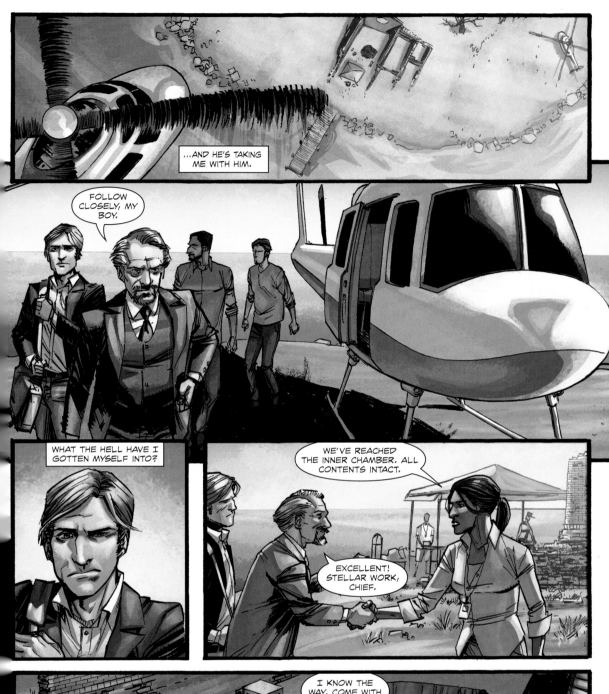

...AND HE'S TAKING ME WITH HIM.

FOLLOW CLOSELY, MY BOY.

WHAT THE HELL HAVE I GOTTEN MYSELF INTO?

WE'VE REACHED THE INNER CHAMBER. ALL CONTENTS INTACT.

EXCELLENT! STELLAR WORK, CHIEF.

I KNOW THE WAY. COME WITH ME, EVAN.

BUT SIR--

HAVE THE MEN PREPARE FOR SHIPPING, JANOS.

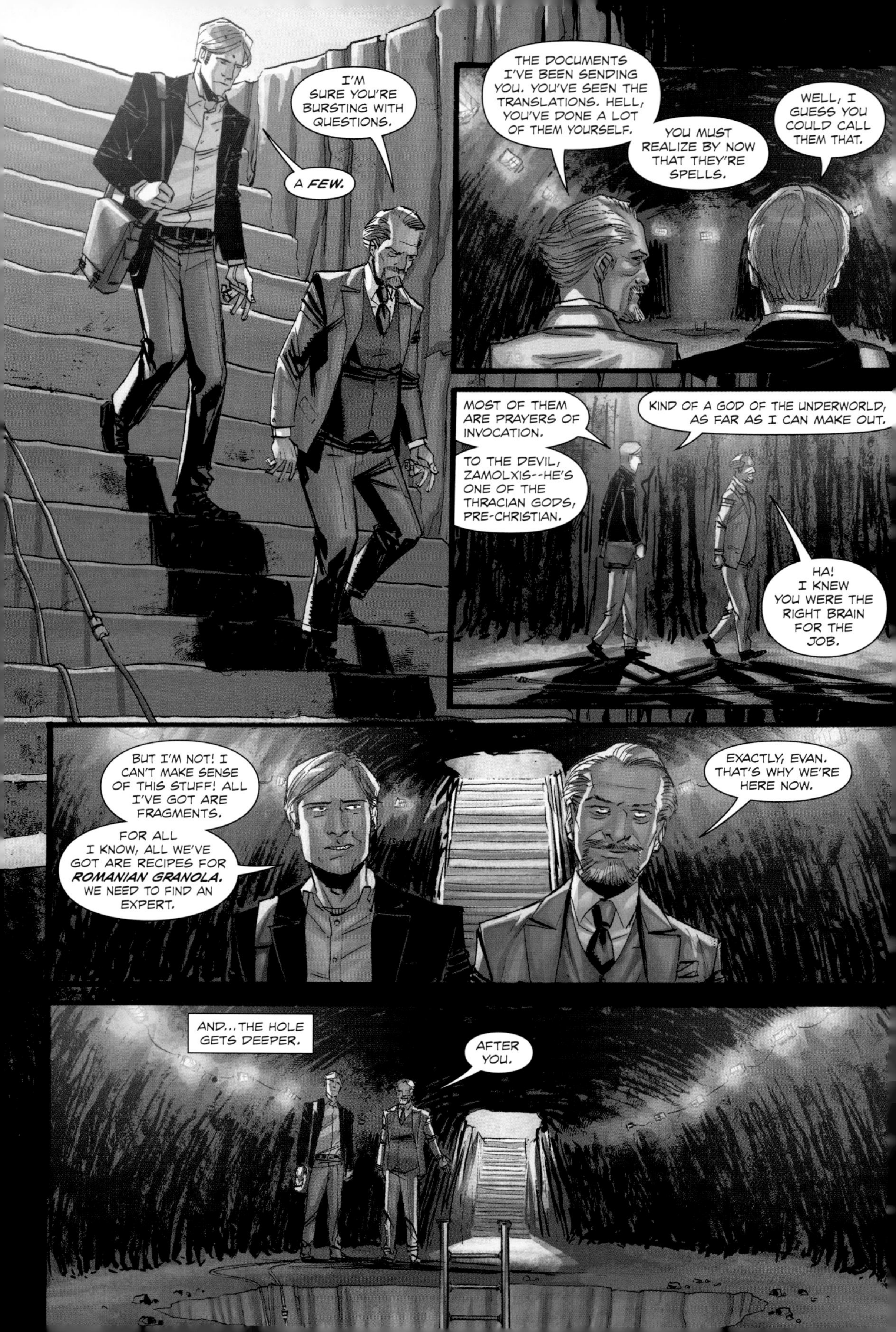
I'M SURE YOU'RE BURSTING WITH QUESTIONS.
A *FEW.*
THE DOCUMENTS I'VE BEEN SENDING YOU. YOU'VE SEEN THE TRANSLATIONS. HELL, YOU'VE DONE A LOT OF THEM YOURSELF.
YOU MUST REALIZE BY NOW THAT THEY'RE SPELLS.
WELL, I GUESS YOU COULD CALL THEM THAT.
MOST OF THEM ARE PRAYERS OF INVOCATION.
TO THE DEVIL, ZAMOLXIS--HE'S ONE OF THE THRACIAN GODS, PRE-CHRISTIAN.
KIND OF A GOD OF THE UNDERWORLD, AS FAR AS I CAN MAKE OUT.
HA! I KNEW YOU WERE THE RIGHT BRAIN FOR THE JOB.
BUT I'M NOT! I CAN'T MAKE SENSE OF THIS STUFF! ALL I'VE GOT ARE FRAGMENTS.
FOR ALL I KNOW, ALL WE'VE GOT ARE RECIPES FOR *ROMANIAN GRANOLA.* WE NEED TO FIND AN EXPERT.
EXACTLY, EVAN. THAT'S WHY WE'RE HERE NOW.
AND...THE HOLE GETS DEEPER.
AFTER YOU.

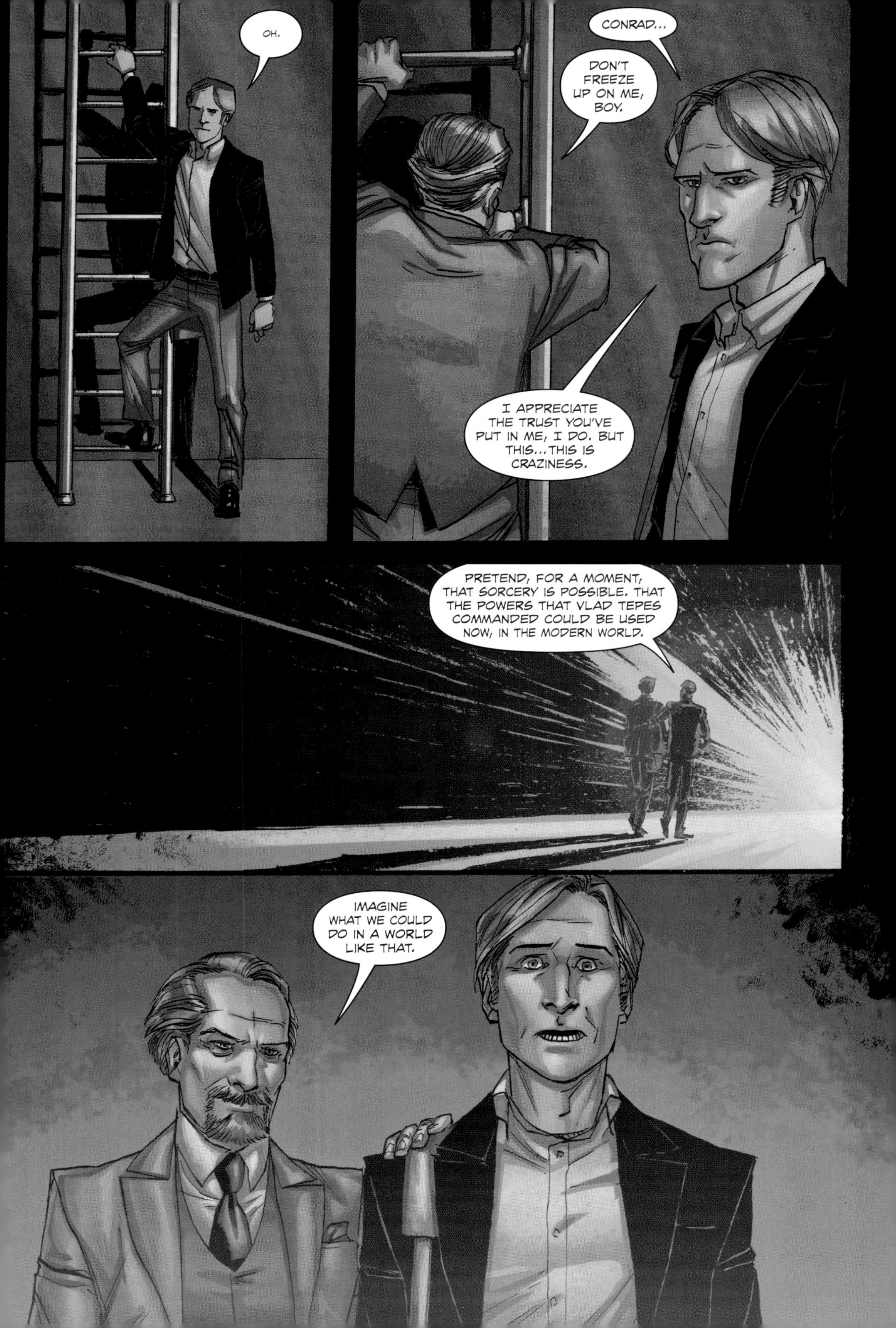
OH.
CONRAD...
DON'T FREEZE UP ON ME, BOY.
I APPRECIATE THE TRUST YOU'VE PUT IN ME, I DO. BUT THIS...THIS IS CRAZINESS.
PRETEND, FOR A MOMENT, THAT SORCERY IS POSSIBLE. THAT THE POWERS THAT VLAD TEPES COMMANDED COULD BE USED NOW, IN THE MODERN WORLD.
IMAGINE WHAT WE COULD DO IN A WORLD LIKE THAT.

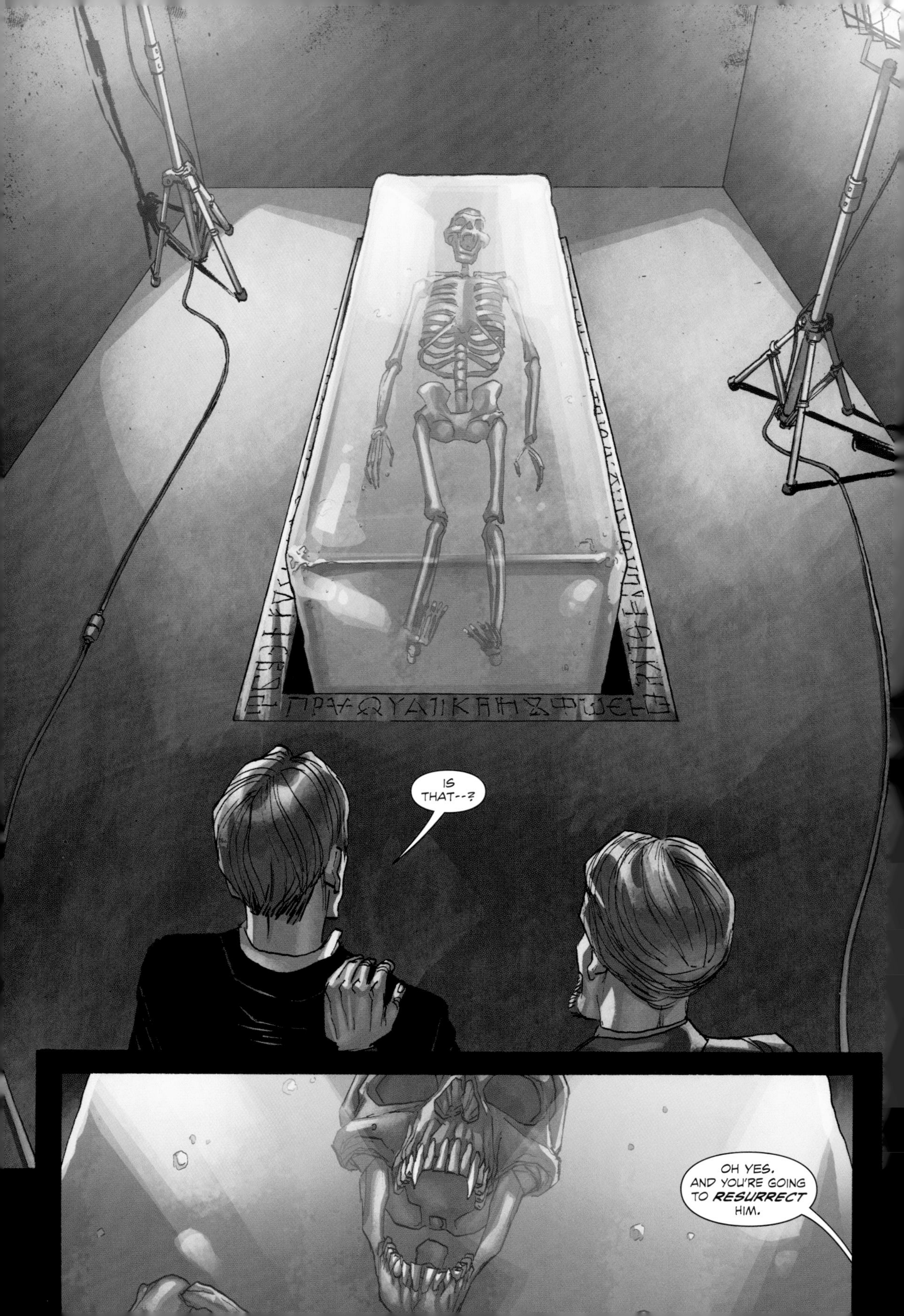
IS THAT--?
OH YES. AND YOU'RE GOING TO ***RESURRECT*** HIM.

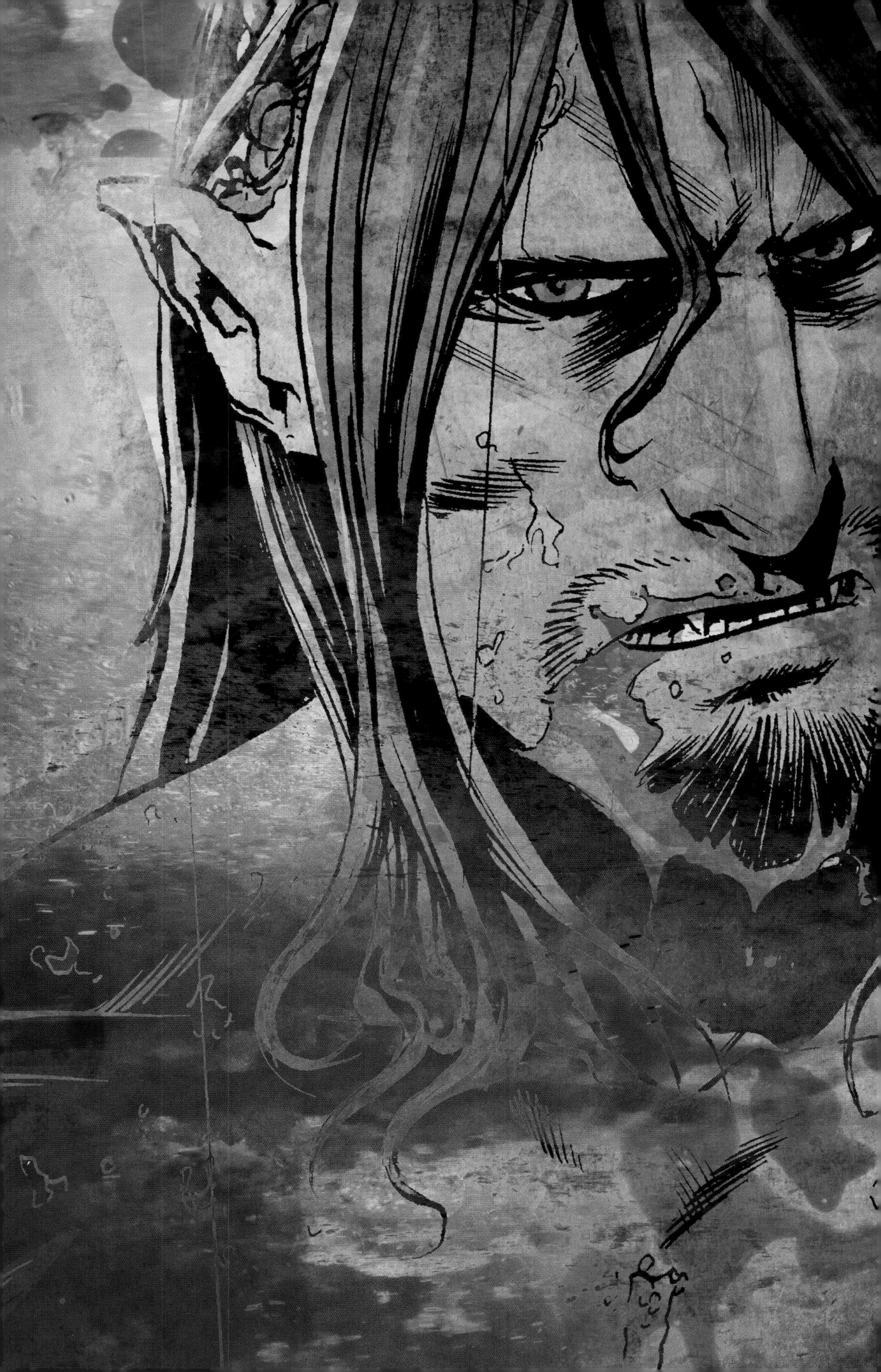

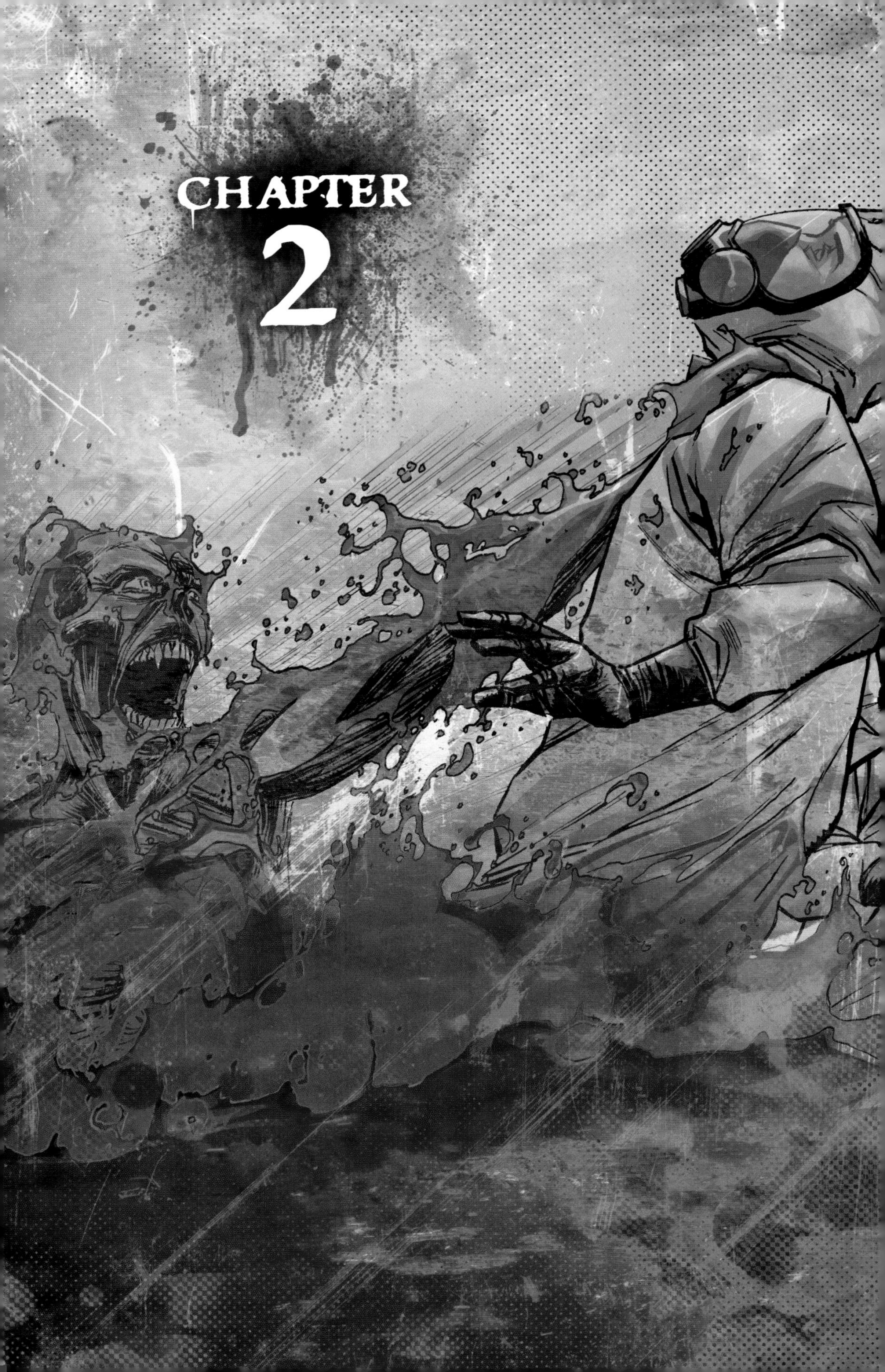
CHAPTER
2

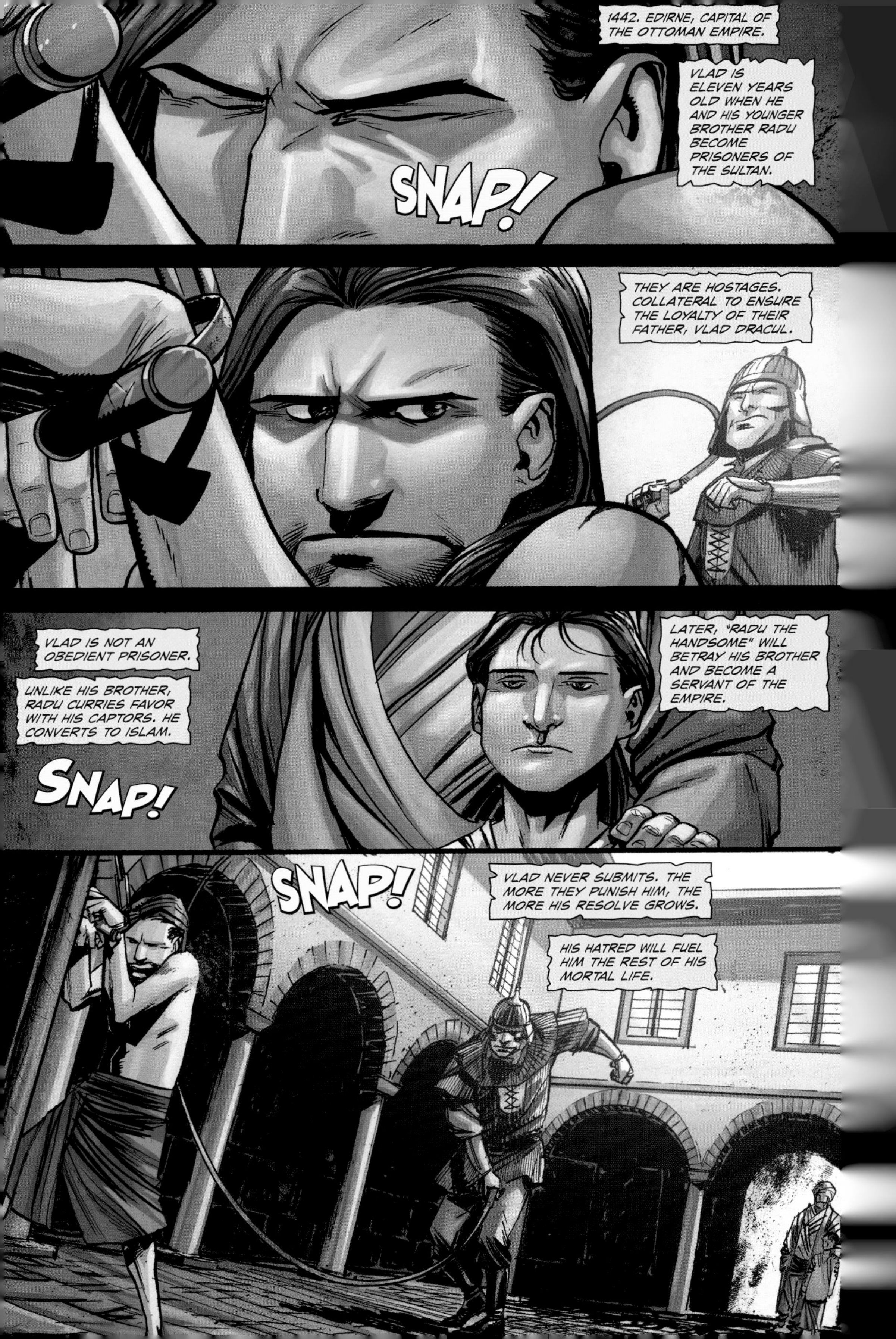

1442. EDIRNE, CAPITAL OF THE OTTOMAN EMPIRE.
VLAD IS ELEVEN YEARS OLD WHEN HE AND HIS YOUNGER BROTHER RADU BECOME PRISONERS OF THE SULTAN.
SNAP!
THEY ARE HOSTAGES. COLLATERAL TO ENSURE THE LOYALTY OF THEIR FATHER, VLAD DRACUL.
VLAD IS NOT AN OBEDIENT PRISONER.
UNLIKE HIS BROTHER, RADU CURRIES FAVOR WITH HIS CAPTORS. HE CONVERTS TO ISLAM.
SNAP!
LATER, "RADU THE HANDSOME" WILL BETRAY HIS BROTHER AND BECOME A SERVANT OF THE EMPIRE.
SNAP!
VLAD NEVER SUBMITS. THE MORE THEY PUNISH HIM, THE MORE HIS RESOLVE GROWS.
HIS HATRED WILL FUEL HIM THE REST OF HIS MORTAL LIFE.

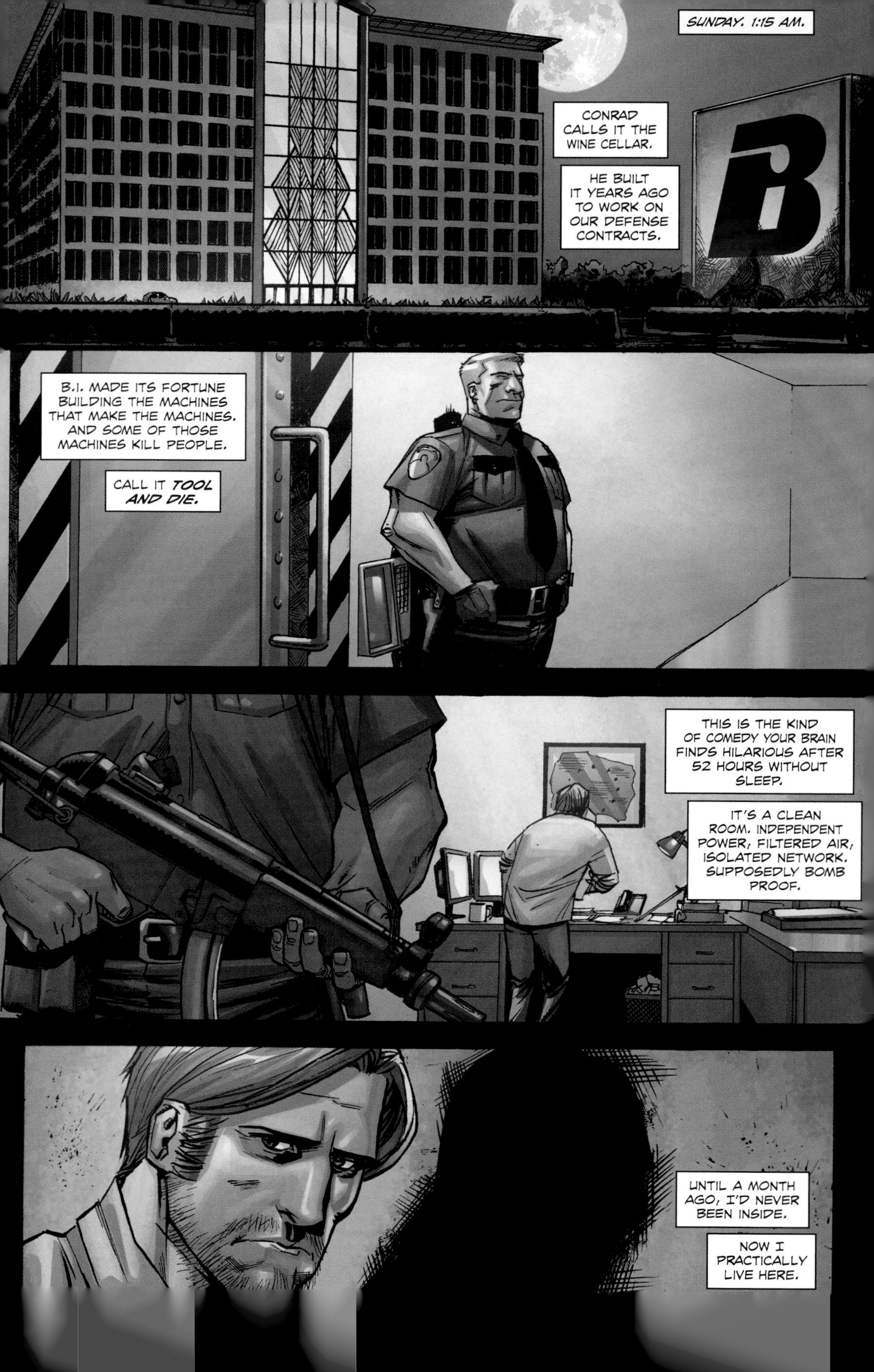
SUNDAY. 1:15 AM.
CONRAD CALLS IT THE WINE CELLAR.
HE BUILT IT YEARS AGO TO WORK ON OUR DEFENSE CONTRACTS.
B.I. MADE ITS FORTUNE BUILDING THE MACHINES THAT MAKE THE MACHINES. AND SOME OF THOSE MACHINES KILL PEOPLE.
CALL IT *TOOL AND DIE.*
THIS IS THE KIND OF COMEDY YOUR BRAIN FINDS HILARIOUS AFTER 52 HOURS WITHOUT SLEEP.
IT'S A CLEAN ROOM. INDEPENDENT POWER, FILTERED AIR, ISOLATED NETWORK. SUPPOSEDLY BOMB PROOF.
UNTIL A MONTH AGO, I'D NEVER BEEN INSIDE.
NOW I PRACTICALLY LIVE HERE.

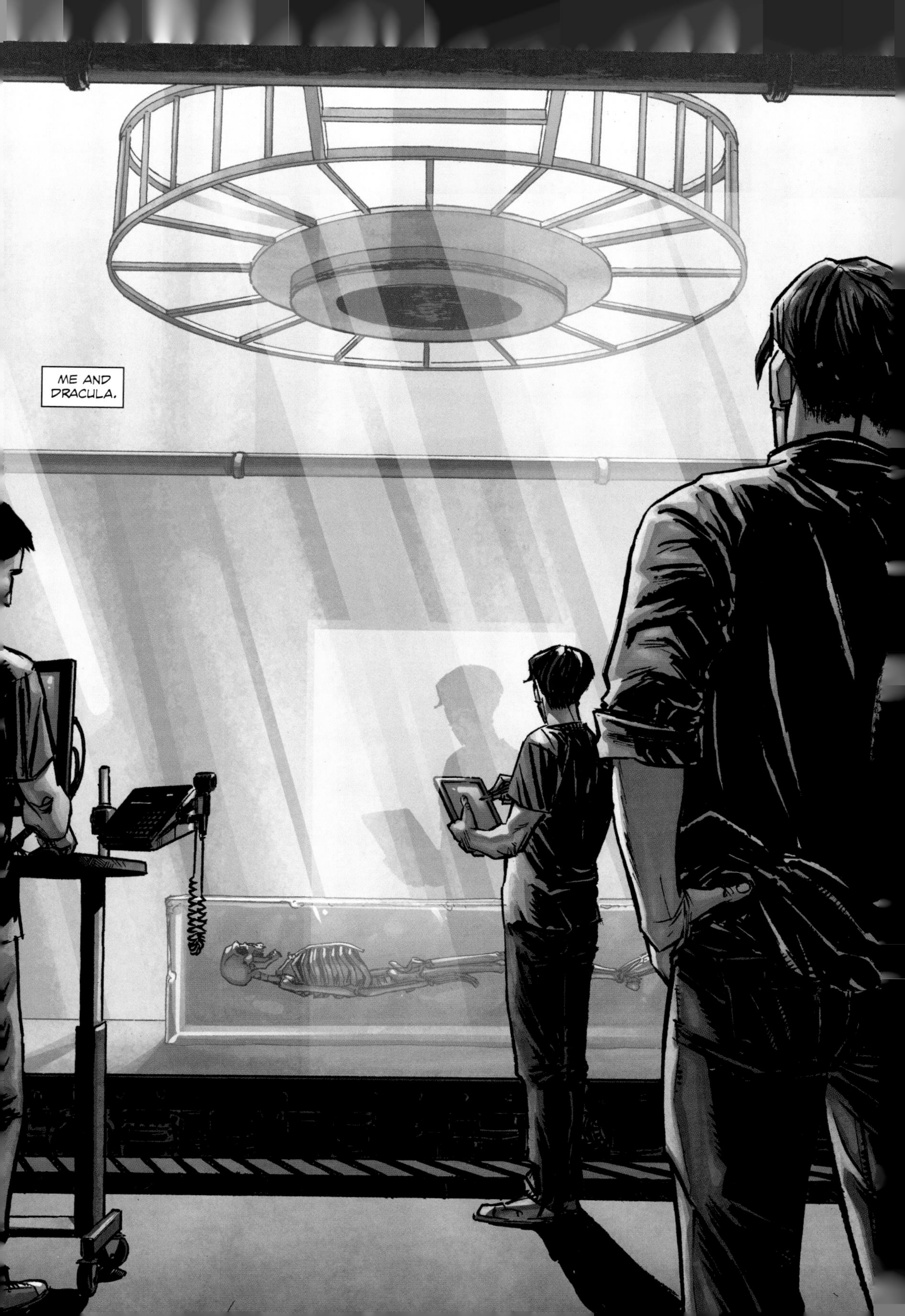
ME AND DRACULA.

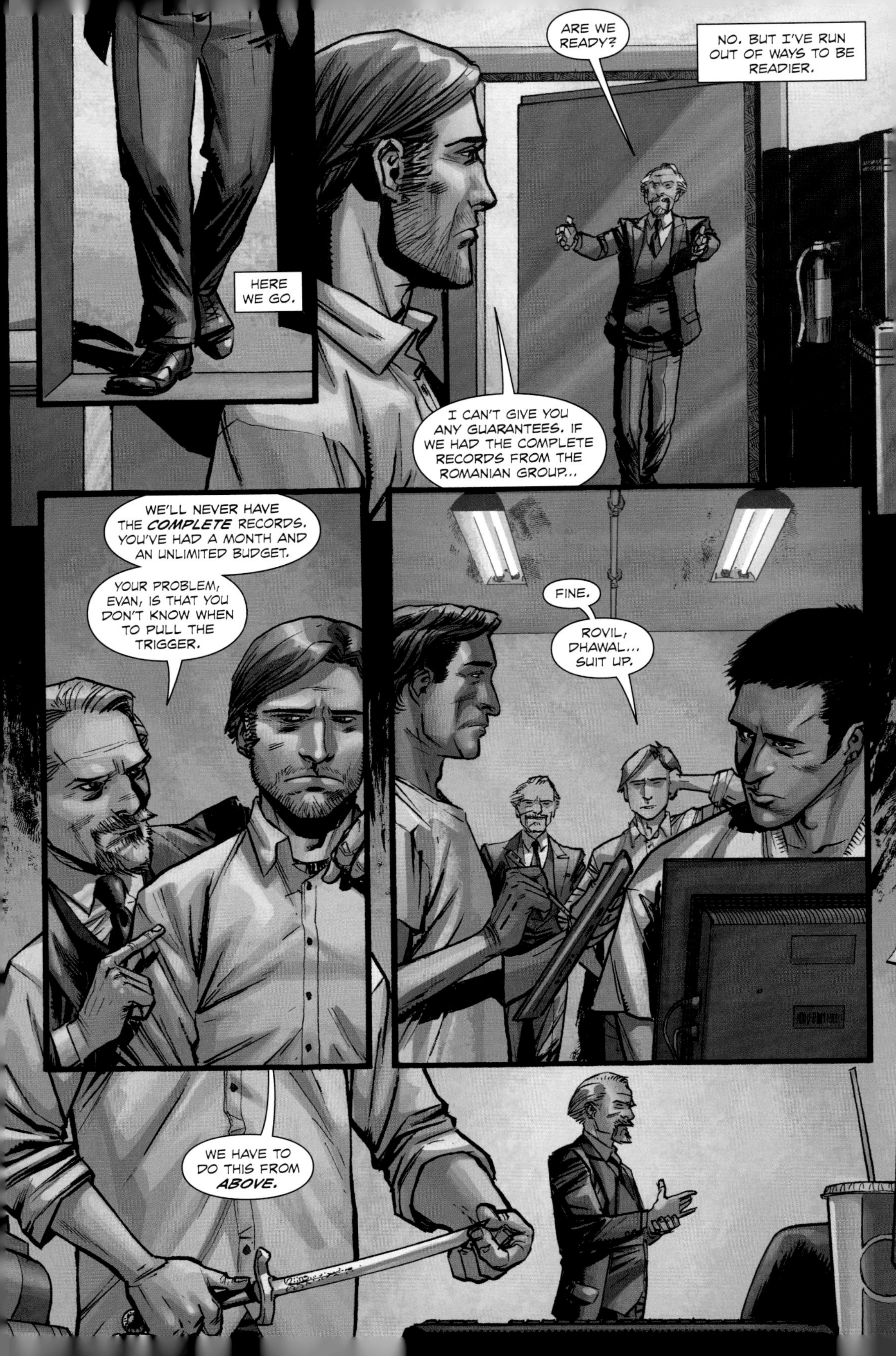
ARE WE READY?
NO. BUT I'VE RUN OUT OF WAYS TO BE READIER.
HERE WE GO.
I CAN'T GIVE YOU ANY GUARANTEES. IF WE HAD THE COMPLETE RECORDS FROM THE ROMANIAN GROUP...
WE'LL NEVER HAVE THE *COMPLETE* RECORDS. YOU'VE HAD A MONTH AND AN UNLIMITED BUDGET.
YOUR PROBLEM, EVAN, IS THAT YOU DON'T KNOW WHEN TO PULL THE TRIGGER.
FINE.
ROVIL, DHAWAL... SUIT UP.
WE HAVE TO DO THIS FROM ***ABOVE.***

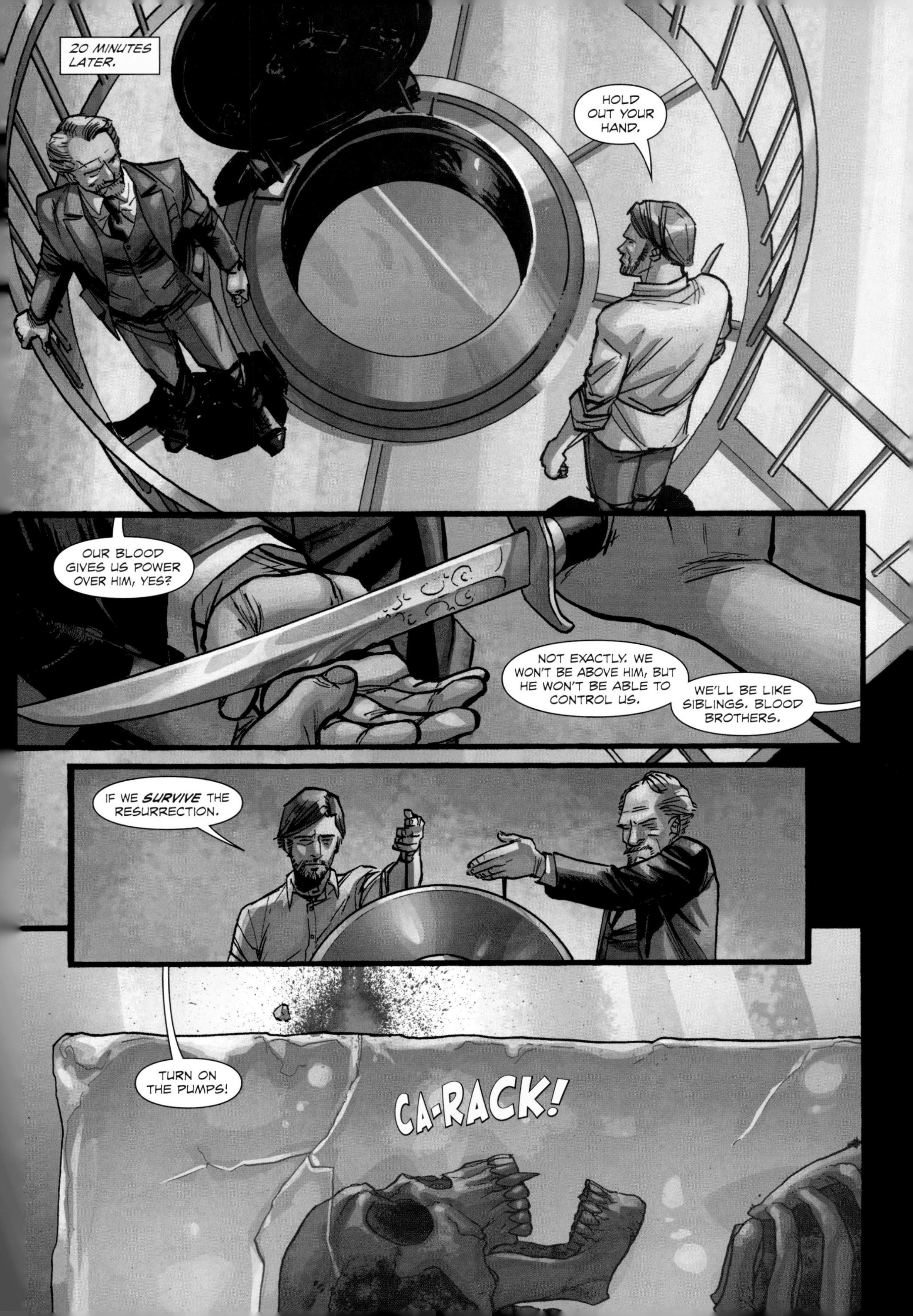
20 MINUTES LATER.
HOLD OUT YOUR HAND.
OUR BLOOD GIVES US POWER OVER HIM, YES?
NOT EXACTLY. WE WON'T BE ABOVE HIM, BUT HE WON'T BE ABLE TO CONTROL US.
WE'LL BE LIKE SIBLINGS. BLOOD BROTHERS.
IF WE *SURVIVE* THE RESURRECTION.
TURN ON THE PUMPS!
CA-RACK!

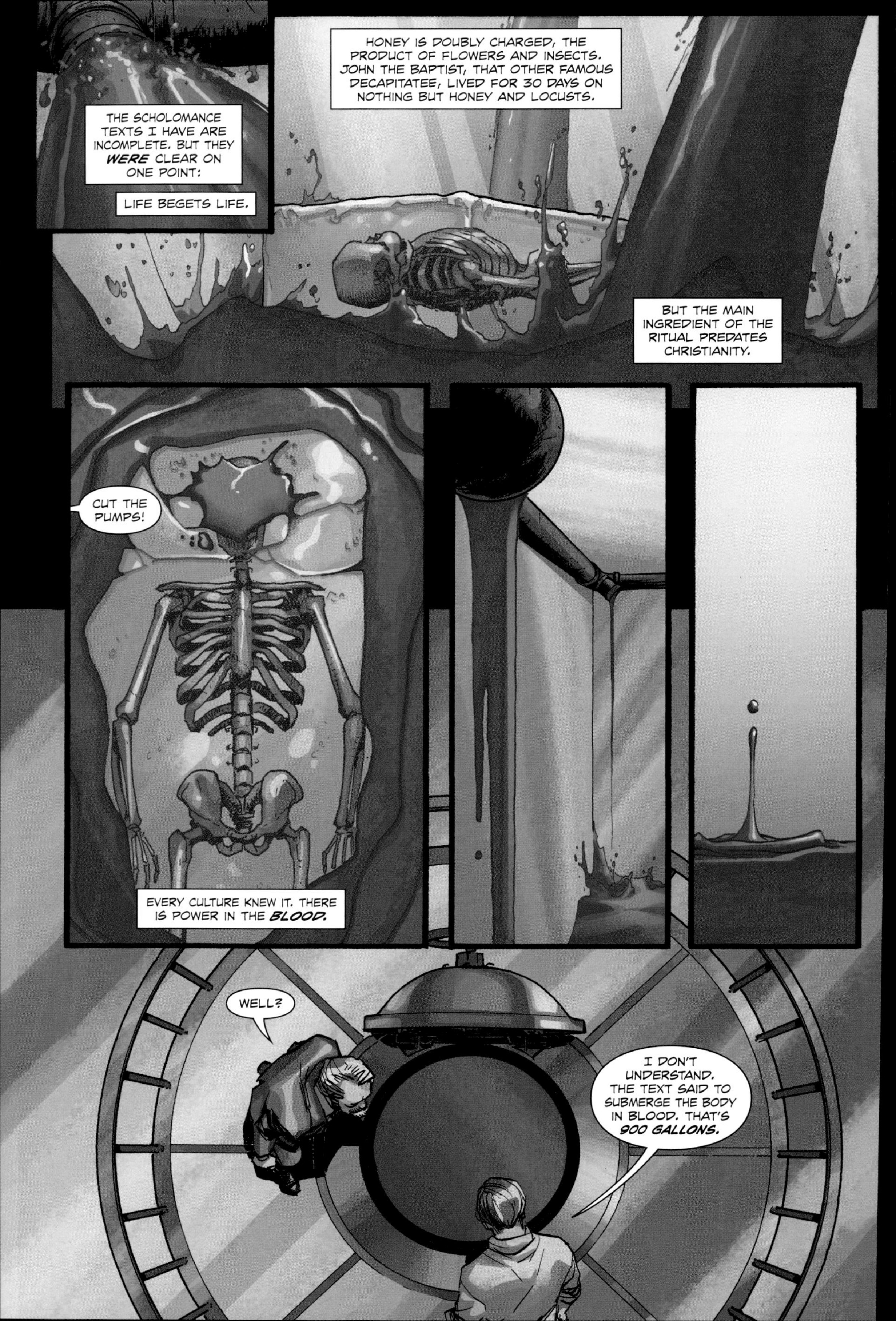
THE SCHOLOMANCE TEXTS I HAVE ARE INCOMPLETE. BUT THEY *WERE* CLEAR ON ONE POINT:
LIFE BEGETS LIFE.
HONEY IS DOUBLY CHARGED, THE PRODUCT OF FLOWERS AND INSECTS. JOHN THE BAPTIST, THAT OTHER FAMOUS DECAPITATEE, LIVED FOR 30 DAYS ON NOTHING BUT HONEY AND LOCUSTS.
BUT THE MAIN INGREDIENT OF THE RITUAL PREDATES CHRISTIANITY.
CUT THE PUMPS!
EVERY CULTURE KNEW IT. THERE IS POWER IN THE *BLOOD.*
WELL?
I DON'T UNDERSTAND. THE TEXT SAID TO SUBMERGE THE BODY IN BLOOD. THAT'S *900 GALLONS.*

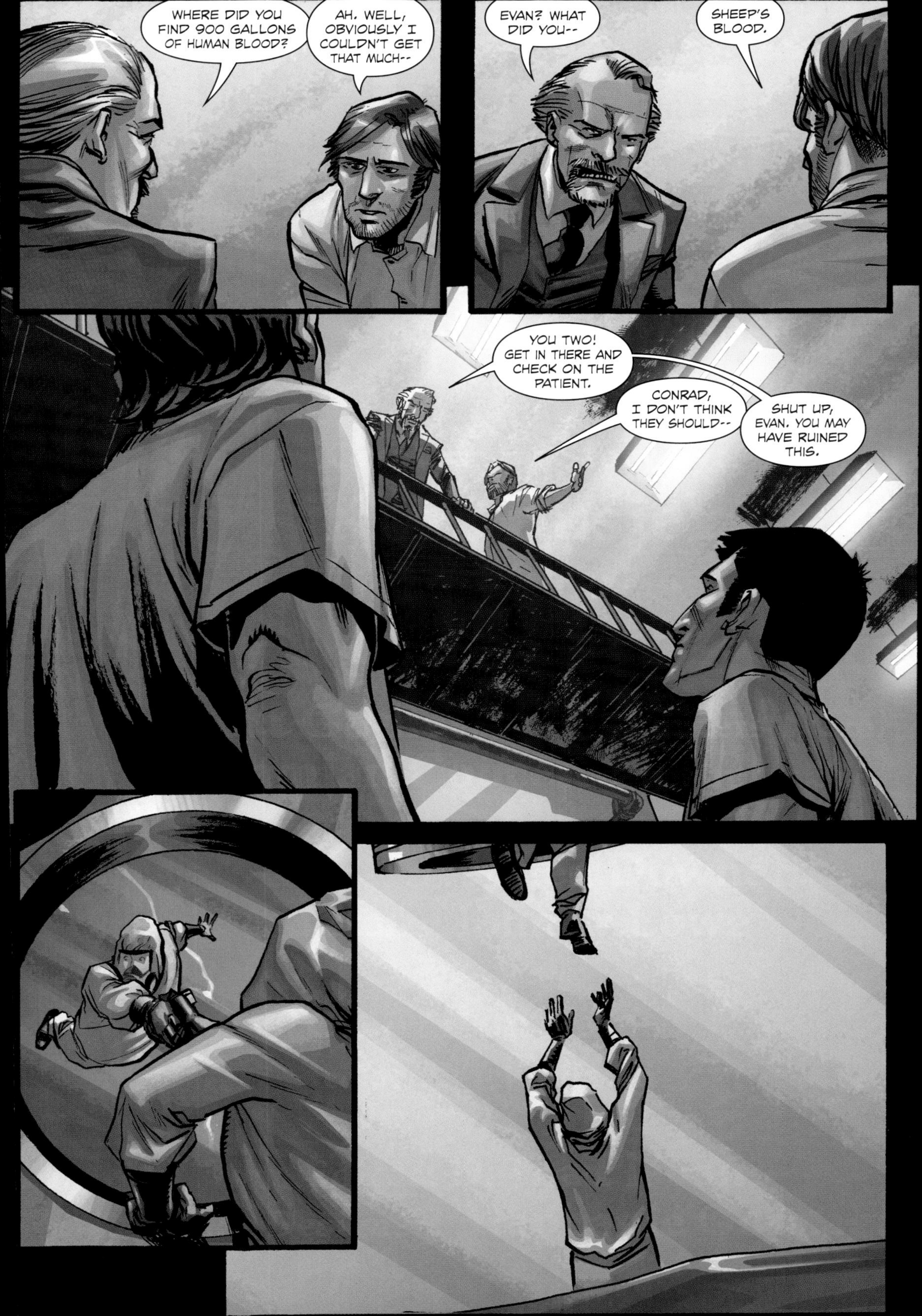
WHERE DID YOU FIND 900 GALLONS OF HUMAN BLOOD?
AH. WELL, OBVIOUSLY I COULDN'T GET THAT MUCH--
EVAN? WHAT DID YOU--
SHEEP'S BLOOD.
YOU TWO! GET IN THERE AND CHECK ON THE PATIENT.
CONRAD, I DON'T THINK THEY SHOULD--
SHUT UP, EVAN. YOU MAY HAVE RUINED THIS.

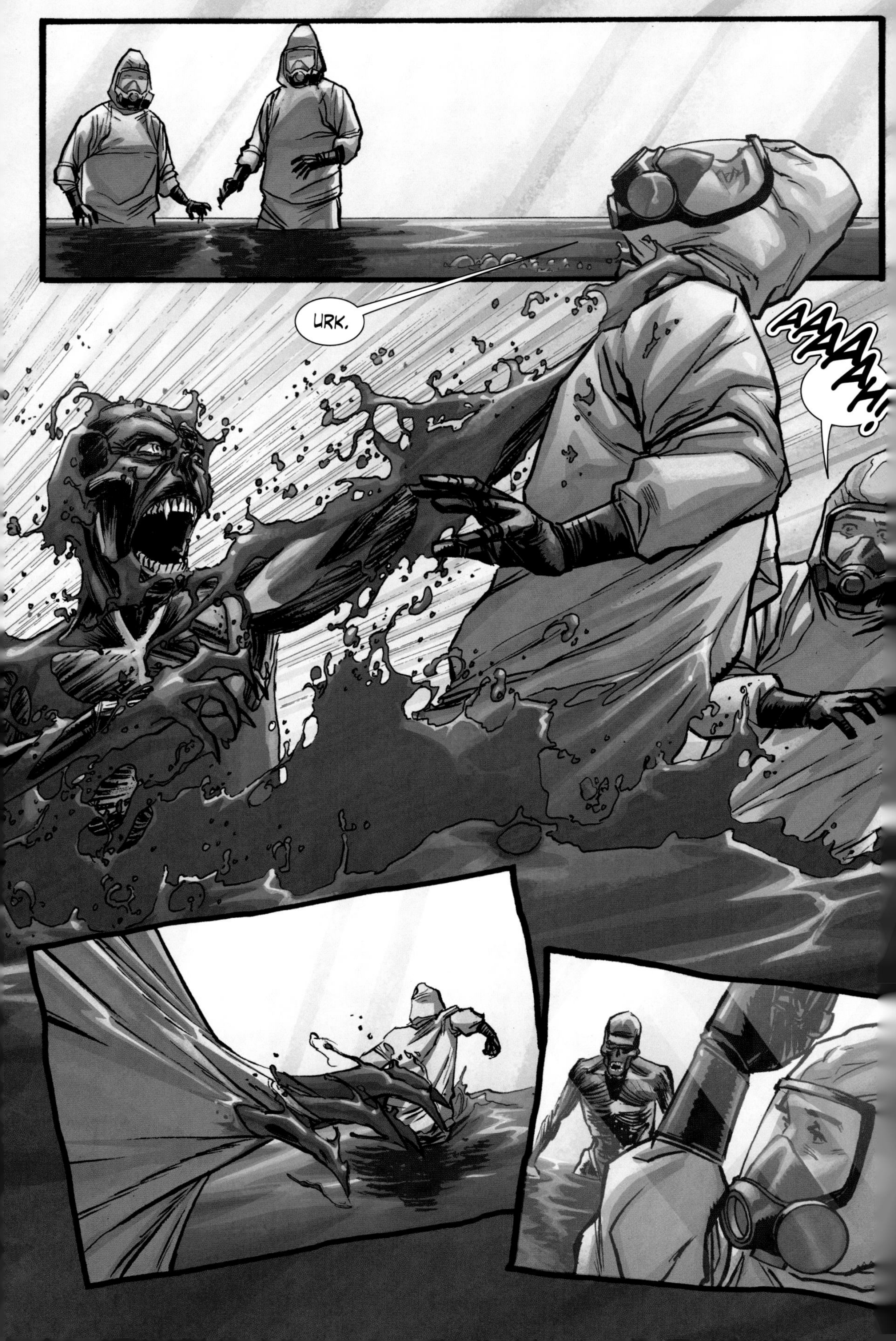

URK.
AAAAAH!

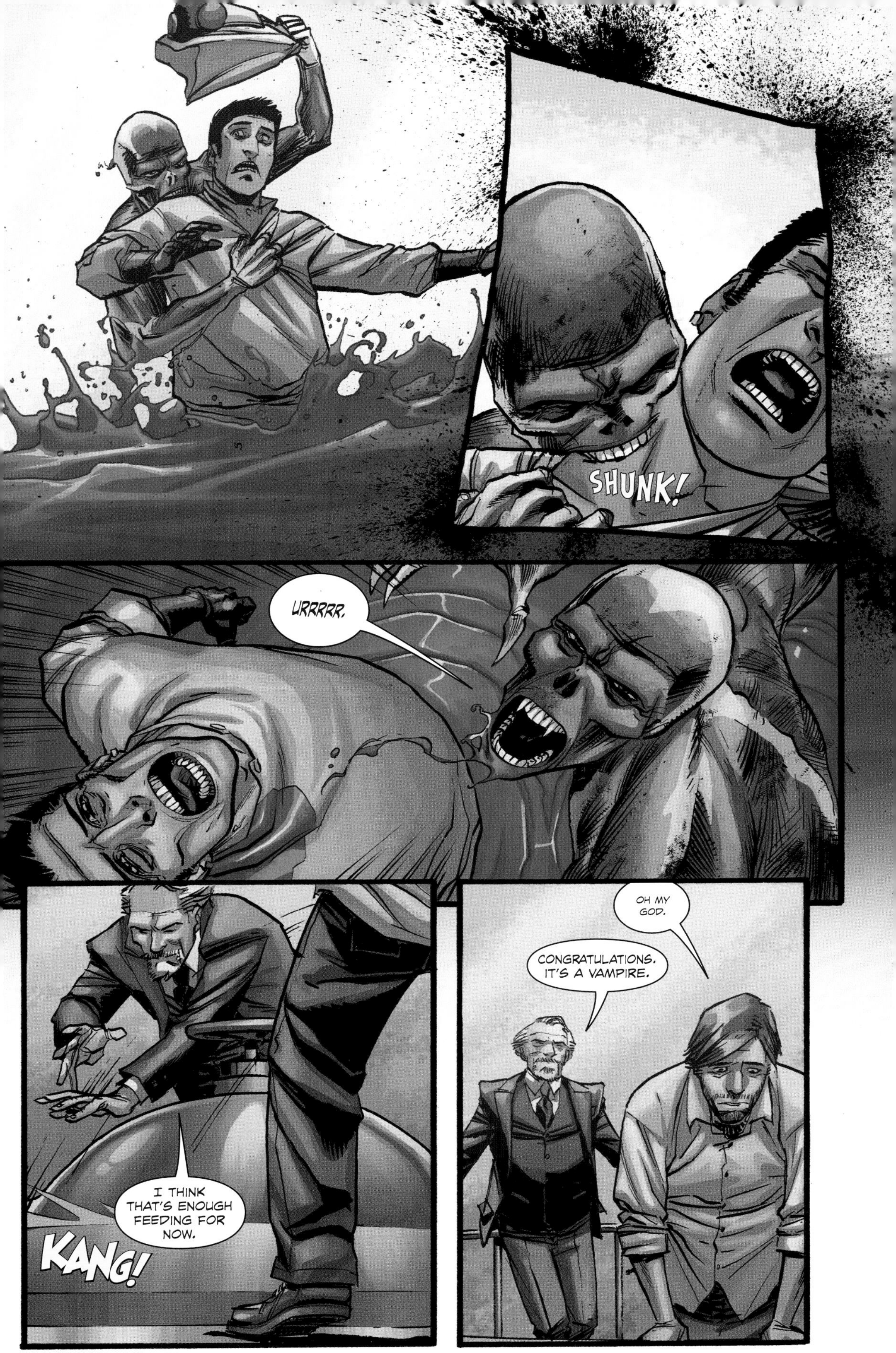
SHUNK!
URRRRR.
I THINK THAT'S ENOUGH FEEDING FOR NOW.
KANG!
OH MY GOD.
CONGRATULATIONS. IT'S A VAMPIRE.

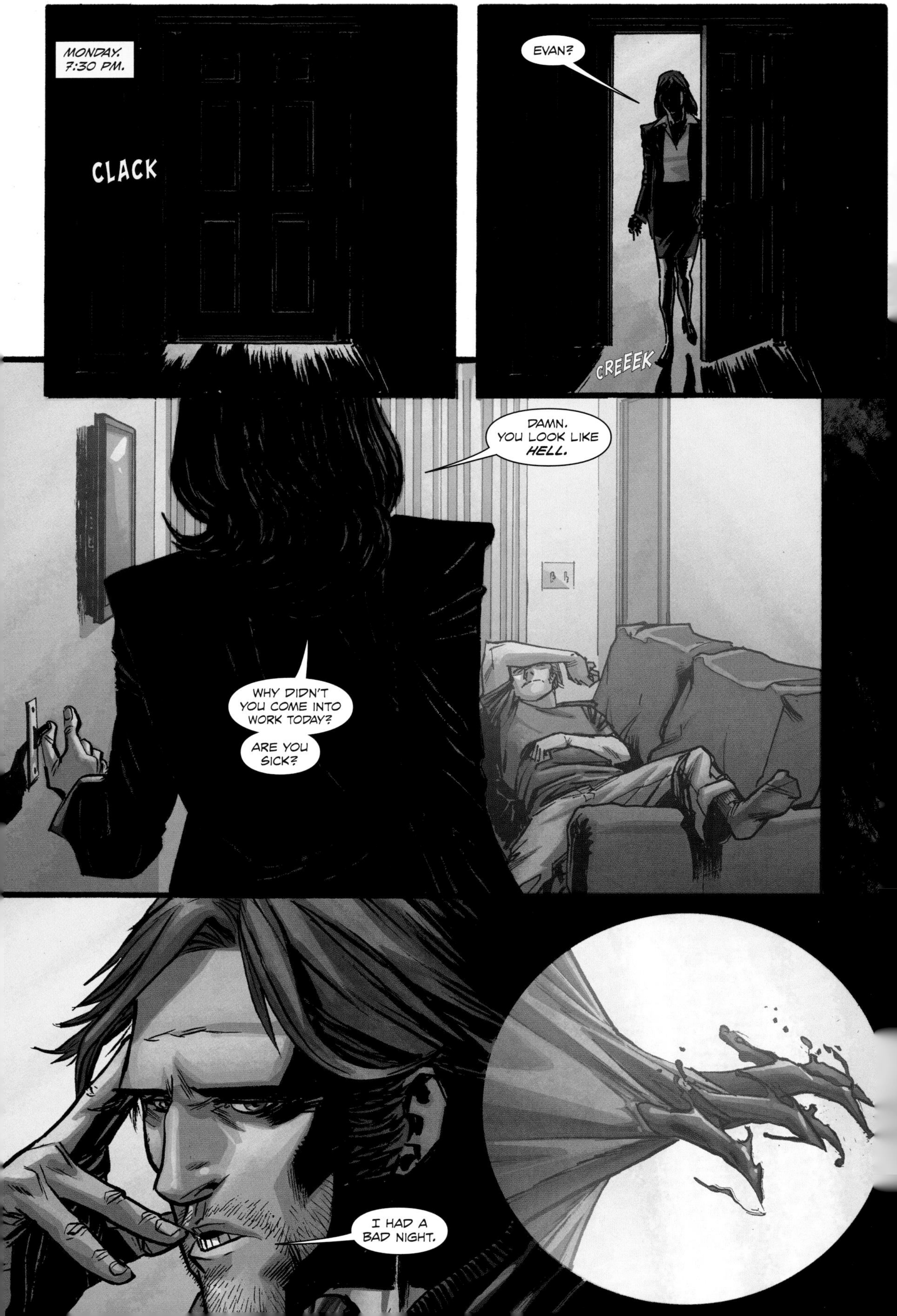
MONDAY.
7:30 PM.
CLACK
EVAN?
CREEEK
DAMN.
YOU LOOK LIKE
HELL.
WHY DIDN'T YOU COME INTO WORK TODAY?
ARE YOU SICK?
I HAD A BAD NIGHT.

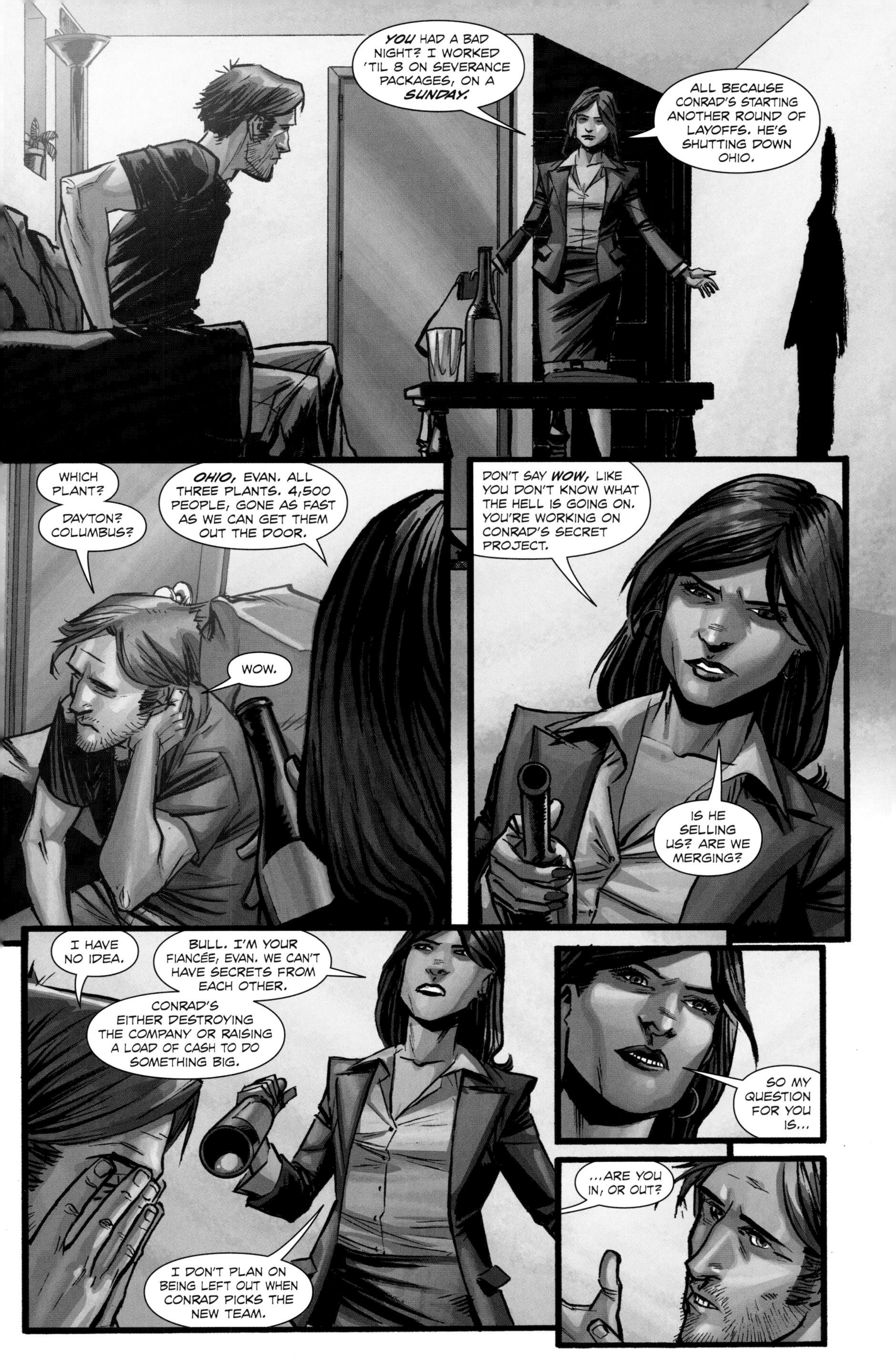
YOU HAD A BAD NIGHT? I WORKED 'TIL 8 ON SEVERANCE PACKAGES, ON A SUNDAY.
ALL BECAUSE CONRAD'S STARTING ANOTHER ROUND OF LAYOFFS. HE'S SHUTTING DOWN OHIO.
WHICH PLANT?
DAYTON? COLUMBUS?
OHIO, EVAN. ALL THREE PLANTS. 4,500 PEOPLE, GONE AS FAST AS WE CAN GET THEM OUT THE DOOR.
WOW.
DON'T SAY WOW, LIKE YOU DON'T KNOW WHAT THE HELL IS GOING ON. YOU'RE WORKING ON CONRAD'S SECRET PROJECT.
IS HE SELLING US? ARE WE MERGING?
I HAVE NO IDEA.
BULL. I'M YOUR FIANCÉE, EVAN. WE CAN'T HAVE SECRETS FROM EACH OTHER.
CONRAD'S EITHER DESTROYING THE COMPANY OR RAISING A LOAD OF CASH TO DO SOMETHING BIG.
I DON'T PLAN ON BEING LEFT OUT WHEN CONRAD PICKS THE NEW TEAM.
SO MY QUESTION FOR YOU IS...
...ARE YOU IN, OR OUT?

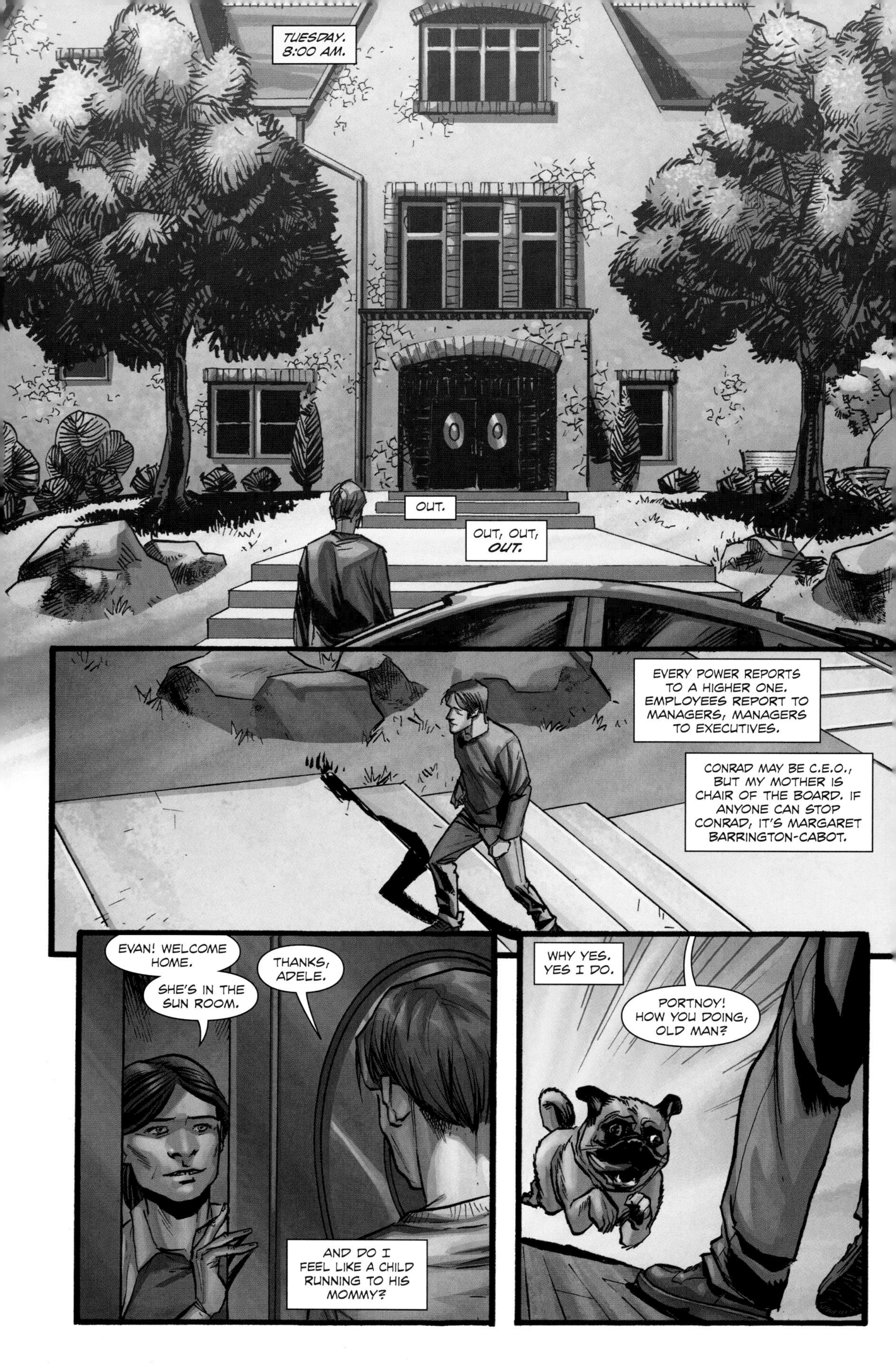
TUESDAY. 8:00 AM.
OUT.
OUT, OUT, OUT.
EVERY POWER REPORTS TO A HIGHER ONE. EMPLOYEES REPORT TO MANAGERS, MANAGERS TO EXECUTIVES.
CONRAD MAY BE C.E.O., BUT MY MOTHER IS CHAIR OF THE BOARD. IF ANYONE CAN STOP CONRAD, IT'S MARGARET BARRINGTON-CABOT.
EVAN! WELCOME HOME.
SHE'S IN THE SUN ROOM.
THANKS, ADELE.
AND DO I FEEL LIKE A CHILD RUNNING TO HIS MOMMY?
WHY YES. YES I DO.
PORTNOY! HOW YOU DOING, OLD MAN?

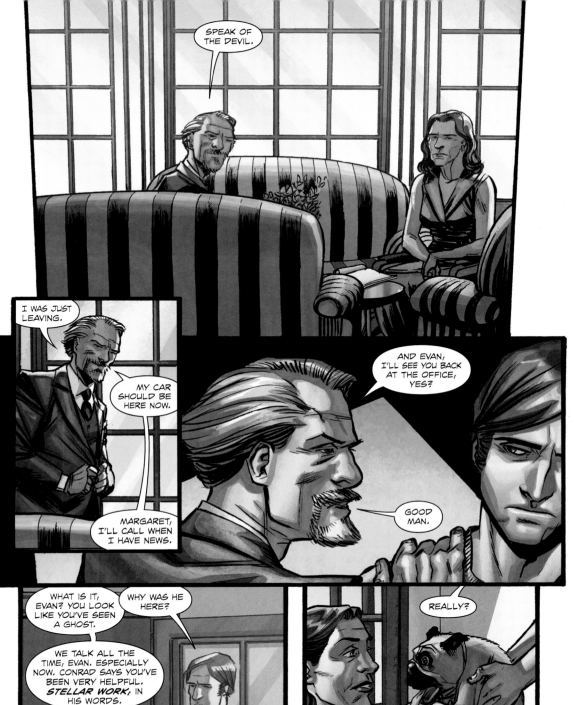

SPEAK OF THE DEVIL.

I WAS JUST LEAVING.

MY CAR SHOULD BE HERE NOW.

MARGARET, I'LL CALL WHEN I HAVE NEWS.

AND EVAN, I'LL SEE YOU BACK AT THE OFFICE, YES?

GOOD MAN.

WHAT IS IT, EVAN? YOU LOOK LIKE YOU'VE SEEN A GHOST.

WHY WAS HE HERE?

WE TALK ALL THE TIME, EVAN. ESPECIALLY NOW. CONRAD SAYS YOU'VE BEEN VERY HELPFUL. *STELLAR WORK*, IN HIS WORDS.

REALLY?

BUT...HE DIDN'T TELL YOU WHAT WE'RE WORKING ON?

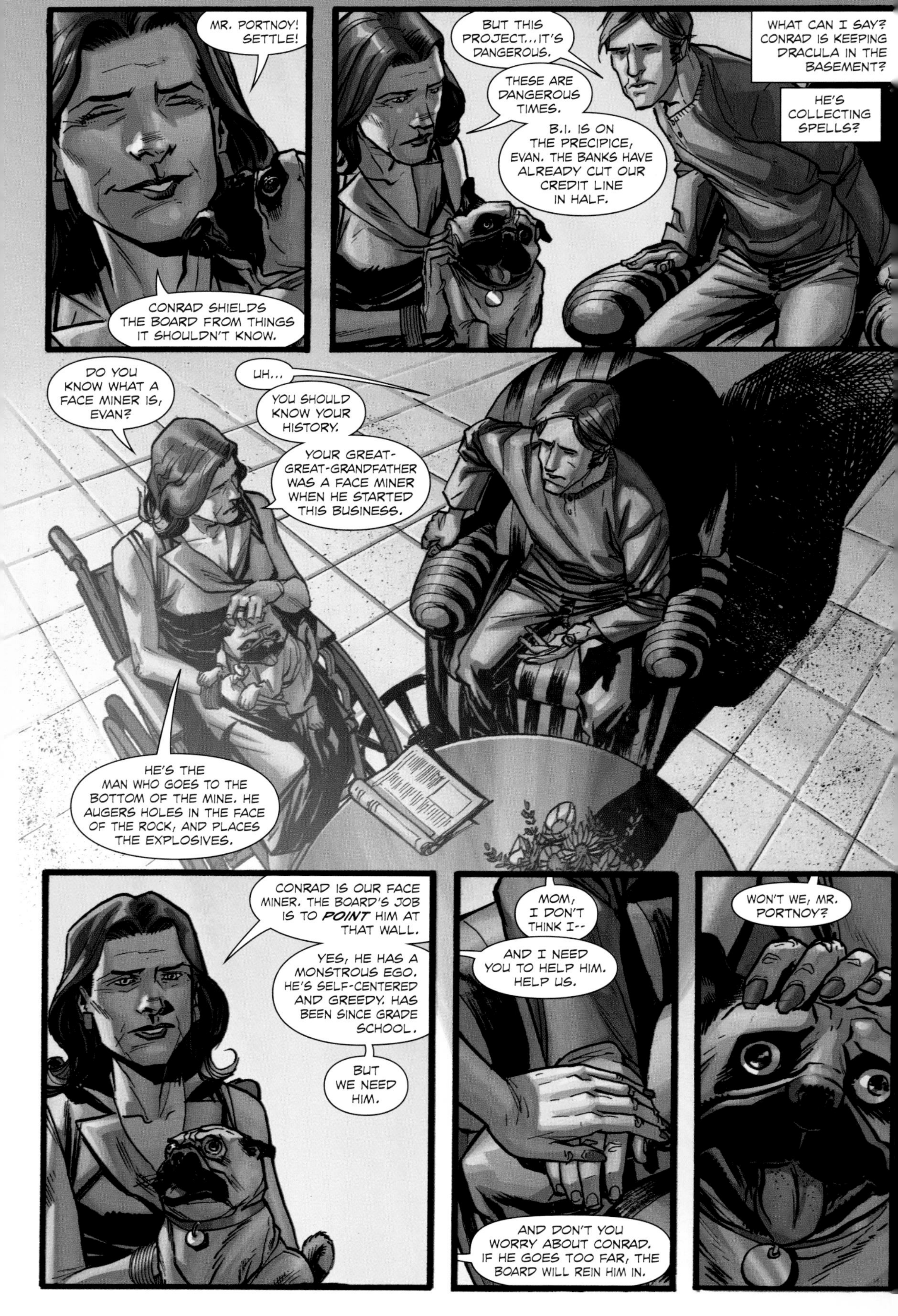
MR. PORTNOY! SETTLE!
CONRAD SHIELDS THE BOARD FROM THINGS IT SHOULDN'T KNOW.
BUT THIS PROJECT...IT'S DANGEROUS.
THESE ARE DANGEROUS TIMES.
B.I. IS ON THE PRECIPICE, EVAN. THE BANKS HAVE ALREADY CUT OUR CREDIT LINE IN HALF.
WHAT CAN I SAY? CONRAD IS KEEPING DRACULA IN THE BASEMENT?
HE'S COLLECTING SPELLS?
DO YOU KNOW WHAT A FACE MINER IS, EVAN?
UH...
YOU SHOULD KNOW YOUR HISTORY.
YOUR GREAT-GREAT-GRANDFATHER WAS A FACE MINER WHEN HE STARTED THIS BUSINESS.
HE'S THE MAN WHO GOES TO THE BOTTOM OF THE MINE. HE AUGERS HOLES IN THE FACE OF THE ROCK, AND PLACES THE EXPLOSIVES.
CONRAD IS OUR FACE MINER. THE BOARD'S JOB IS TO *POINT* HIM AT THAT WALL.
YES, HE HAS A MONSTROUS EGO. HE'S SELF-CENTERED AND GREEDY. HAS BEEN SINCE GRADE SCHOOL.
BUT WE NEED HIM.
MOM, I DON'T THINK I--
AND I NEED YOU TO HELP HIM. HELP US.
AND DON'T YOU WORRY ABOUT CONRAD. IF HE GOES TOO FAR, THE BOARD WILL REIN HIM IN.
WON'T WE, MR. PORTNOY?

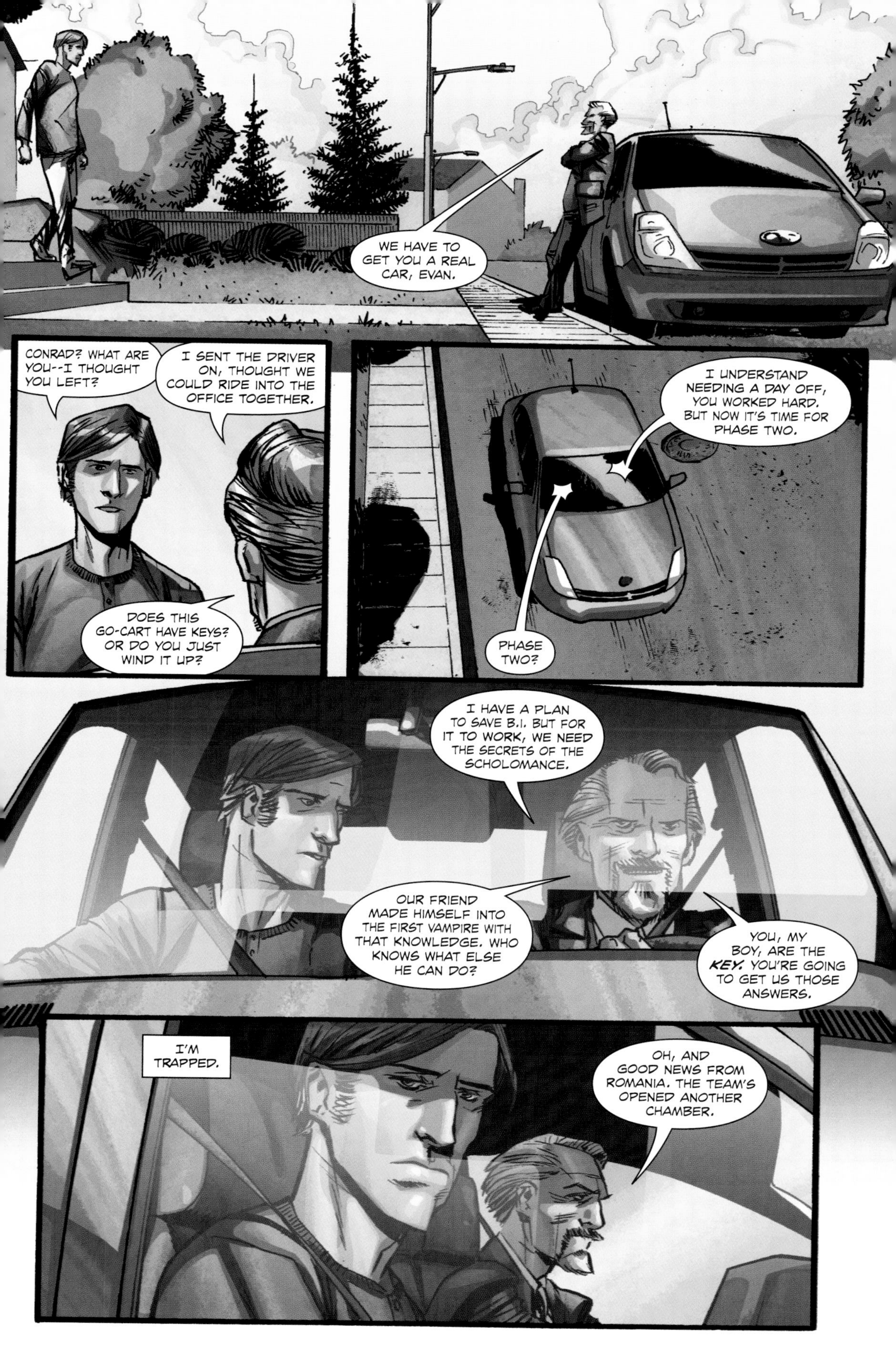
WE HAVE TO GET YOU A REAL CAR, EVAN.
CONRAD? WHAT ARE YOU--I THOUGHT YOU LEFT?
I SENT THE DRIVER ON, THOUGHT WE COULD RIDE INTO THE OFFICE TOGETHER.
DOES THIS GO-CART HAVE KEYS? OR DO YOU JUST WIND IT UP?
I UNDERSTAND NEEDING A DAY OFF, YOU WORKED HARD. BUT NOW IT'S TIME FOR PHASE TWO.
PHASE TWO?
I HAVE A PLAN TO SAVE B.I. BUT FOR IT TO WORK, WE NEED THE SECRETS OF THE SCHOLOMANCE.
OUR FRIEND MADE HIMSELF INTO THE FIRST VAMPIRE WITH THAT KNOWLEDGE. WHO KNOWS WHAT ELSE HE CAN DO?
YOU, MY BOY, ARE THE ***KEY.*** YOU'RE GOING TO GET US THOSE ANSWERS.
I'M TRAPPED.
OH, AND GOOD NEWS FROM ROMANIA. THE TEAM'S OPENED ANOTHER CHAMBER.

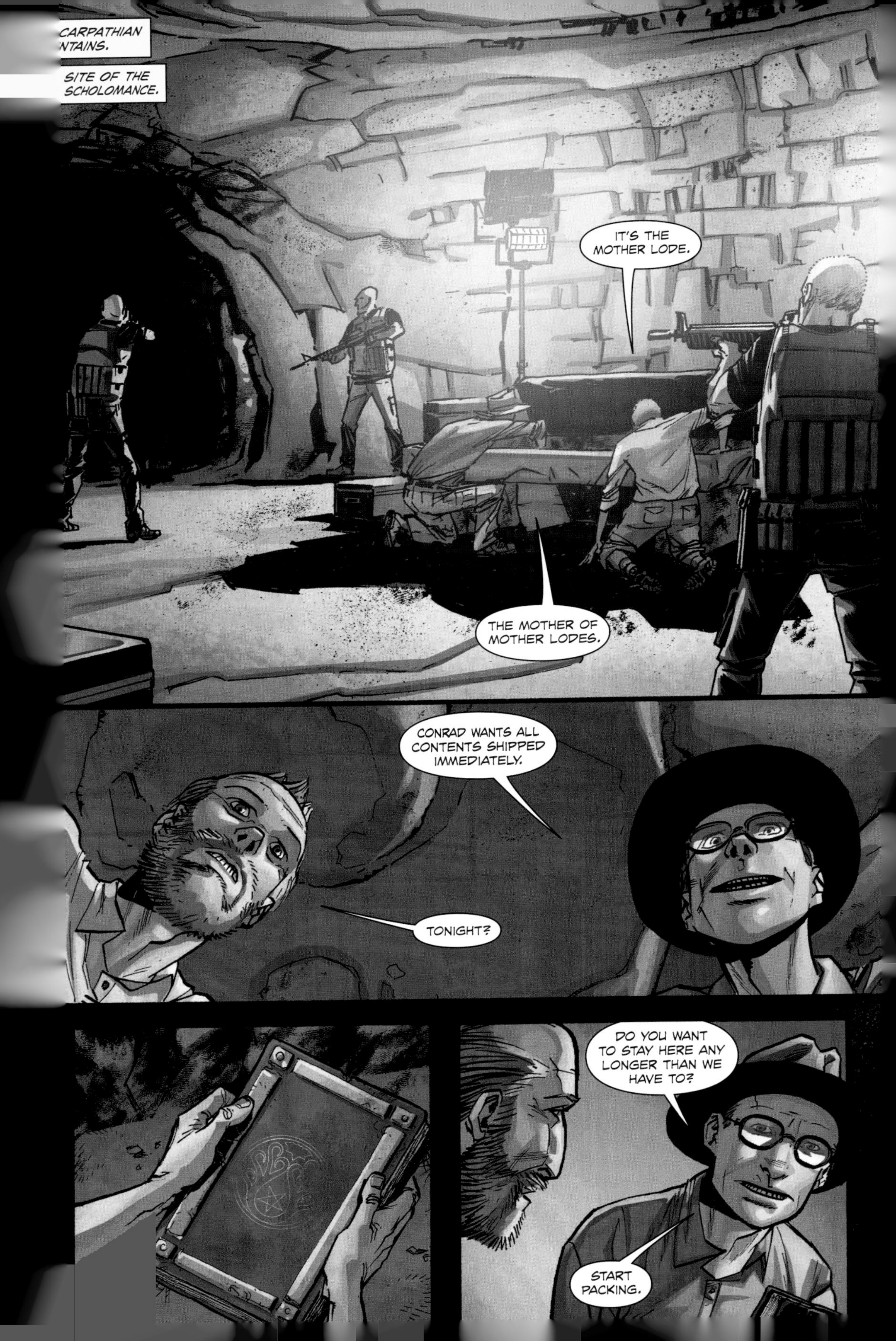
CARPATHIAN
NTAINS.
SITE OF THE SCHOLOMANCE.
IT'S THE MOTHER LODE.
THE MOTHER OF MOTHER LODES.
CONRAD WANTS ALL CONTENTS SHIPPED IMMEDIATELY.
TONIGHT?
DO YOU WANT TO STAY HERE ANY LONGER THAN WE HAVE TO?
START PACKING.

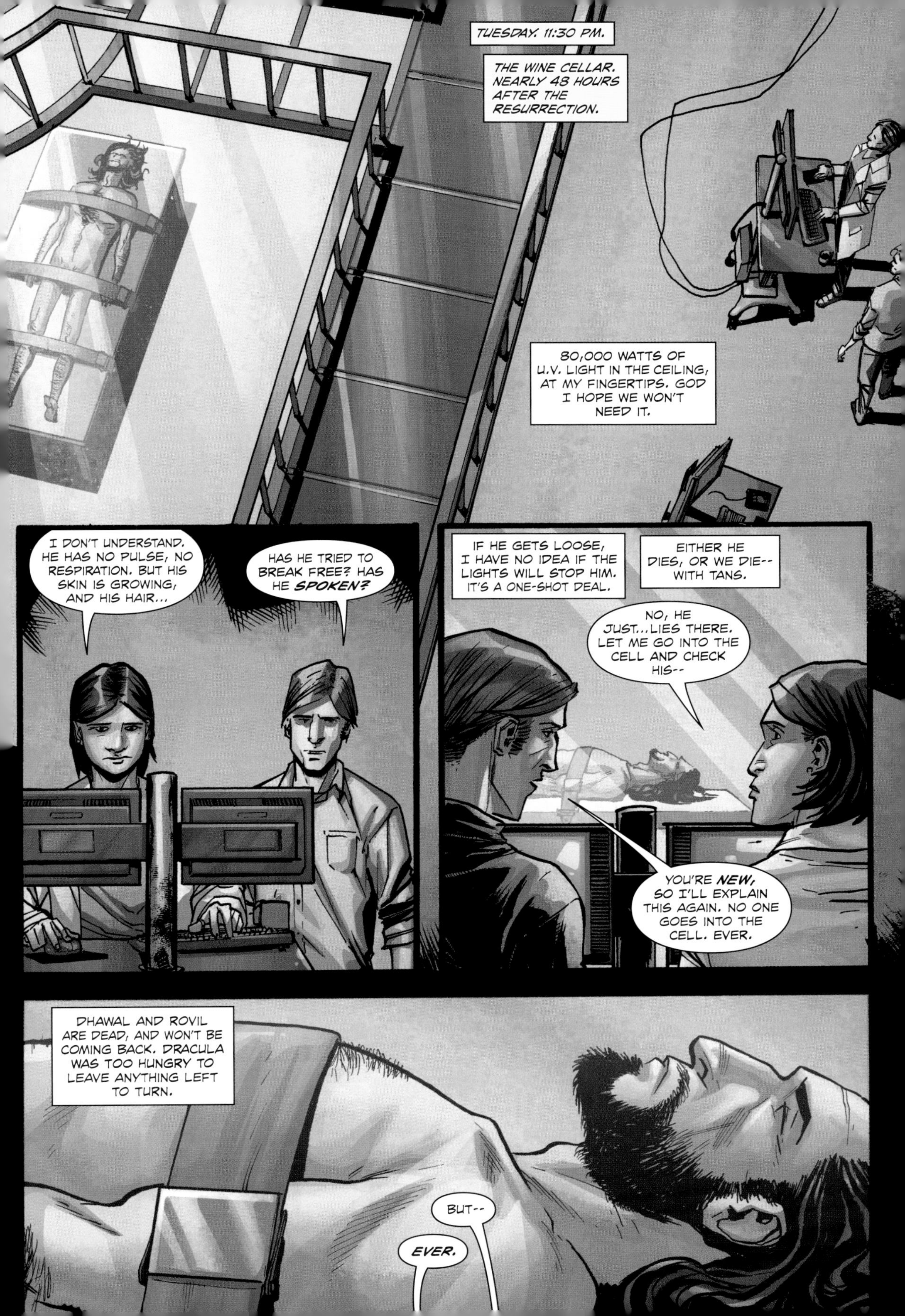
TUESDAY. 11:30 PM.
THE WINE CELLAR. NEARLY 48 HOURS AFTER THE RESURRECTION.
80,000 WATTS OF U.V. LIGHT IN THE CEILING, AT MY FINGERTIPS. GOD I HOPE WE WON'T NEED IT.
I DON'T UNDERSTAND. HE HAS NO PULSE, NO RESPIRATION. BUT HIS SKIN IS GROWING, AND HIS HAIR...
HAS HE TRIED TO BREAK FREE? HAS HE *SPOKEN?*
IF HE GETS LOOSE, I HAVE NO IDEA IF THE LIGHTS WILL STOP HIM. IT'S A ONE-SHOT DEAL.
EITHER HE DIES, OR WE DIE-- WITH TANS.
NO, HE JUST...LIES THERE. LET ME GO INTO THE CELL AND CHECK HIS--
YOU'RE *NEW,* SO I'LL EXPLAIN THIS AGAIN. NO ONE GOES INTO THE CELL. EVER.
DHAWAL AND ROVIL ARE DEAD, AND WON'T BE COMING BACK. DRACULA WAS TOO HUNGRY TO LEAVE ANYTHING LEFT TO TURN.
BUT--
EVER.

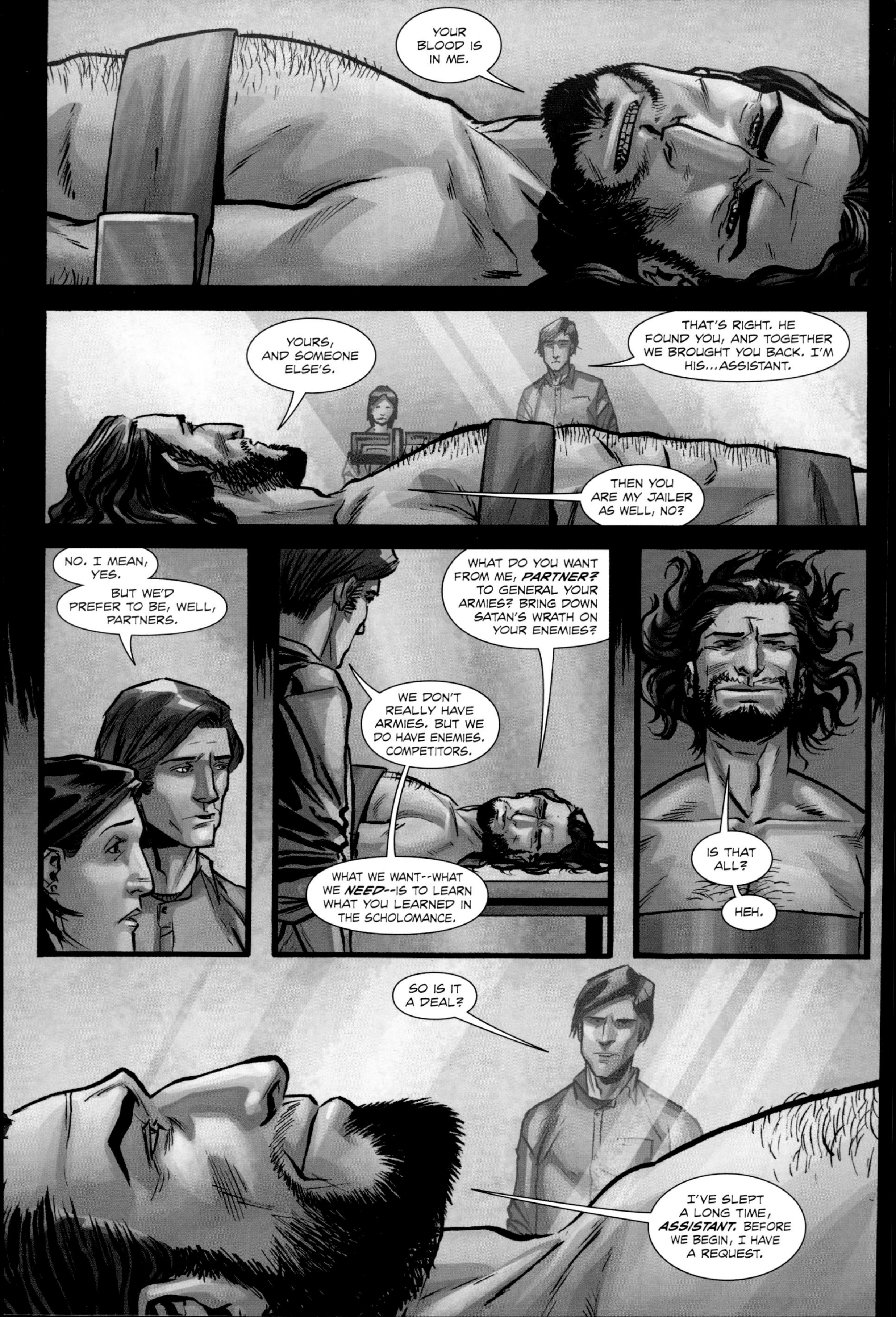
YOUR BLOOD IS IN ME.
YOURS, AND SOMEONE ELSE'S.
THAT'S RIGHT. HE FOUND YOU, AND TOGETHER WE BROUGHT YOU BACK. I'M HIS...ASSISTANT.
THEN YOU ARE MY JAILER AS WELL, NO?
NO. I MEAN, YES.
BUT WE'D PREFER TO BE, WELL, PARTNERS.
WHAT DO YOU WANT FROM ME, ***PARTNER?*** TO GENERAL YOUR ARMIES? BRING DOWN SATAN'S WRATH ON YOUR ENEMIES?
WE DON'T REALLY HAVE ARMIES. BUT WE DO HAVE ENEMIES. COMPETITORS.
WHAT WE WANT--WHAT WE ***NEED***--IS TO LEARN WHAT YOU LEARNED IN THE SCHOLOMANCE.
IS THAT ALL?
HEH.
SO IS IT A DEAL?
I'VE SLEPT A LONG TIME, ***ASSISTANT.*** BEFORE WE BEGIN, I HAVE A REQUEST.

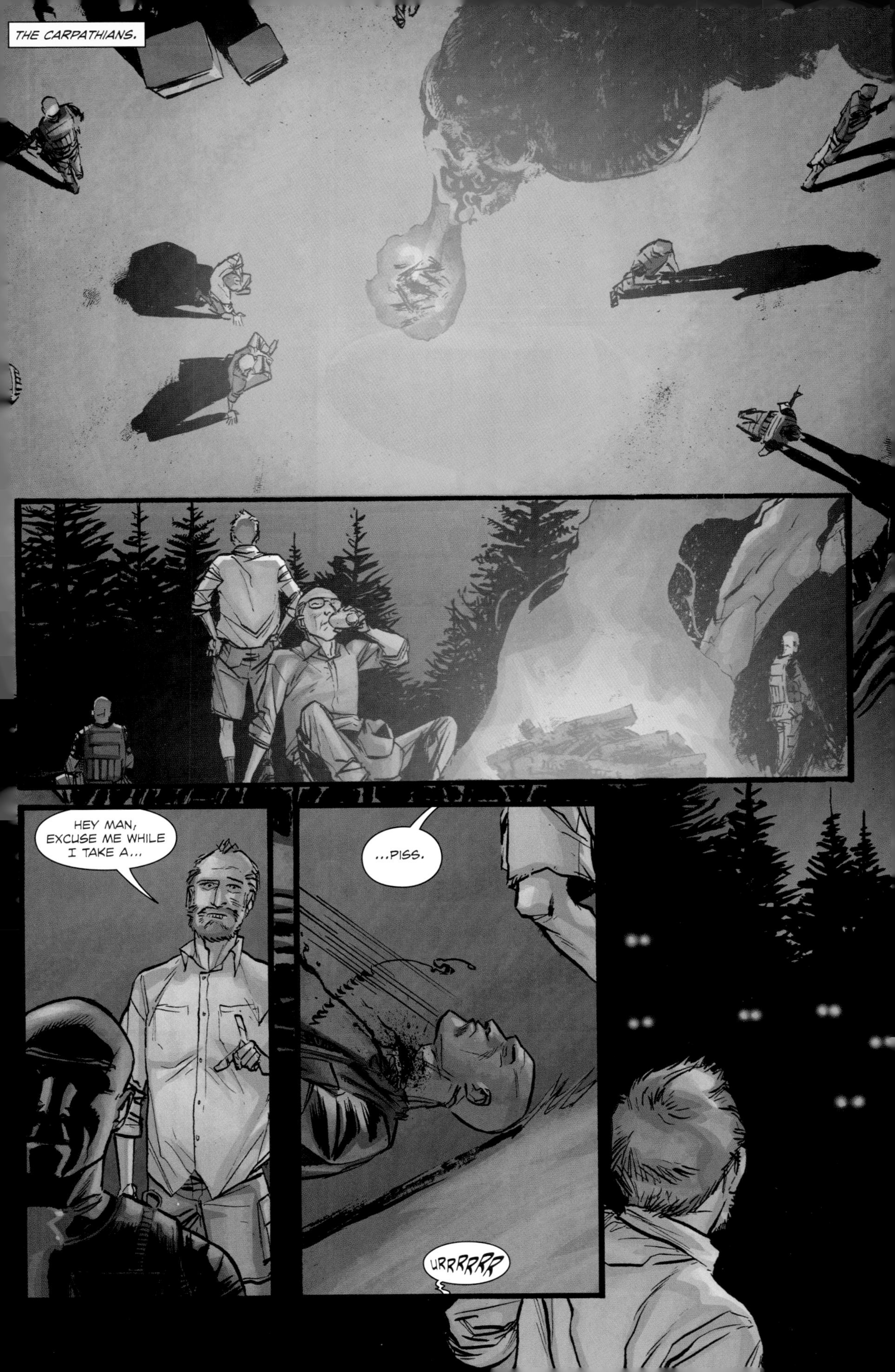
THE CARPATHIANS.
HEY MAN, EXCUSE ME WHILE I TAKE A...
...PISS.
URRRRRR

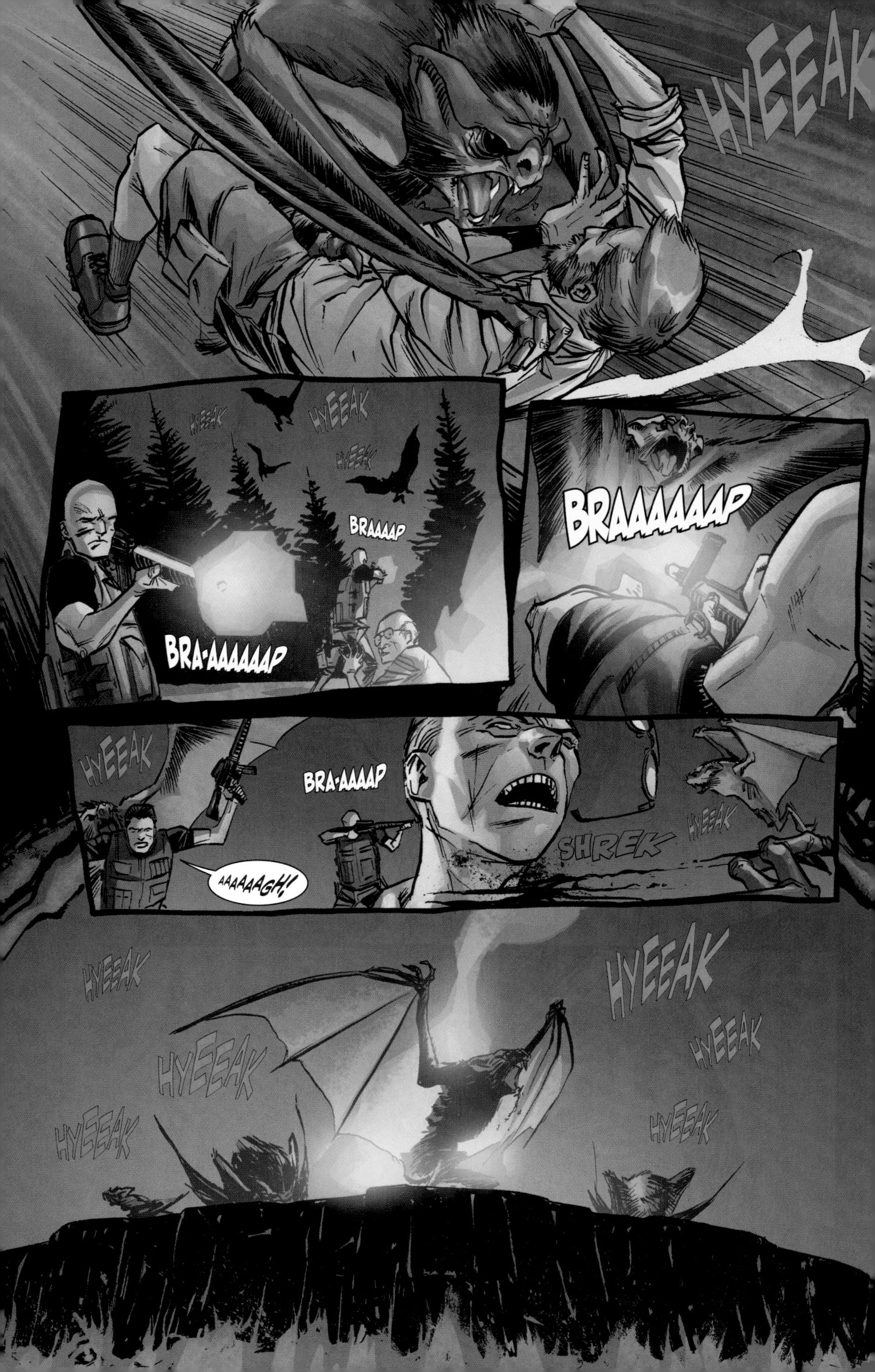
HYEEAK
HYEEAK
HYEEAK
HYEEAK
BRAAAAP
BRA-AAAAAAP
BRAAAAAAAP
HYEEAK
BRA-AAAAP
AAAAAAGH!
SHREK
HYEEAK
HYEEAK
HYEEAK
HYEEAK
HYEEAK
HYEEAK
HYEEAK

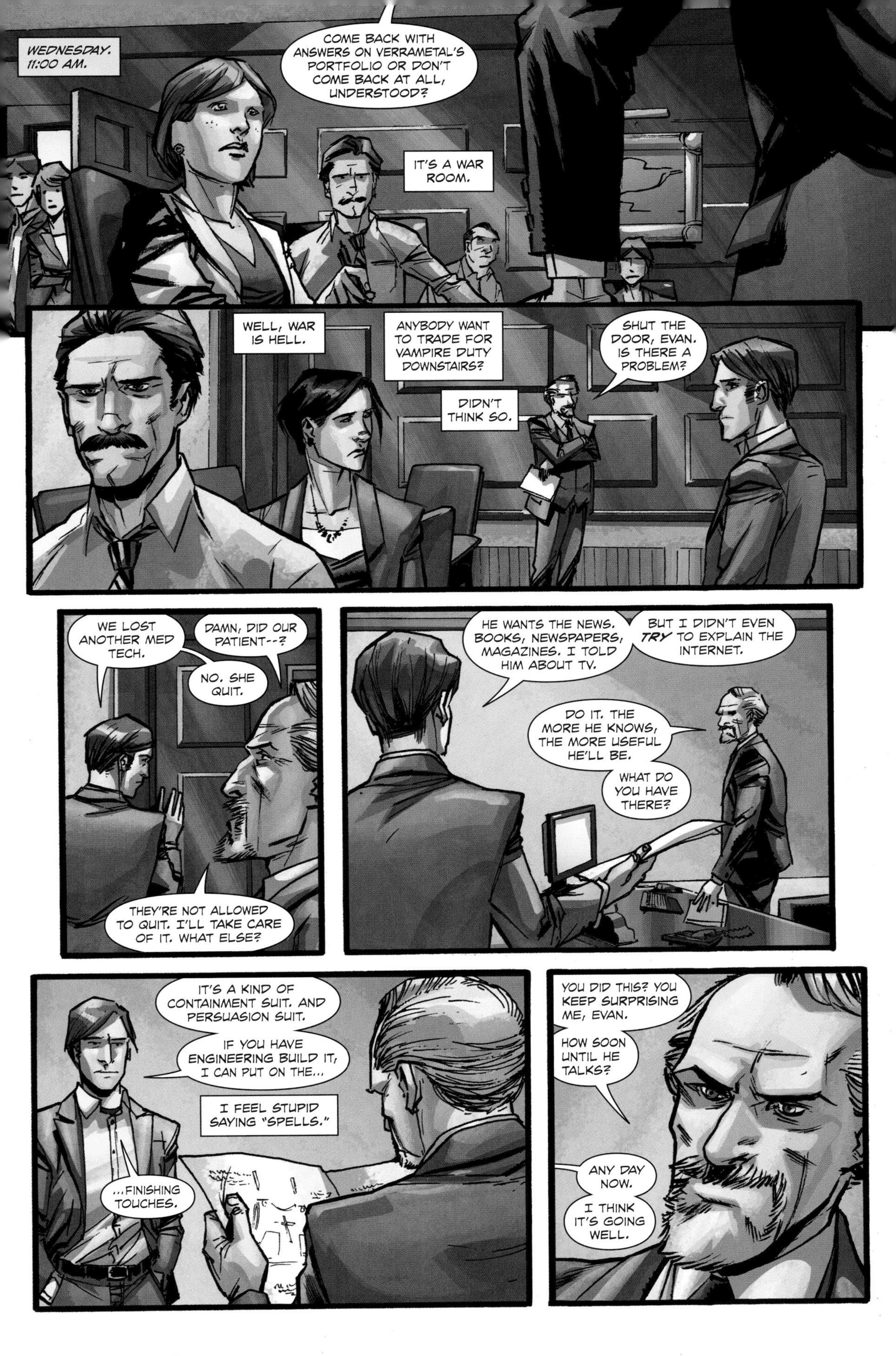
WEDNESDAY. 11:00 AM.
COME BACK WITH ANSWERS ON VERRAMETAL'S PORTFOLIO OR DON'T COME BACK AT ALL, UNDERSTOOD?
IT'S A WAR ROOM.
WELL, WAR IS HELL.
ANYBODY WANT TO TRADE FOR VAMPIRE DUTY DOWNSTAIRS?
DIDN'T THINK SO.
SHUT THE DOOR, EVAN. IS THERE A PROBLEM?
WE LOST ANOTHER MED TECH.
DAMN, DID OUR PATIENT--?
NO. SHE QUIT.
THEY'RE NOT ALLOWED TO QUIT. I'LL TAKE CARE OF IT. WHAT ELSE?
HE WANTS THE NEWS. BOOKS, NEWSPAPERS, MAGAZINES. I TOLD HIM ABOUT TV.
BUT I DIDN'T EVEN *TRY* TO EXPLAIN THE INTERNET.
DO IT. THE MORE HE KNOWS, THE MORE USEFUL HE'LL BE.
WHAT DO YOU HAVE THERE?
IT'S A KIND OF CONTAINMENT SUIT. AND PERSUASION SUIT.
IF YOU HAVE ENGINEERING BUILD IT, I CAN PUT ON THE...
I FEEL STUPID SAYING "SPELLS."
...FINISHING TOUCHES.
YOU DID THIS? YOU KEEP SURPRISING ME, EVAN.
HOW SOON UNTIL HE TALKS?
ANY DAY NOW.
I THINK IT'S GOING WELL.

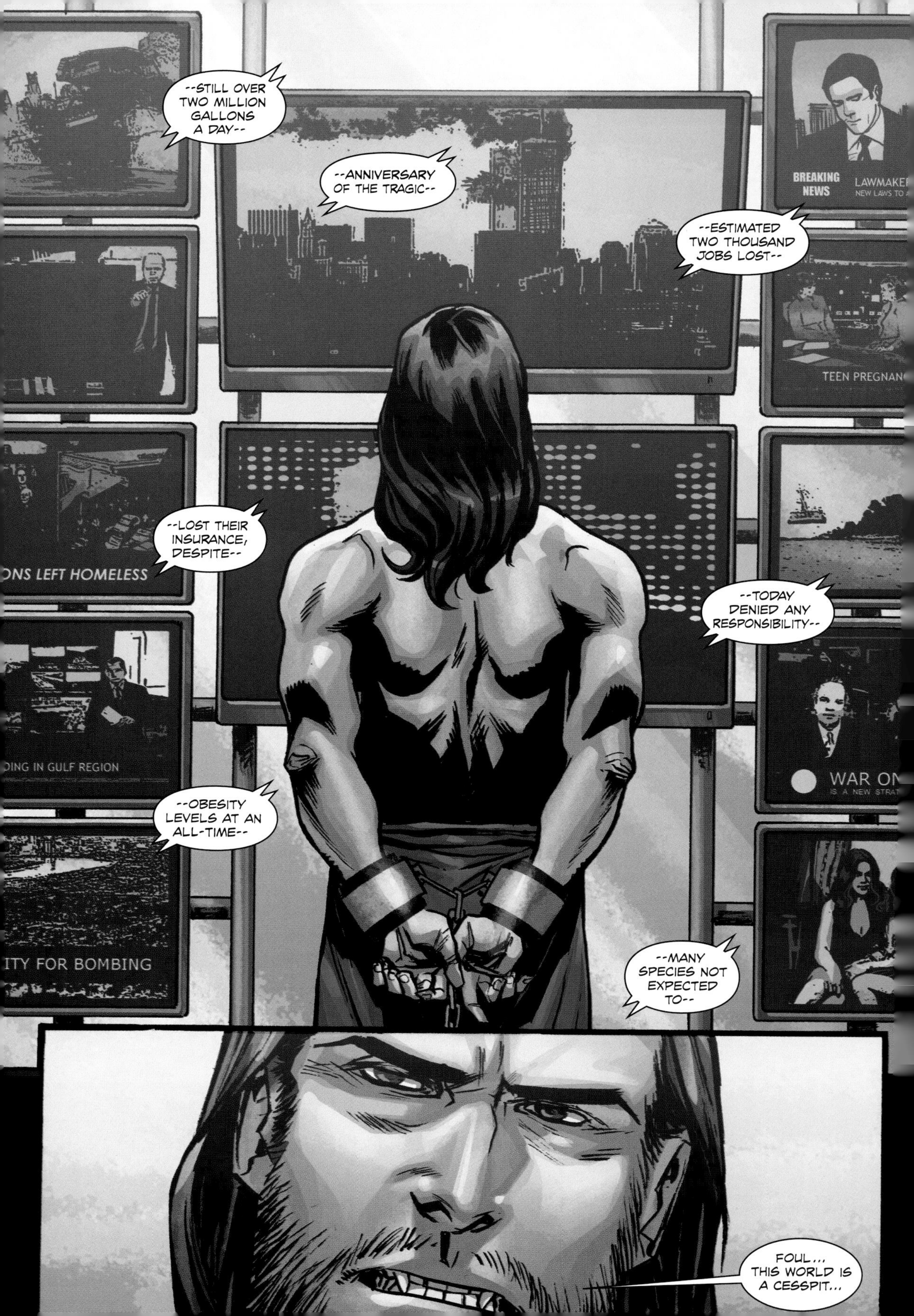
--STILL OVER TWO MILLION GALLONS A DAY--
--ANNIVERSARY OF THE TRAGIC--
BREAKING NEWS
LAWMAKER
NEW LAWS TO A
--ESTIMATED TWO THOUSAND JOBS LOST--
TEEN PREGNANC
--LOST THEIR INSURANCE, DESPITE--
ONS LEFT HOMELESS
--TODAY DENIED ANY RESPONSIBILITY--
DING IN GULF REGION
WAR ON
IS A NEW STRAT
--OBESITY LEVELS AT AN ALL-TIME--
ITY FOR BOMBING
--MANY SPECIES NOT EXPECTED TO--
FOUL... THIS WORLD IS A CESSPIT...

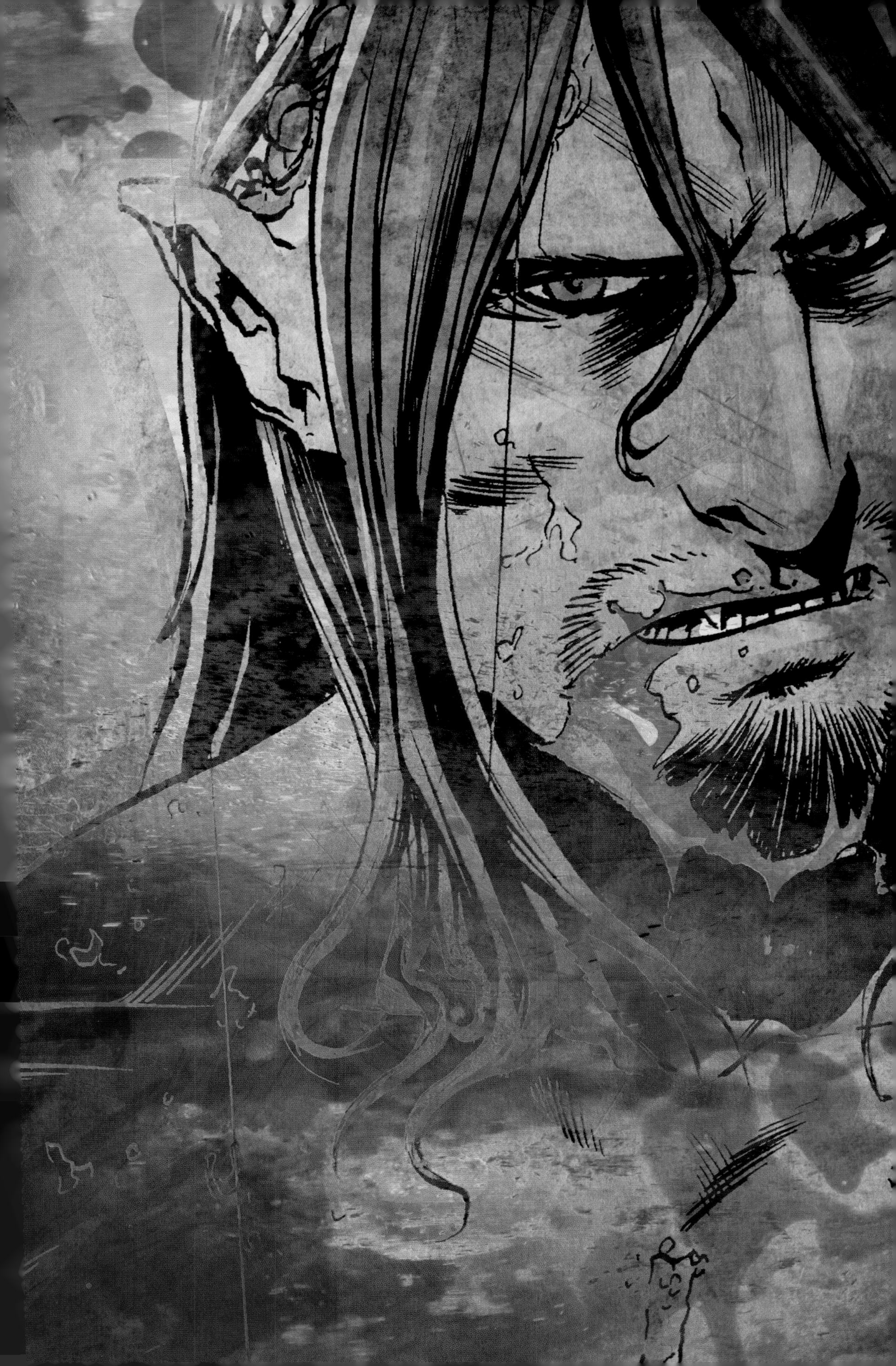

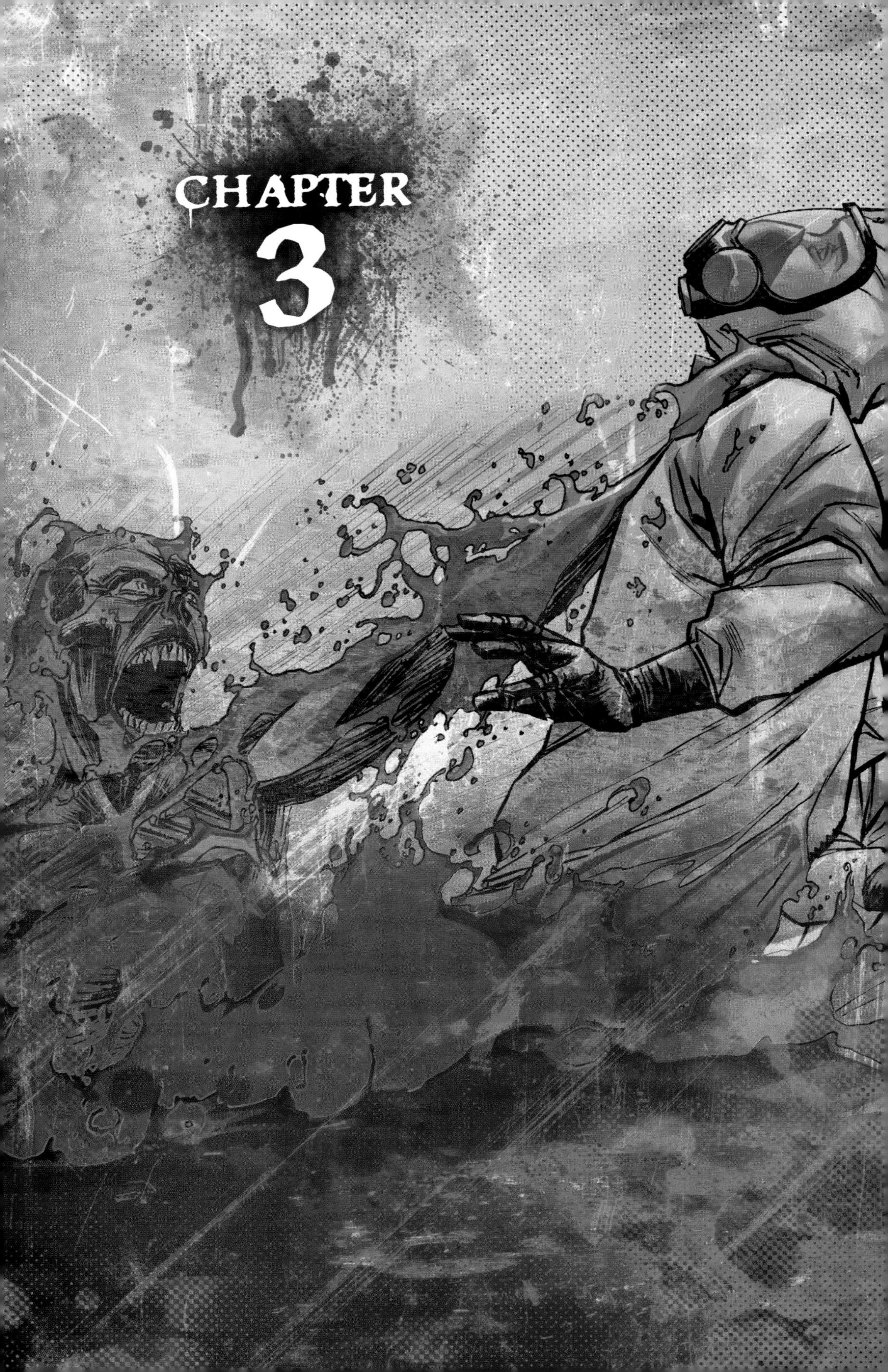
CHAPTER
3

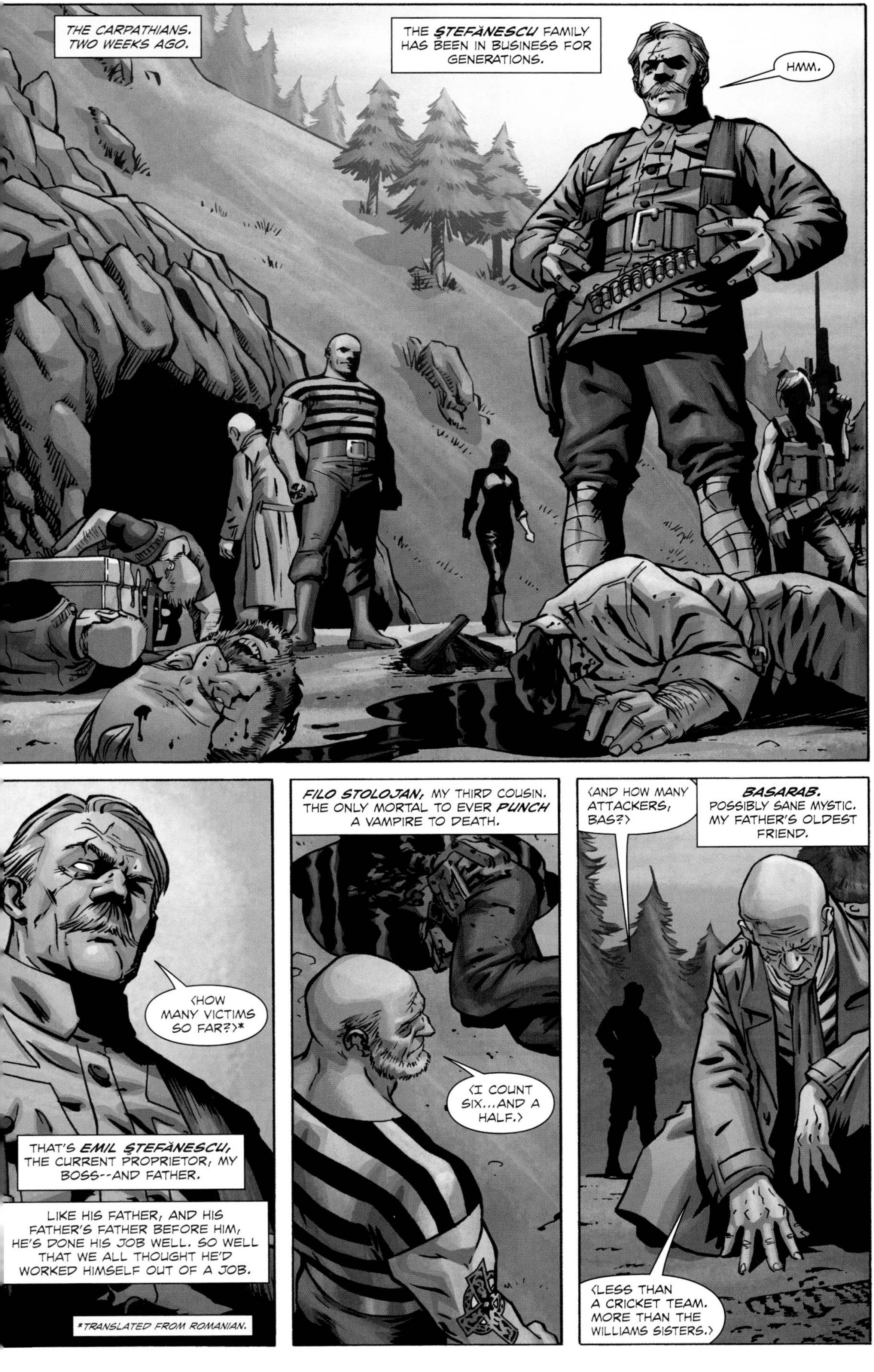
THE CARPATHIANS. TWO WEEKS AGO.
THE ȘTEFĂNESCU FAMILY HAS BEEN IN BUSINESS FOR GENERATIONS.
HMM.
<HOW MANY VICTIMS SO FAR?>*
THAT'S EMIL ȘTEFĂNESCU, THE CURRENT PROPRIETOR, MY BOSS--AND FATHER.
LIKE HIS FATHER, AND HIS FATHER'S FATHER BEFORE HIM, HE'S DONE HIS JOB WELL. SO WELL THAT WE ALL THOUGHT HE'D WORKED HIMSELF OUT OF A JOB.
*TRANSLATED FROM ROMANIAN.
FILO STOLOJAN, MY THIRD COUSIN. THE ONLY MORTAL TO EVER PUNCH A VAMPIRE TO DEATH.
<I COUNT SIX...AND A HALF.>
BASARAB. POSSIBLY SANE MYSTIC. MY FATHER'S OLDEST FRIEND.
<AND HOW MANY ATTACKERS, BAS?>
<LESS THAN A CRICKET TEAM. MORE THAN THE WILLIAMS SISTERS.>

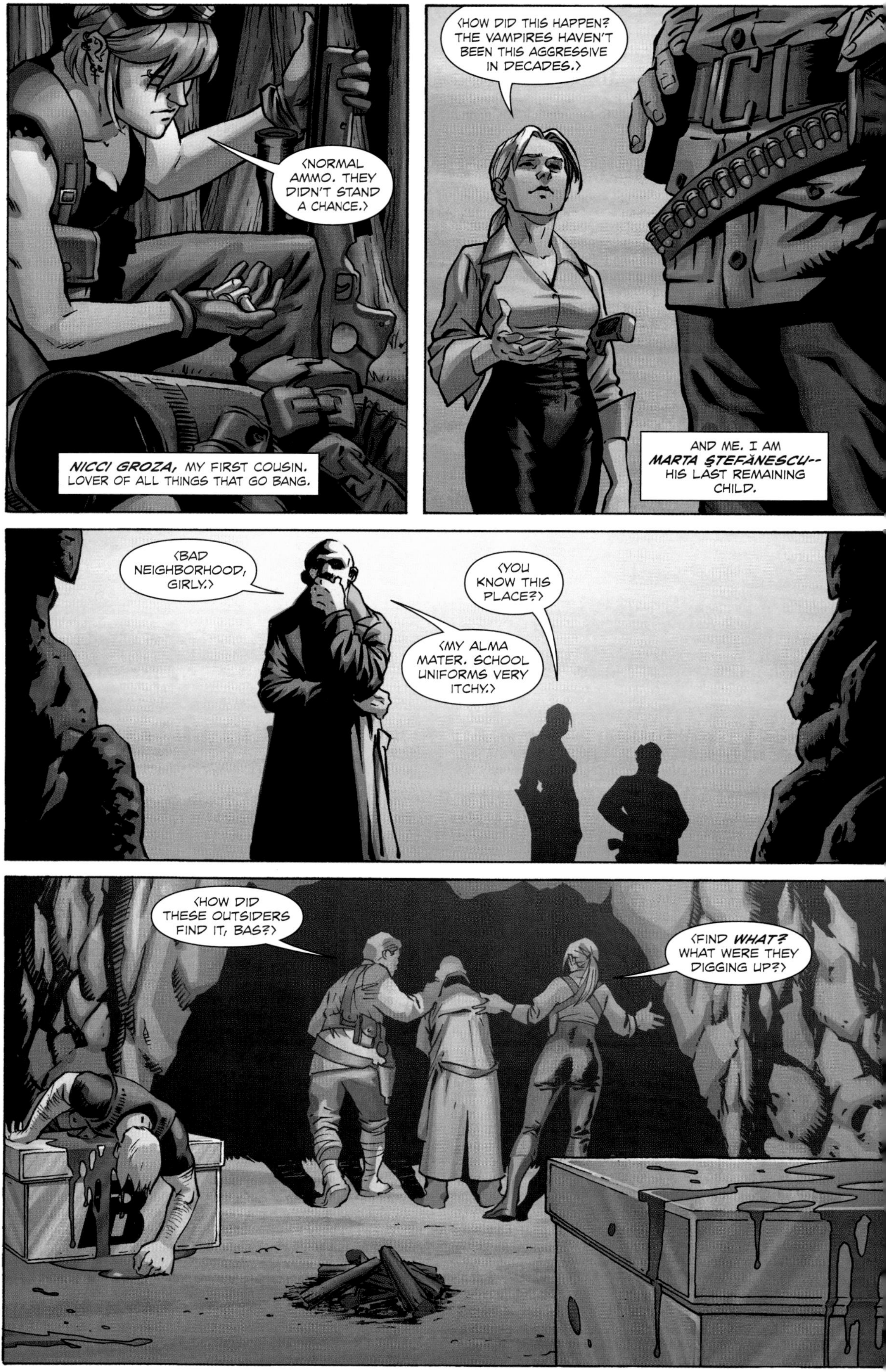

<NORMAL AMMO. THEY DIDN'T STAND A CHANCE.>
NICCI GROZA, MY FIRST COUSIN. LOVER OF ALL THINGS THAT GO BANG.
<HOW DID THIS HAPPEN? THE VAMPIRES HAVEN'T BEEN THIS AGGRESSIVE IN DECADES.>
AND ME. I AM MARTA ŞTEFĂNESCU-- HIS LAST REMAINING CHILD.
<BAD NEIGHBORHOOD, GIRLY.>
<YOU KNOW THIS PLACE?>
<MY ALMA MATER. SCHOOL UNIFORMS VERY ITCHY.>
<HOW DID THESE OUTSIDERS FIND IT, BAS?>
<FIND WHAT? WHAT WERE THEY DIGGING UP?>

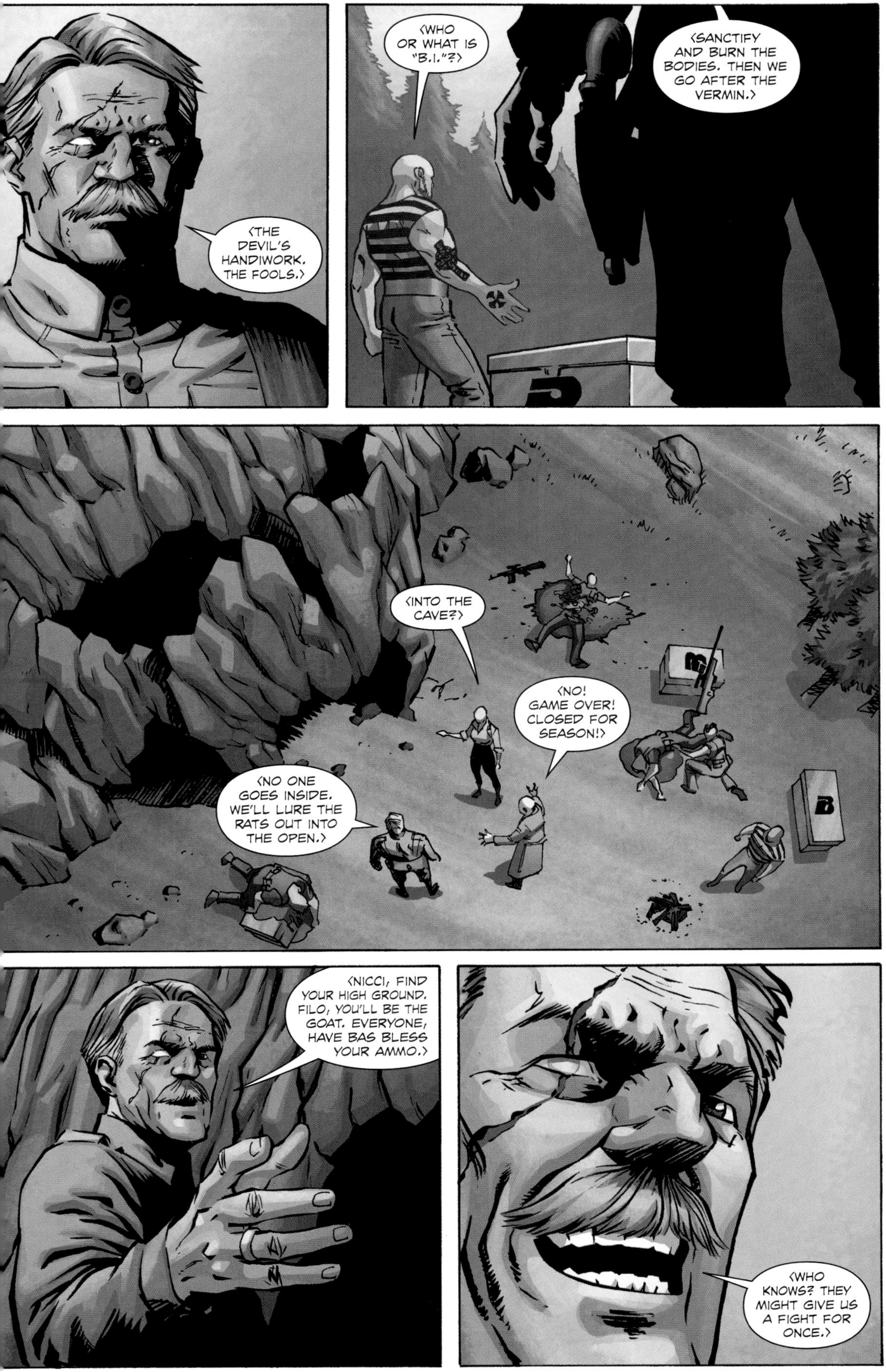
<THE DEVIL'S HANDIWORK. THE FOOLS.>
<WHO OR WHAT IS "B.I."?>
<SANCTIFY AND BURN THE BODIES. THEN WE GO AFTER THE VERMIN.>
<INTO THE CAVE?>
<NO! GAME OVER! CLOSED FOR SEASON!>
<NO ONE GOES INSIDE. WE'LL LURE THE RATS OUT INTO THE OPEN.>
<NICCI, FIND YOUR HIGH GROUND. FILO, YOU'LL BE THE GOAT. EVERYONE, HAVE BAS BLESS YOUR AMMO.>
<WHO KNOWS? THEY MIGHT GIVE US A FIGHT FOR ONCE.>

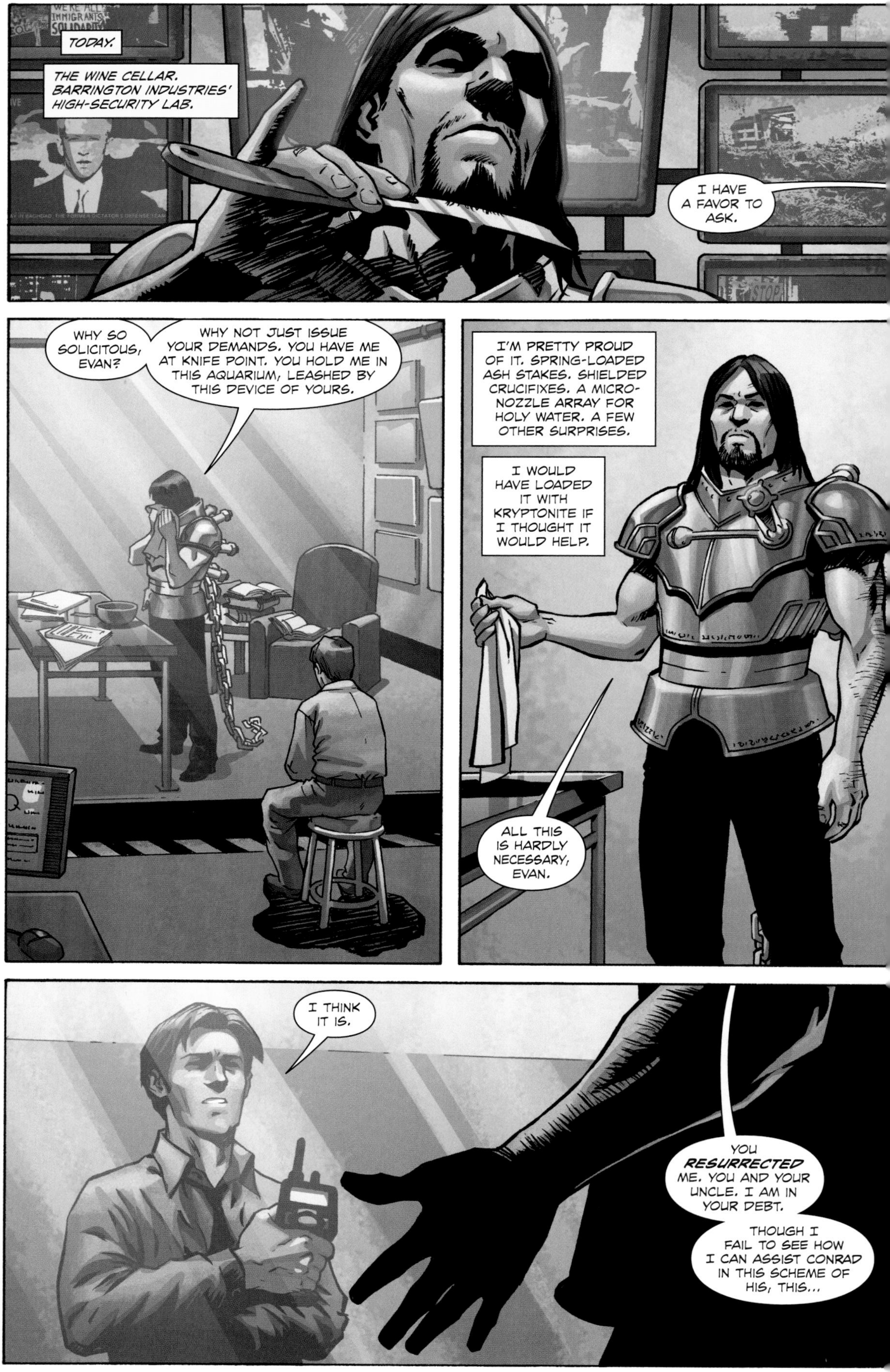

TODAY.
THE WINE CELLAR. BARRINGTON INDUSTRIES' HIGH-SECURITY LAB.
I HAVE A FAVOR TO ASK.
WHY SO SOLICITOUS, EVAN?
WHY NOT JUST ISSUE YOUR DEMANDS. YOU HAVE ME AT KNIFE POINT. YOU HOLD ME IN THIS AQUARIUM, LEASHED BY THIS DEVICE OF YOURS.
I'M PRETTY PROUD OF IT. SPRING-LOADED ASH STAKES. SHIELDED CRUCIFIXES. A MICRO-NOZZLE ARRAY FOR HOLY WATER. A FEW OTHER SURPRISES.
I WOULD HAVE LOADED IT WITH KRYPTONITE IF I THOUGHT IT WOULD HELP.
ALL THIS IS HARDLY NECESSARY, EVAN.
I THINK IT IS.
YOU **RESURRECTED** ME. YOU AND YOUR UNCLE. I AM IN YOUR DEBT.
THOUGH I FAIL TO SEE HOW I CAN ASSIST CONRAD IN THIS SCHEME OF HIS, THIS...

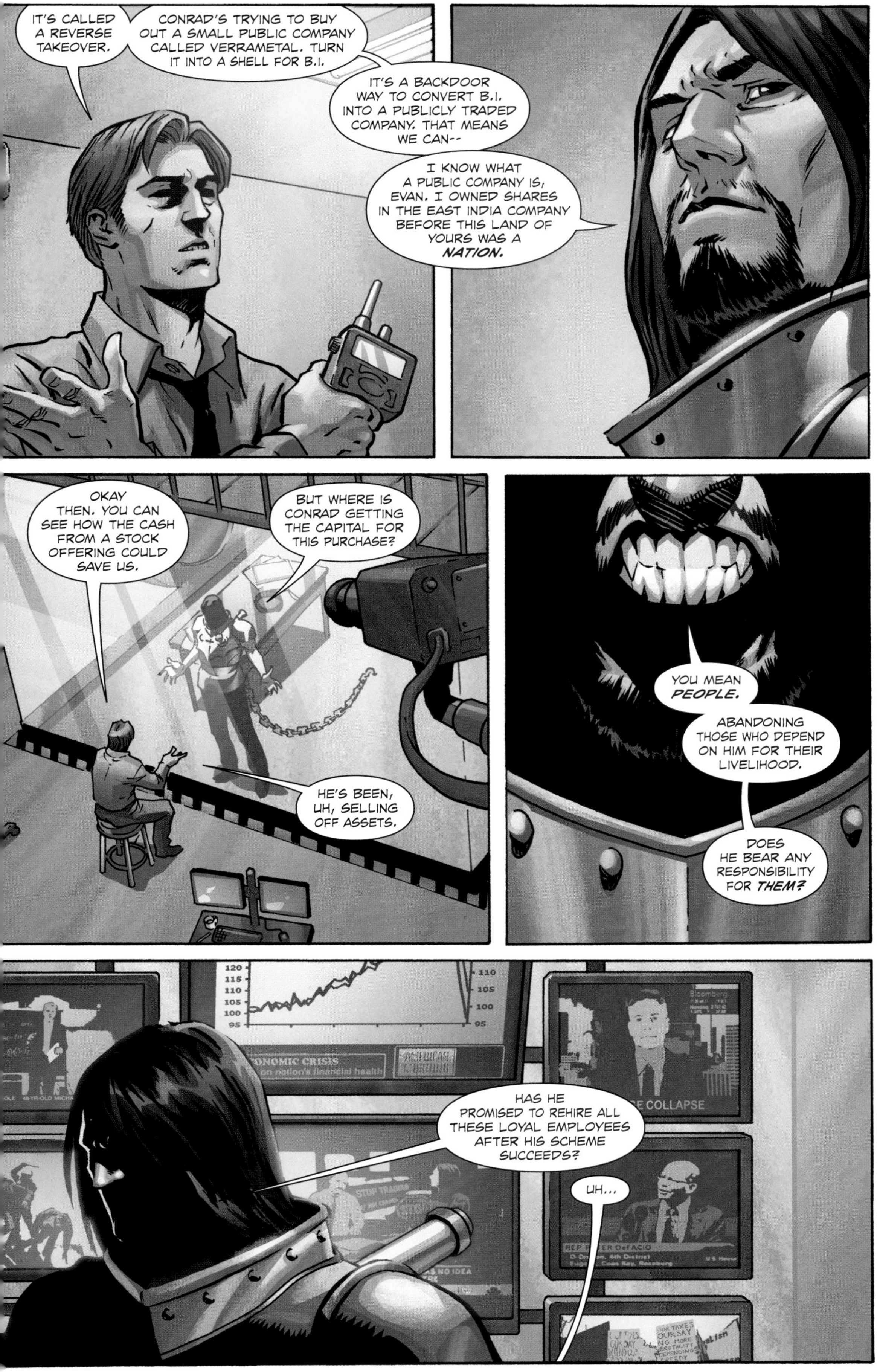
IT'S CALLED A REVERSE TAKEOVER.
CONRAD'S TRYING TO BUY OUT A SMALL PUBLIC COMPANY CALLED VERRAMETAL. TURN IT INTO A SHELL FOR B.I.
IT'S A BACKDOOR WAY TO CONVERT B.I. INTO A PUBLICLY TRADED COMPANY. THAT MEANS WE CAN--
I KNOW WHAT A PUBLIC COMPANY IS, EVAN. I OWNED SHARES IN THE EAST INDIA COMPANY BEFORE THIS LAND OF YOURS WAS A *NATION.*
OKAY THEN. YOU CAN SEE HOW THE CASH FROM A STOCK OFFERING COULD SAVE US.
BUT WHERE IS CONRAD GETTING THE CAPITAL FOR THIS PURCHASE?
HE'S BEEN, UH, SELLING OFF ASSETS.
YOU MEAN *PEOPLE.*
ABANDONING THOSE WHO DEPEND ON HIM FOR THEIR LIVELIHOOD.
DOES HE BEAR ANY RESPONSIBILITY FOR *THEM?*
ECONOMIC CRISIS
on nation's financial health
HAS HE PROMISED TO REHIRE ALL THESE LOYAL EMPLOYEES AFTER HIS SCHEME SUCCEEDS?
UH...

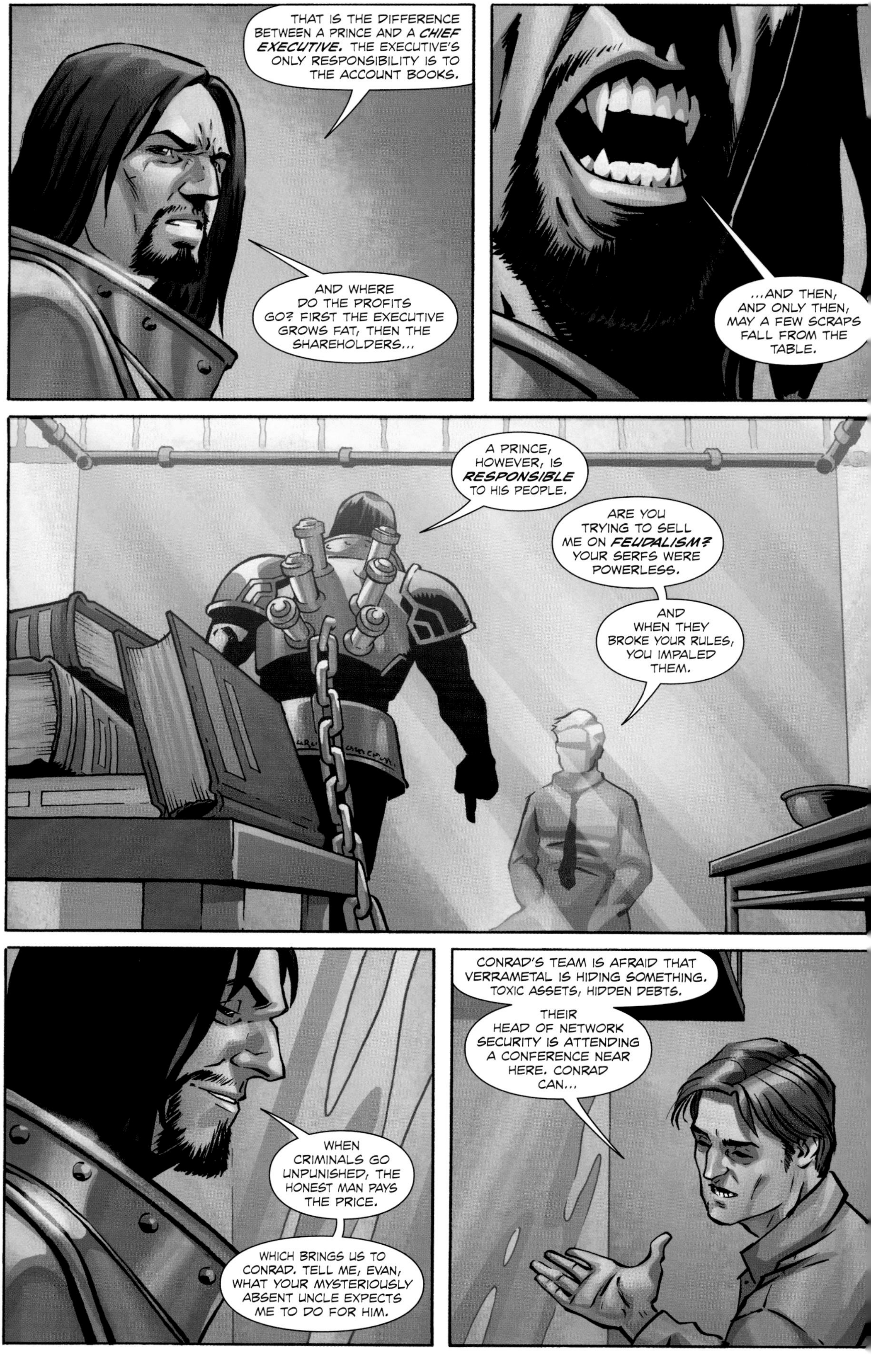
THAT IS THE DIFFERENCE BETWEEN A PRINCE AND A *CHIEF EXECUTIVE.* THE EXECUTIVE'S ONLY RESPONSIBILITY IS TO THE ACCOUNT BOOKS.
AND WHERE DO THE PROFITS GO? FIRST THE EXECUTIVE GROWS FAT, THEN THE SHAREHOLDERS...
...AND THEN, AND ONLY THEN, MAY A FEW SCRAPS FALL FROM THE TABLE.
A PRINCE, HOWEVER, IS ***RESPONSIBLE*** TO HIS PEOPLE.
ARE YOU TRYING TO SELL ME ON ***FEUDALISM?*** YOUR SERFS WERE POWERLESS.
AND WHEN THEY BROKE YOUR RULES, YOU IMPALED THEM.
WHEN CRIMINALS GO UNPUNISHED, THE HONEST MAN PAYS THE PRICE.
WHICH BRINGS US TO CONRAD. TELL ME, EVAN, WHAT YOUR MYSTERIOUSLY ABSENT UNCLE EXPECTS ME TO DO FOR HIM.
CONRAD'S TEAM IS AFRAID THAT VERRAMETAL IS HIDING SOMETHING. TOXIC ASSETS, HIDDEN DEBTS.
THEIR HEAD OF NETWORK SECURITY IS ATTENDING A CONFERENCE NEAR HERE. CONRAD CAN...

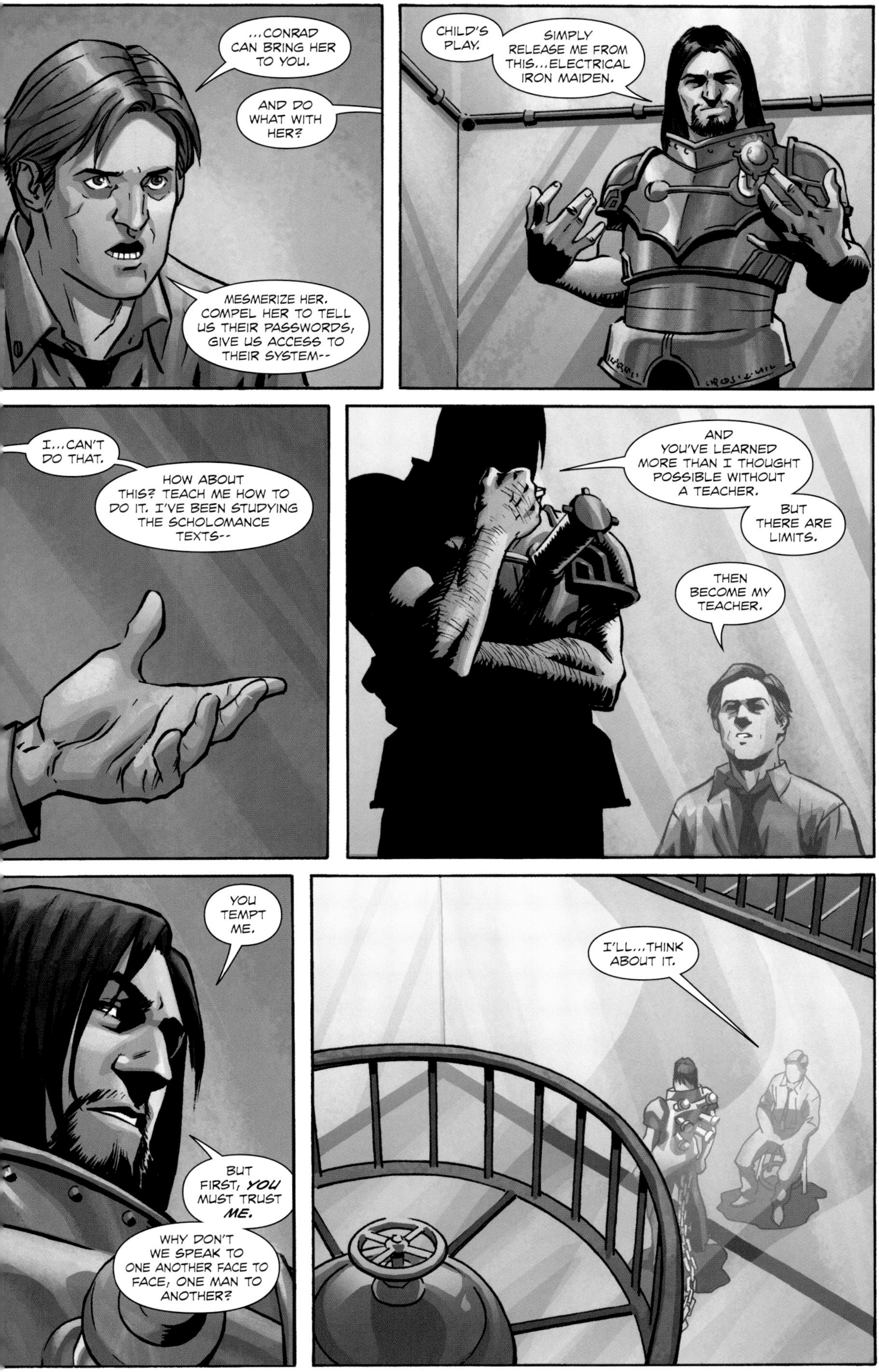
...CONRAD CAN BRING HER TO YOU.
AND DO WHAT WITH HER?
MESMERIZE HER. COMPEL HER TO TELL US THEIR PASSWORDS, GIVE US ACCESS TO THEIR SYSTEM--
CHILD'S PLAY.
SIMPLY RELEASE ME FROM THIS...ELECTRICAL IRON MAIDEN.
I...CAN'T DO THAT.
HOW ABOUT THIS? TEACH ME HOW TO DO IT. I'VE BEEN STUDYING THE SCHOLOMANCE TEXTS--
AND YOU'VE LEARNED MORE THAN I THOUGHT POSSIBLE WITHOUT A TEACHER.
BUT THERE ARE LIMITS.
THEN BECOME MY TEACHER.
YOU TEMPT ME.
BUT FIRST, *YOU* MUST TRUST *ME.*
WHY DON'T WE SPEAK TO ONE ANOTHER FACE TO FACE, ONE MAN TO ANOTHER?
I'LL...THINK ABOUT IT.

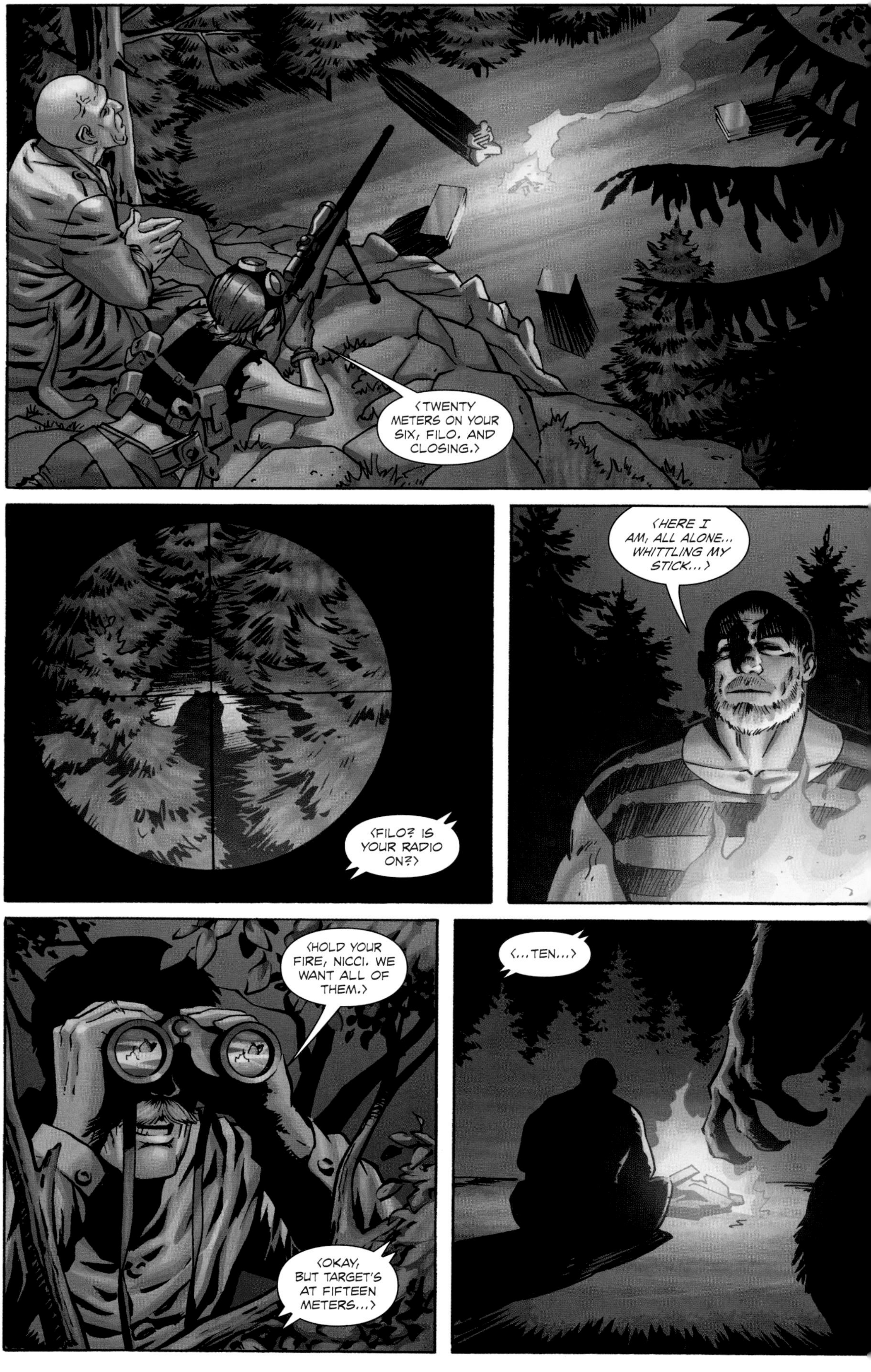
‹TWENTY METERS ON YOUR SIX, FILO. AND CLOSING.›
‹FILO? IS YOUR RADIO ON?›
‹HERE I AM, ALL ALONE... WHITTLING MY STICK...›
‹HOLD YOUR FIRE, NICCI. WE WANT ALL OF THEM.›
‹OKAY, BUT TARGET'S AT FIFTEEN METERS...›
‹...TEN...›

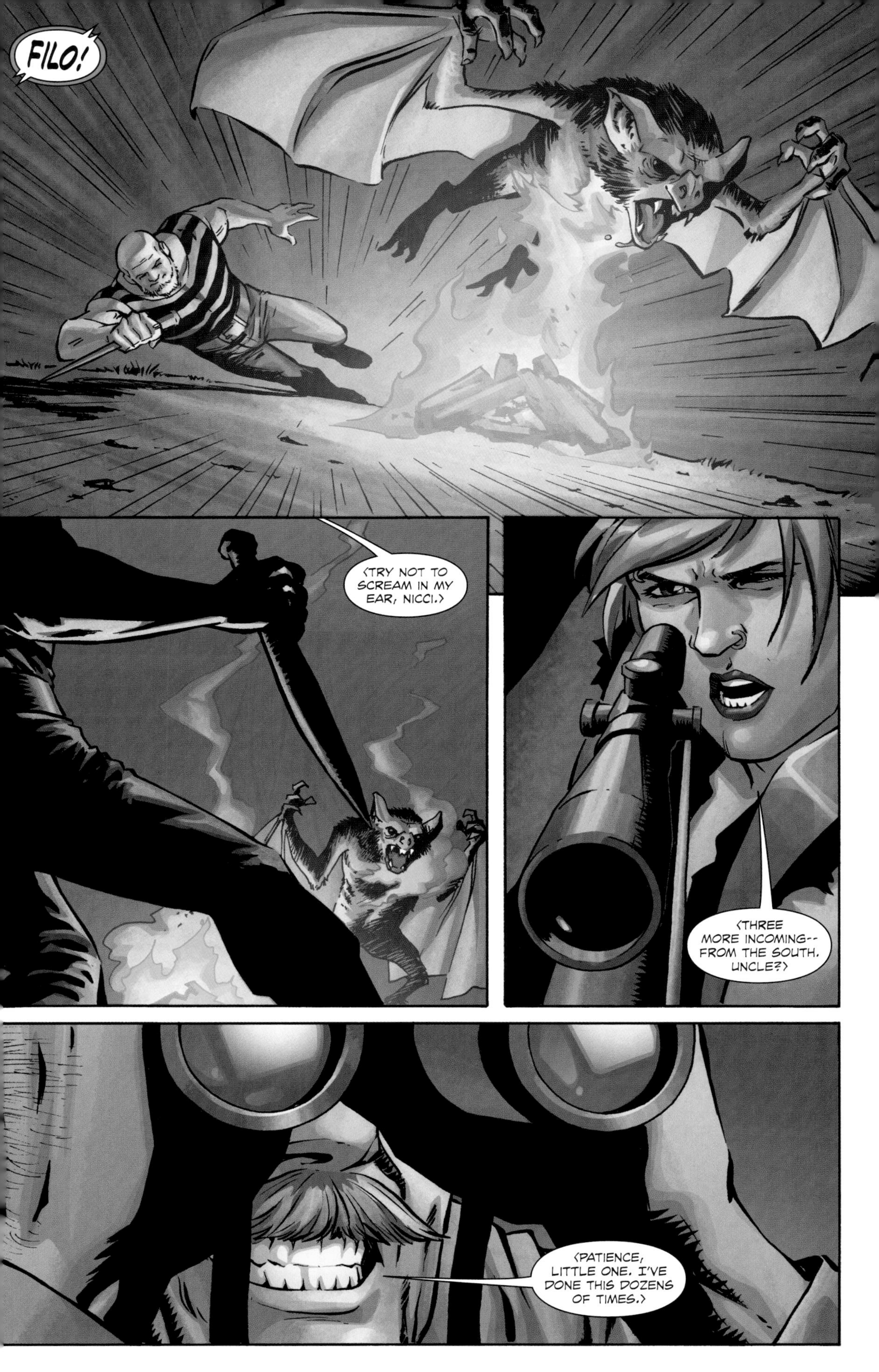
FILO!
〈TRY NOT TO SCREAM IN MY EAR, NICCI.〉
〈THREE MORE INCOMING-- FROM THE SOUTH. UNCLE?〉
〈PATIENCE, LITTLE ONE. I'VE DONE THIS DOZENS OF TIMES.〉

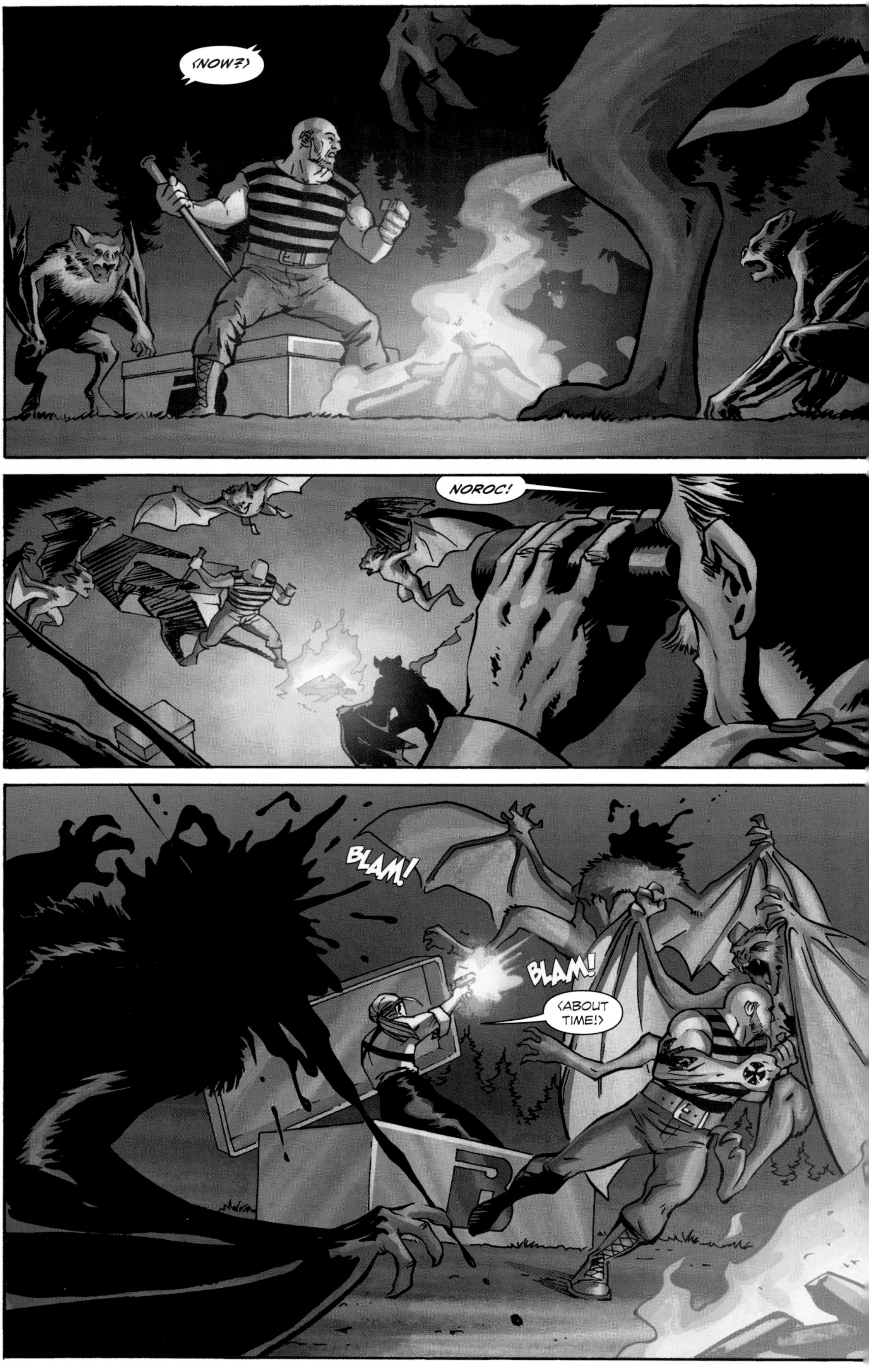

‹NOW?›
NOROC!
BLAM!
BLAM!
‹ABOUT TIME!›

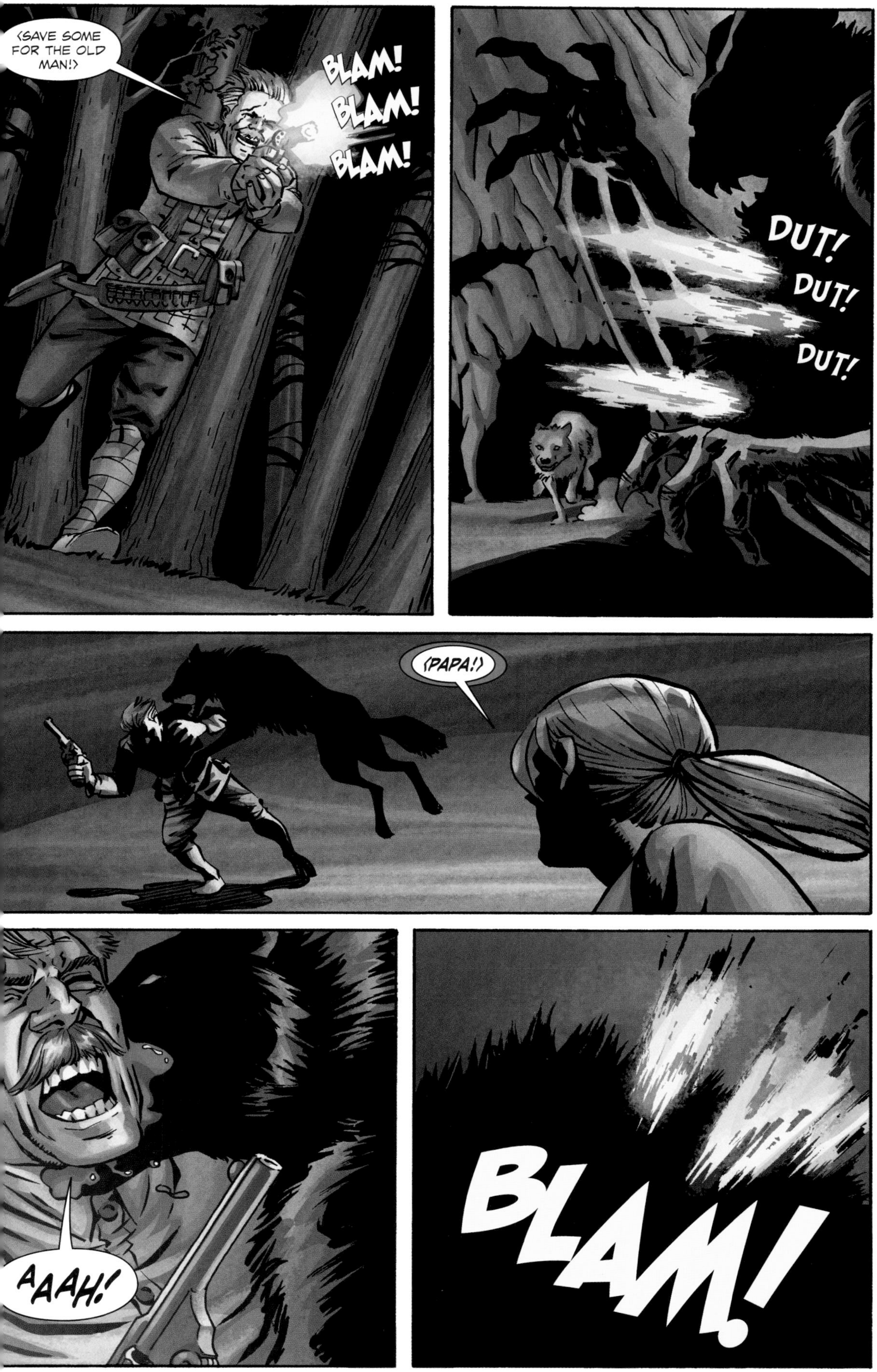

‹SAVE SOME FOR THE OLD MAN!›
BLAM! BLAM! BLAM!
DUT! DUT! DUT!
‹PAPA!›
AAAH!
BLAM!

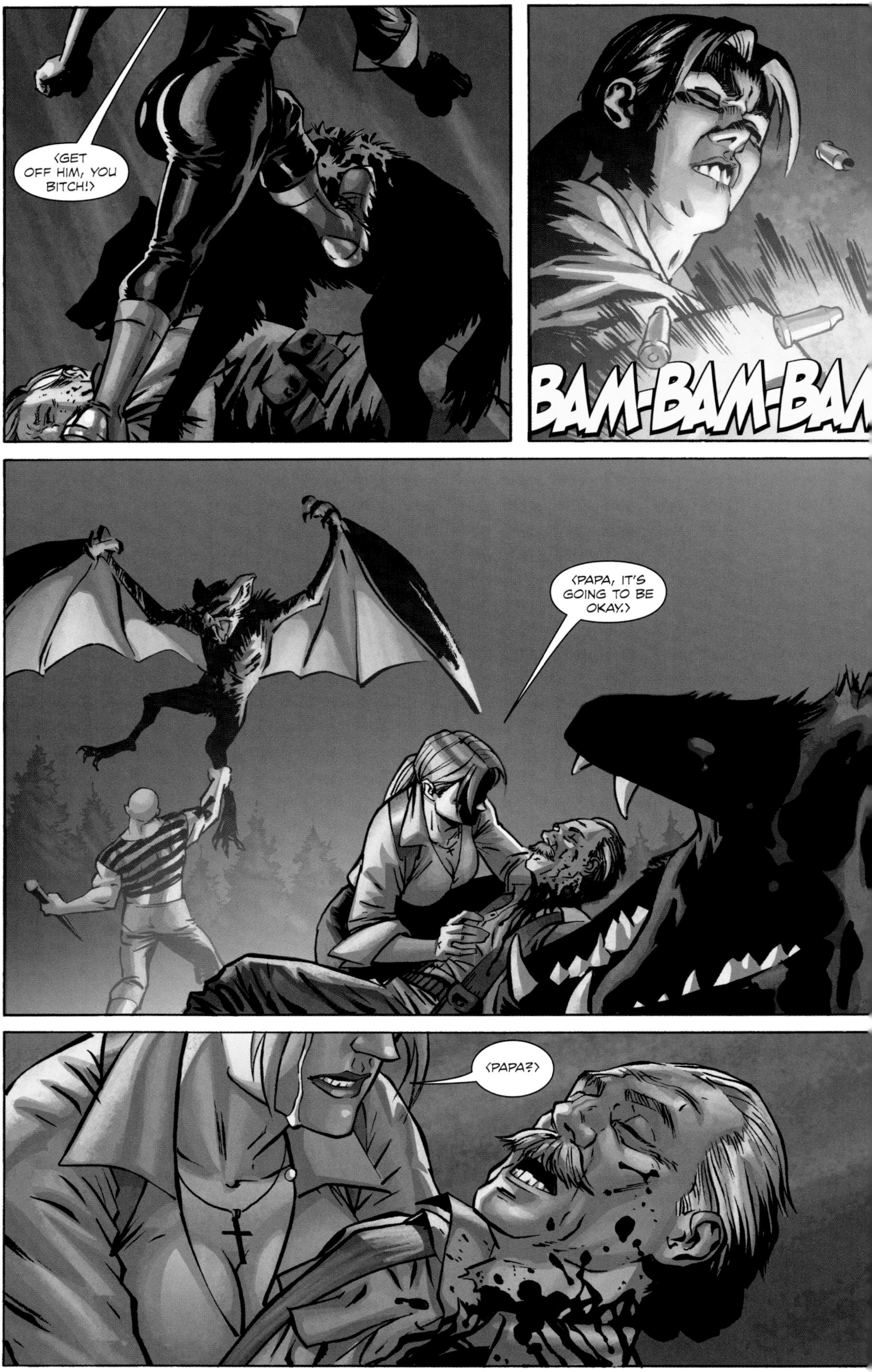
⟨GET OFF HIM, YOU BITCH!⟩
BAM-BAM-BAM
⟨PAPA, IT'S GOING TO BE OKAY.⟩
⟨PAPA?⟩

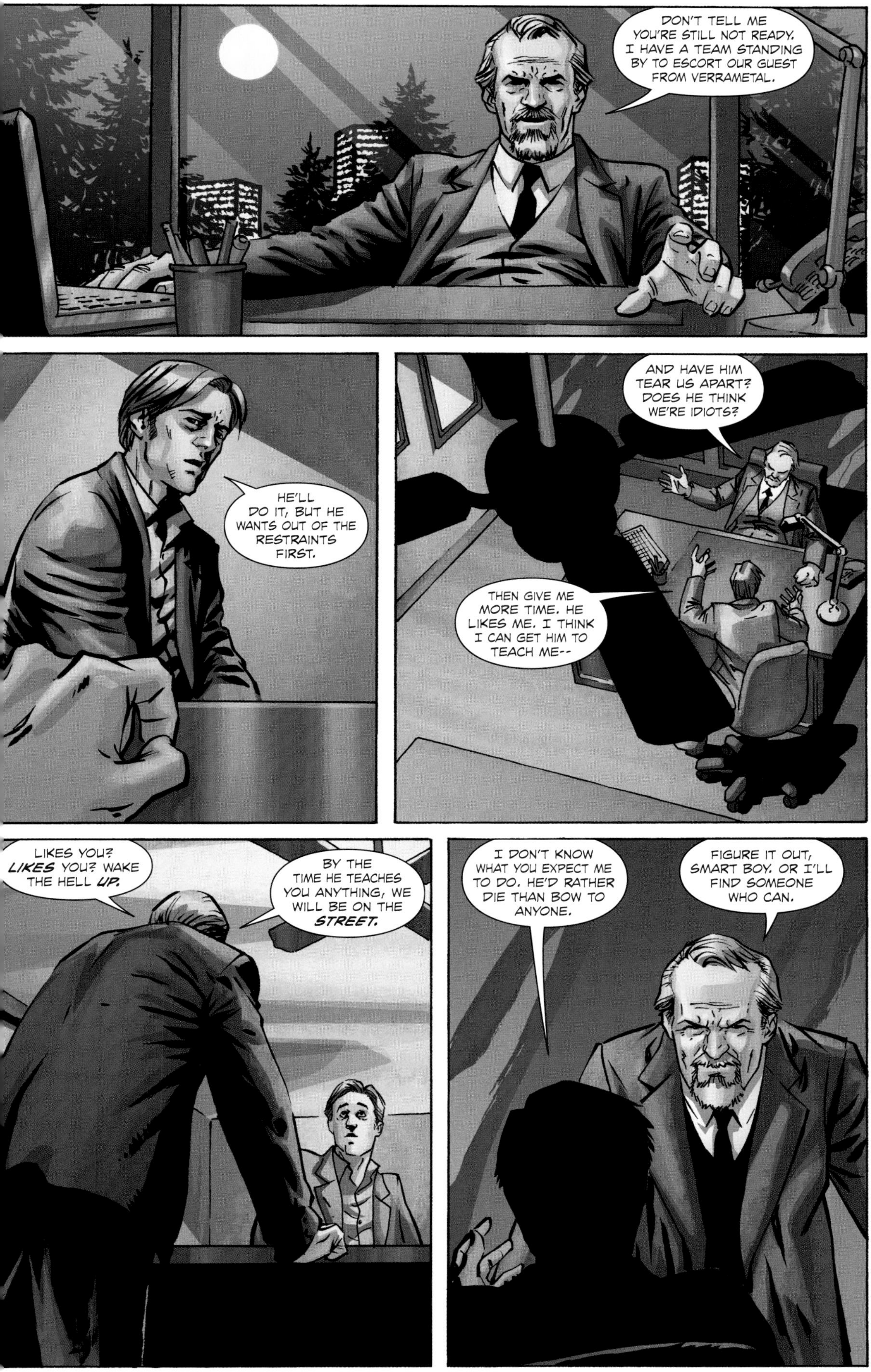
DON'T TELL ME YOU'RE STILL NOT READY. I HAVE A TEAM STANDING BY TO ESCORT OUR GUEST FROM VERRAMETAL.
HE'LL DO IT, BUT HE WANTS OUT OF THE RESTRAINTS FIRST.
AND HAVE HIM TEAR US APART? DOES HE THINK WE'RE IDIOTS?
THEN GIVE ME MORE TIME. HE LIKES ME. I THINK I CAN GET HIM TO TEACH ME--
LIKES YOU? *LIKES* YOU? WAKE THE HELL *UP*.
BY THE TIME HE TEACHES YOU ANYTHING, WE WILL BE ON THE *STREET*.
I DON'T KNOW WHAT YOU EXPECT ME TO DO. HE'D RATHER DIE THAN BOW TO ANYONE.
FIGURE IT OUT, SMART BOY. OR I'LL FIND SOMEONE WHO CAN.

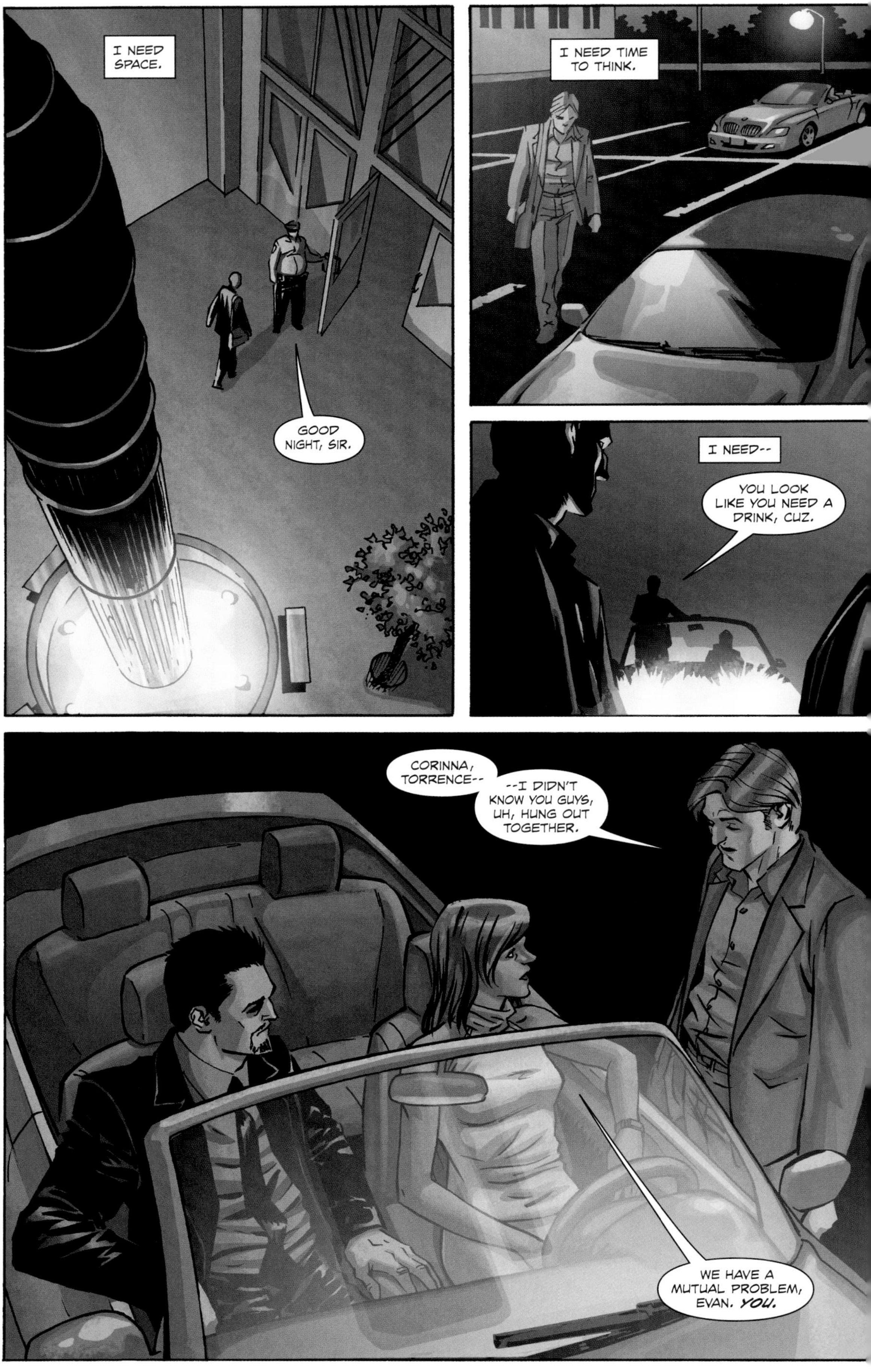
I NEED SPACE.
GOOD NIGHT, SIR.
I NEED TIME TO THINK.
I NEED--
YOU LOOK LIKE YOU NEED A DRINK, CUZ.
CORINNA, TORRENCE--
--I DIDN'T KNOW YOU GUYS, UH, HUNG OUT TOGETHER.
WE HAVE A MUTUAL PROBLEM, EVAN. *YOU.*

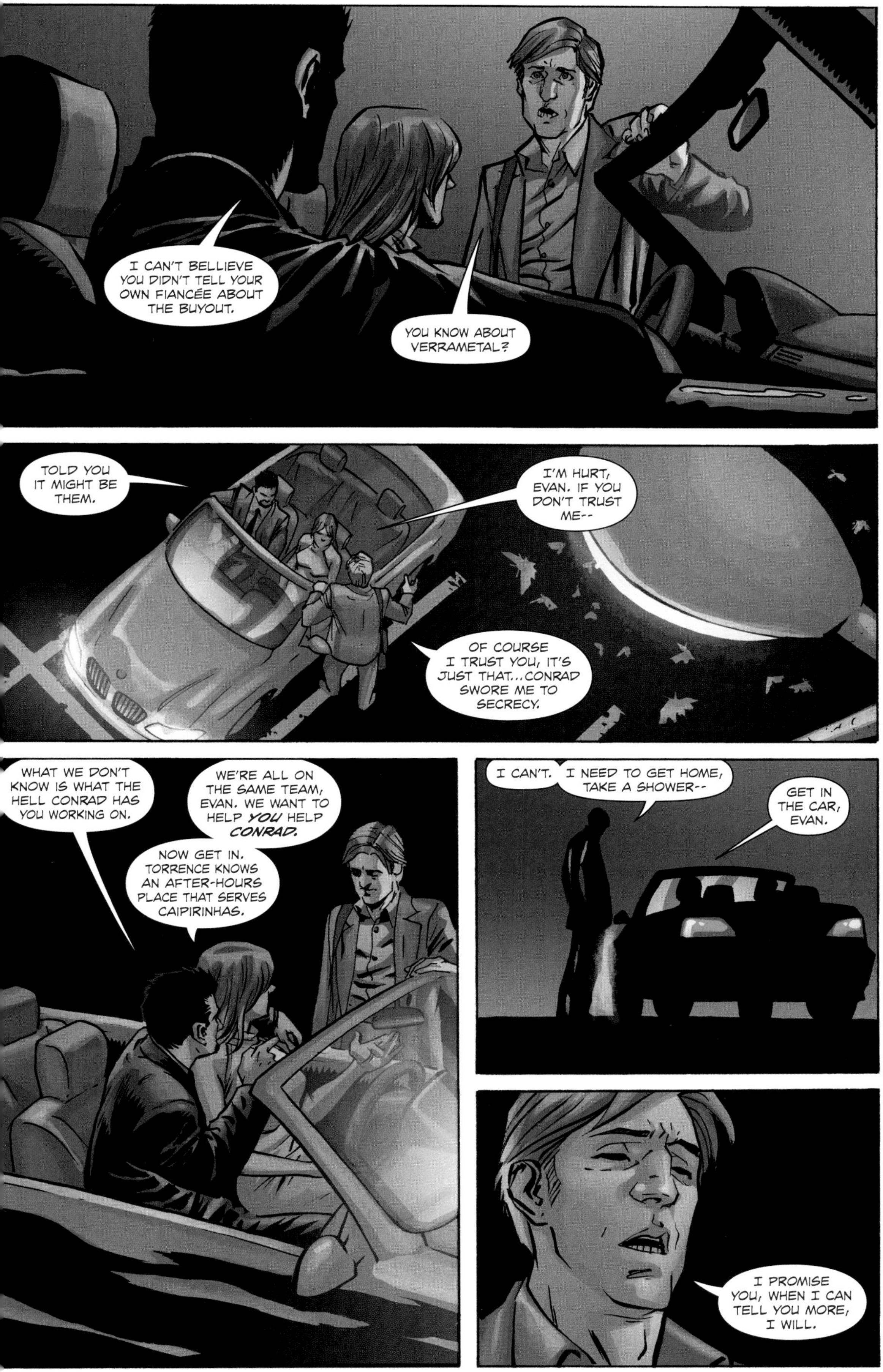

I CAN'T BELLIEVE YOU DIDN'T TELL YOUR OWN FIANCÉE ABOUT THE BUYOUT.
YOU KNOW ABOUT VERRAMETAL?
TOLD YOU IT MIGHT BE THEM.
I'M HURT, EVAN. IF YOU DON'T TRUST ME--
OF COURSE I TRUST YOU, IT'S JUST THAT...CONRAD SWORE ME TO SECRECY.
WHAT WE DON'T KNOW IS WHAT THE HELL CONRAD HAS YOU WORKING ON.
WE'RE ALL ON THE SAME TEAM, EVAN. WE WANT TO HELP *YOU* HELP *CONRAD.*
NOW GET IN. TORRENCE KNOWS AN AFTER-HOURS PLACE THAT SERVES CAIPIRINHAS.
I CAN'T.
I NEED TO GET HOME, TAKE A SHOWER--
GET IN THE CAR, EVAN.
I PROMISE YOU, WHEN I CAN TELL YOU MORE, I WILL.

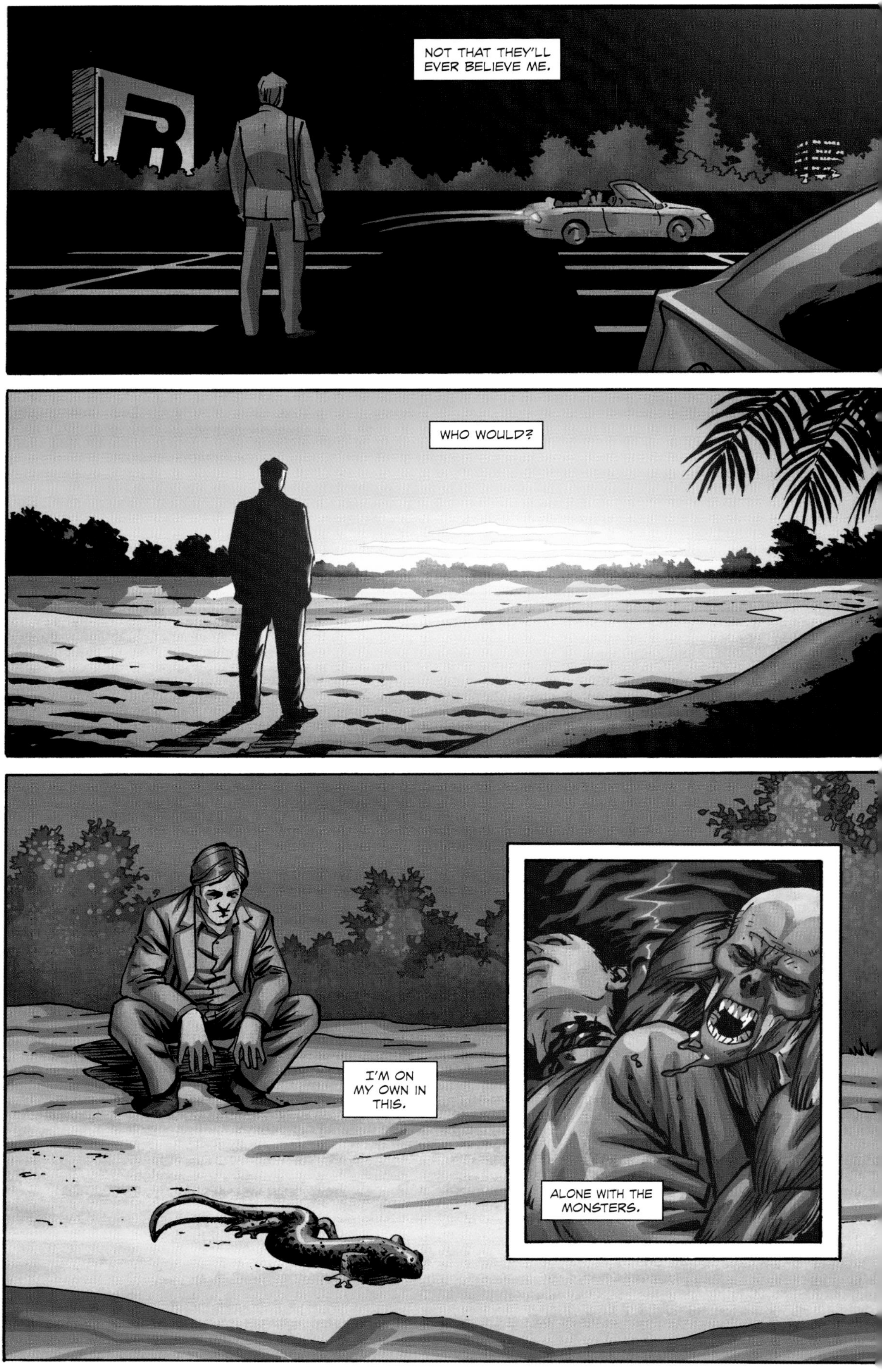
NOT THAT THEY'LL EVER BELIEVE ME.
WHO WOULD?
I'M ON MY OWN IN THIS.
ALONE WITH THE MONSTERS.

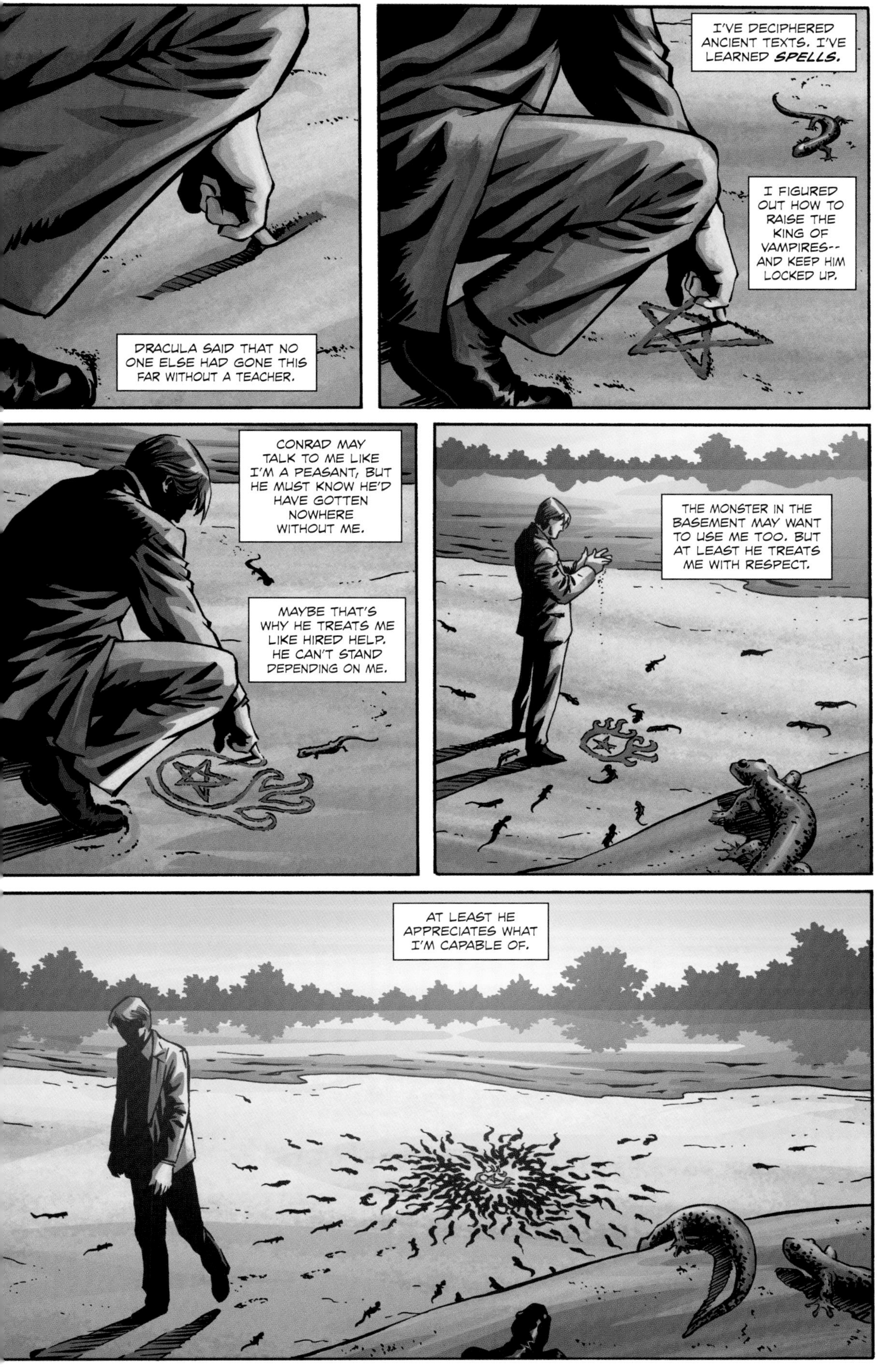
DRACULA SAID THAT NO ONE ELSE HAD GONE THIS FAR WITHOUT A TEACHER.
I'VE DECIPHERED ANCIENT TEXTS. I'VE LEARNED *SPELLS.*
I FIGURED OUT HOW TO RAISE THE KING OF VAMPIRES-- AND KEEP HIM LOCKED UP.
CONRAD MAY TALK TO ME LIKE I'M A PEASANT, BUT HE MUST KNOW HE'D HAVE GOTTEN NOWHERE WITHOUT ME.
MAYBE THAT'S WHY HE TREATS ME LIKE HIRED HELP. HE CAN'T STAND DEPENDING ON ME.
THE MONSTER IN THE BASEMENT MAY WANT TO USE ME TOO. BUT AT LEAST HE TREATS ME WITH RESPECT.
AT LEAST HE APPRECIATES WHAT I'M CAPABLE OF.

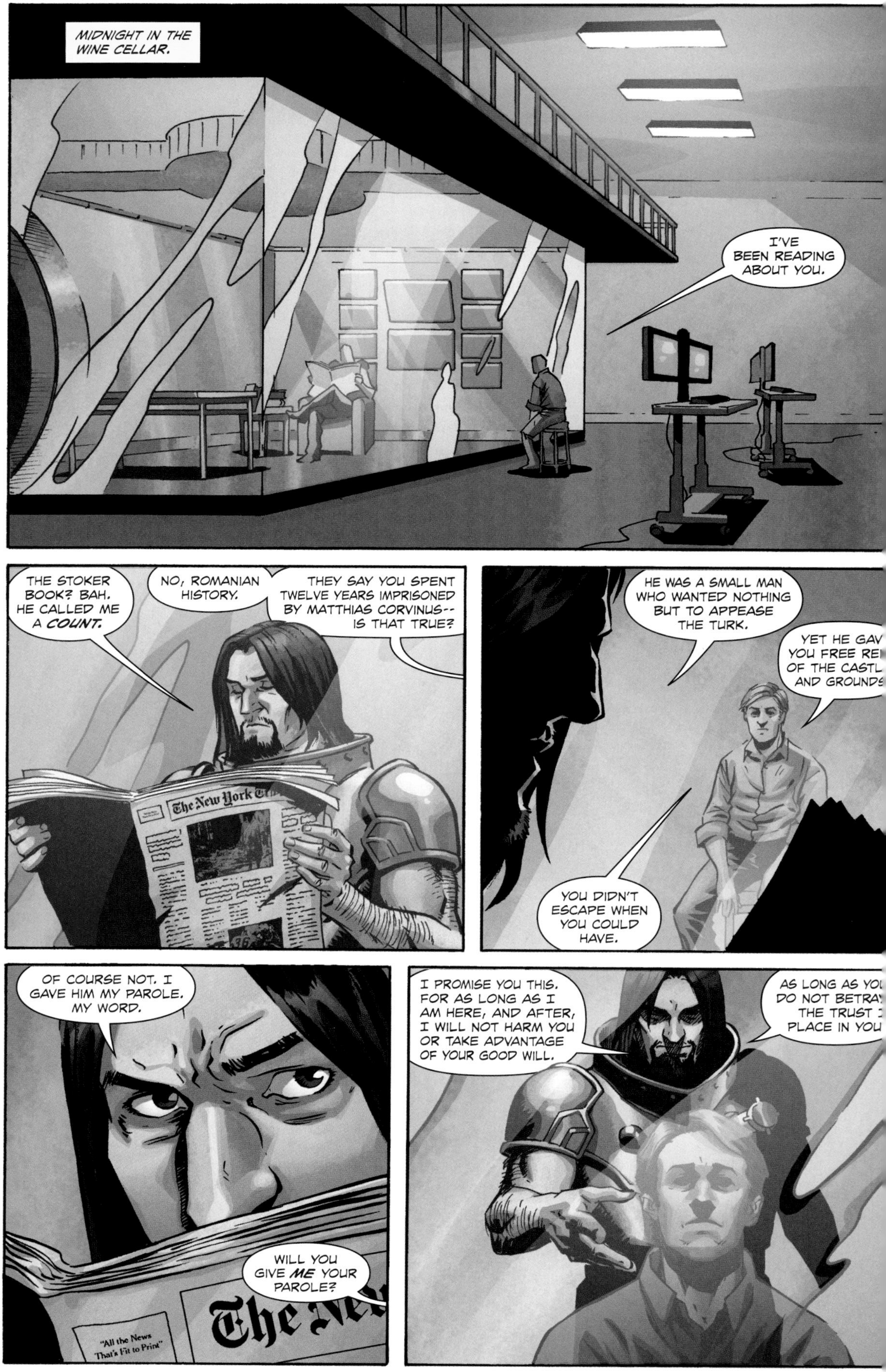
MIDNIGHT IN THE WINE CELLAR.
I'VE BEEN READING ABOUT YOU.
THE STOKER BOOK? BAH. HE CALLED ME A COUNT.
NO, ROMANIAN HISTORY.
THEY SAY YOU SPENT TWELVE YEARS IMPRISONED BY MATTHIAS CORVINUS-- IS THAT TRUE?
HE WAS A SMALL MAN WHO WANTED NOTHING BUT TO APPEASE THE TURK.
YET HE GAV YOU FREE RE OF THE CASTL AND GROUNDS
YOU DIDN'T ESCAPE WHEN YOU COULD HAVE.
OF COURSE NOT. I GAVE HIM MY PAROLE. MY WORD.
WILL YOU GIVE ME YOUR PAROLE?
"All the News That's Fit to Print"
I PROMISE YOU THIS. FOR AS LONG AS I AM HERE, AND AFTER, I WILL NOT HARM YOU OR TAKE ADVANTAGE OF YOUR GOOD WILL.
AS LONG AS YO DO NOT BETRA THE TRUST I PLACE IN YOU

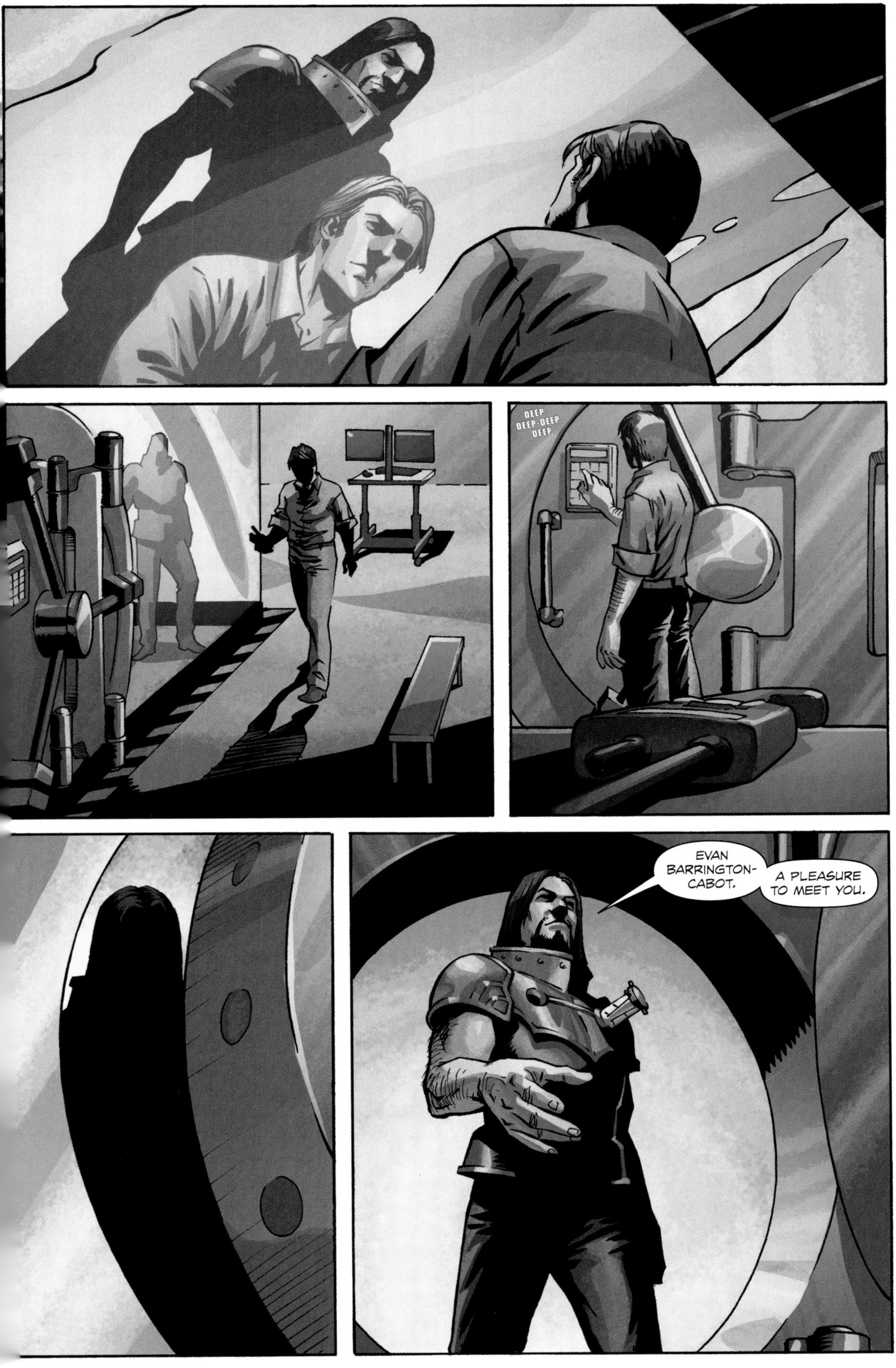
DEEP. DEEP-DEEP. DEEP.
EVAN BARRINGTON-CABOT.
A PLEASURE TO MEET YOU.

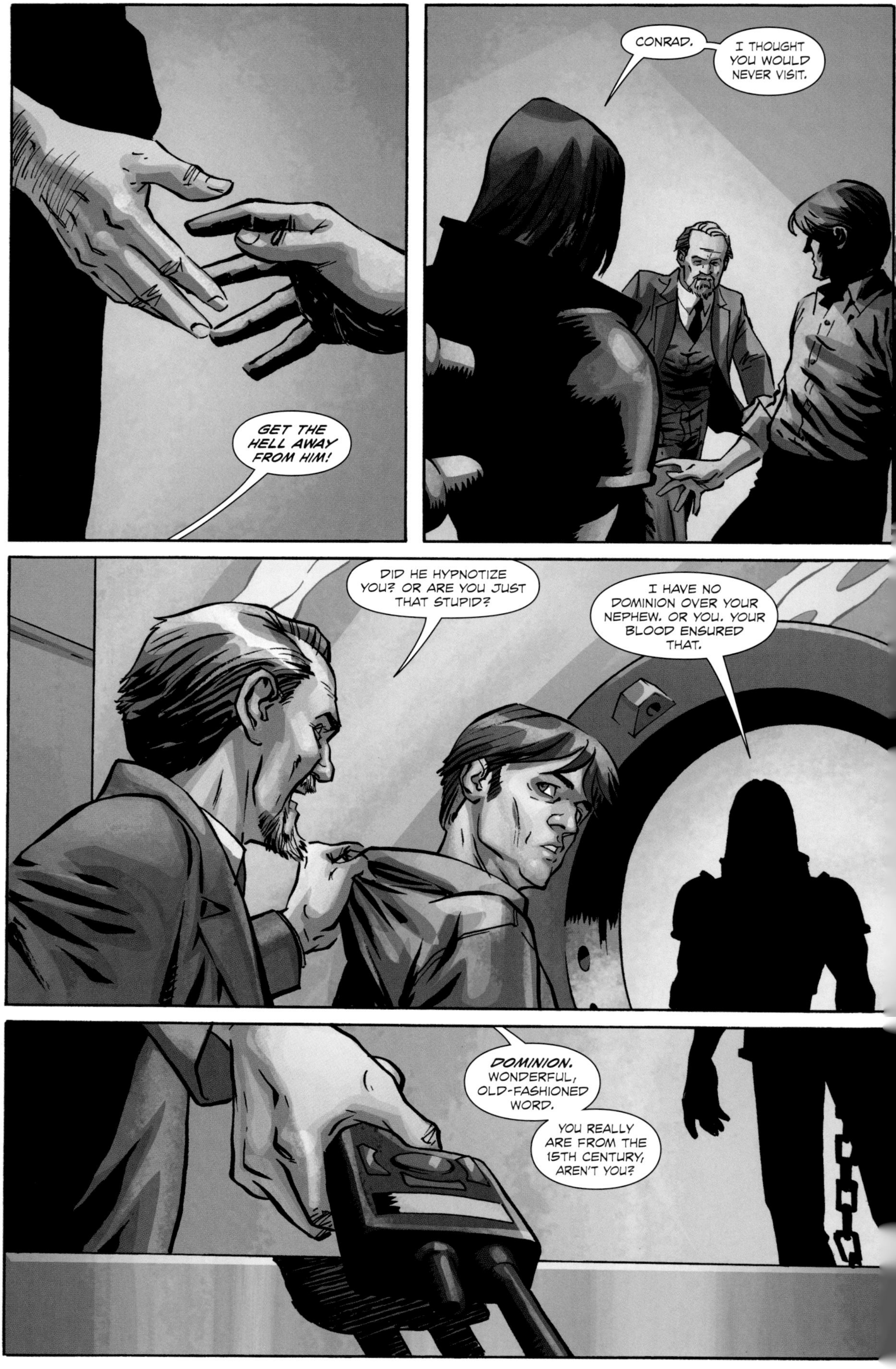

GET THE HELL AWAY FROM HIM!
CONRAD.
I THOUGHT YOU WOULD NEVER VISIT.
DID HE HYPNOTIZE YOU? OR ARE YOU JUST THAT STUPID?
I HAVE NO DOMINION OVER YOUR NEPHEW. OR YOU. YOUR BLOOD ENSURED THAT.
DOMINION. WONDERFUL, OLD-FASHIONED WORD.
YOU REALLY ARE FROM THE 15TH CENTURY, AREN'T YOU?

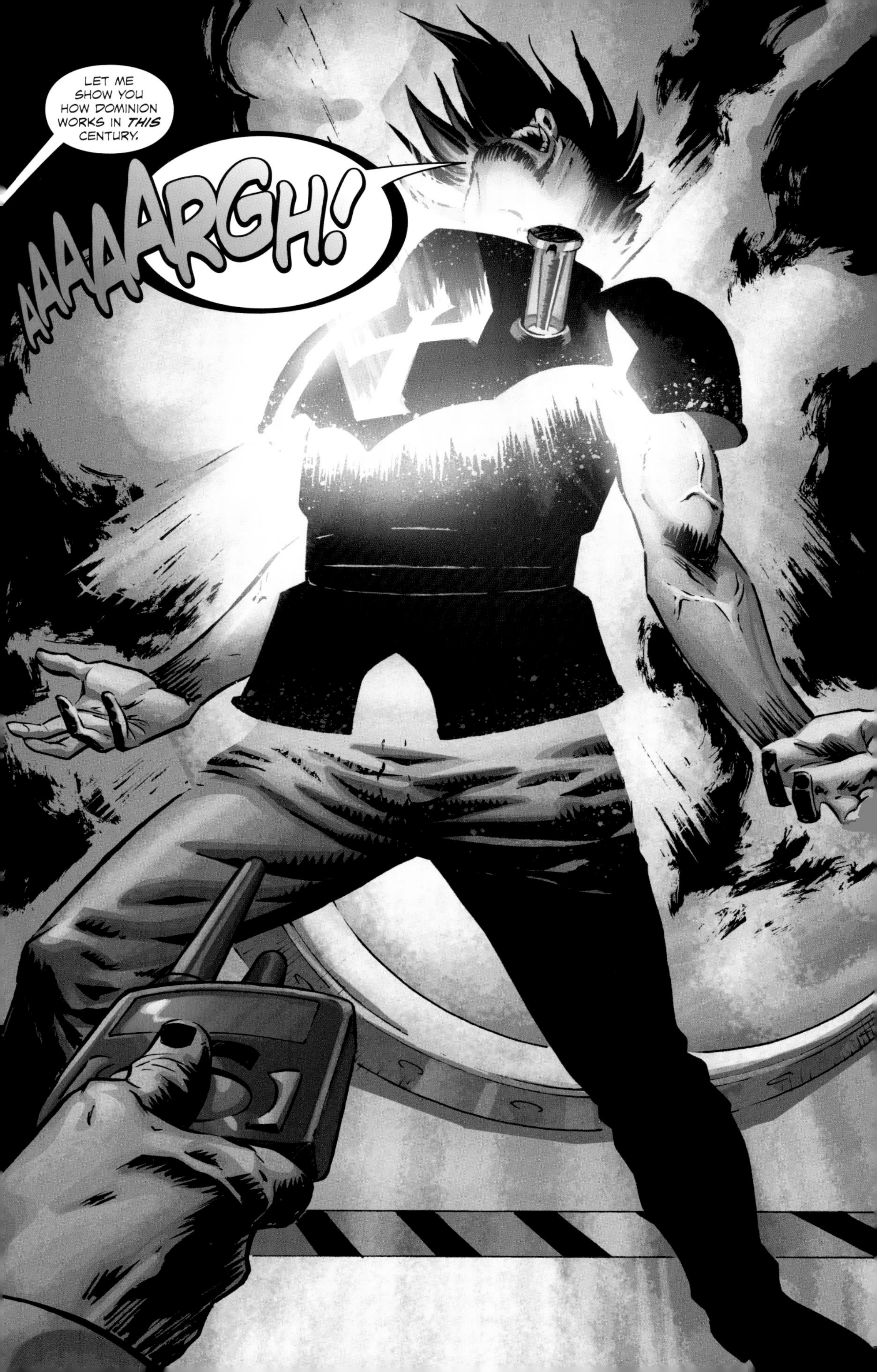
LET ME SHOW YOU HOW DOMINION WORKS IN *THIS* CENTURY.
AAAAARGH!

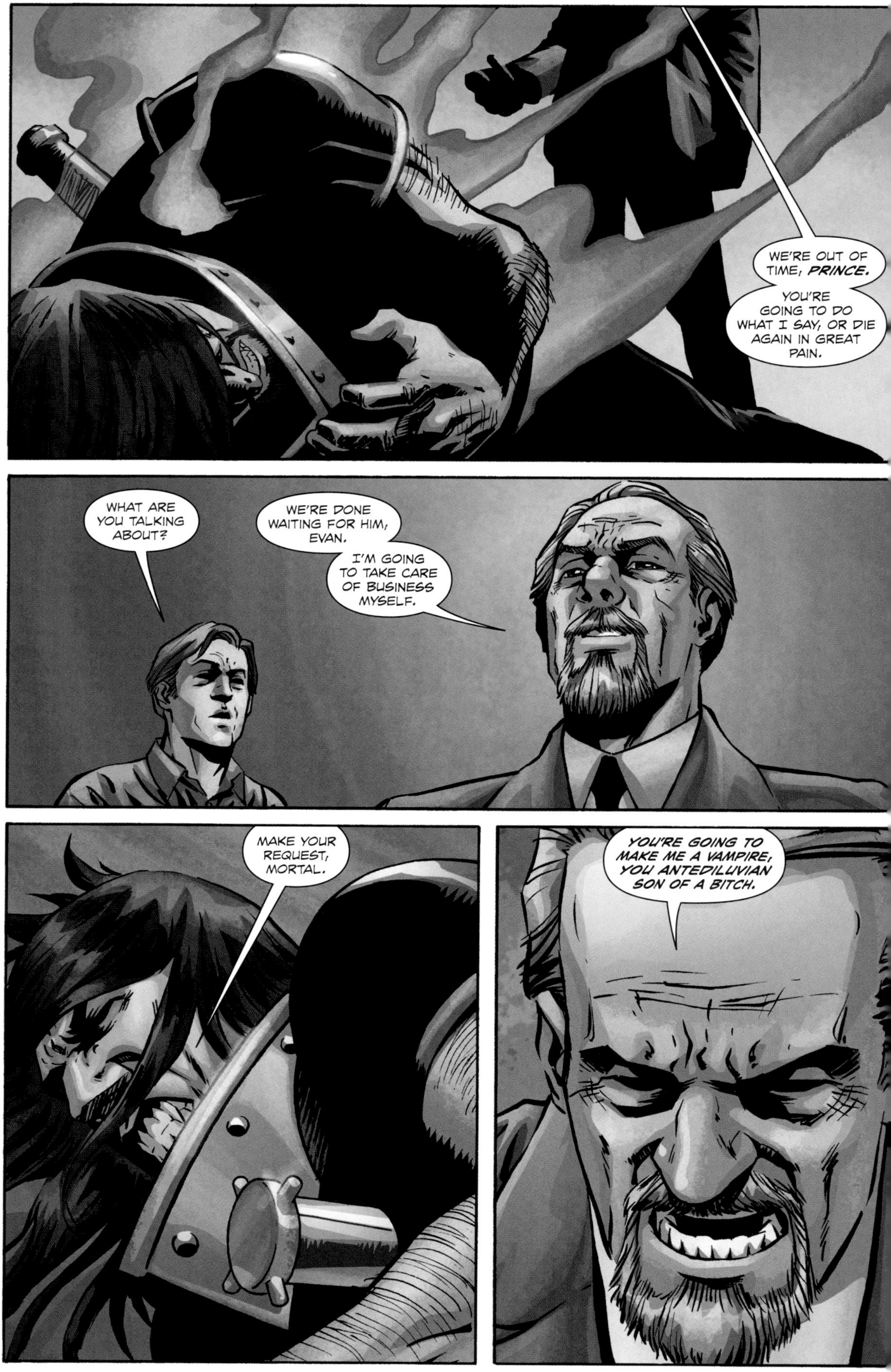
WE'RE OUT OF TIME, *PRINCE.*
YOU'RE GOING TO DO WHAT I SAY, OR DIE AGAIN IN GREAT PAIN.
WHAT ARE YOU TALKING ABOUT?
WE'RE DONE WAITING FOR HIM, EVAN.
I'M GOING TO TAKE CARE OF BUSINESS MYSELF.
MAKE YOUR REQUEST, MORTAL.
YOU'RE GOING TO MAKE ME A VAMPIRE, YOU ANTEDILUVIAN SON OF A BITCH.

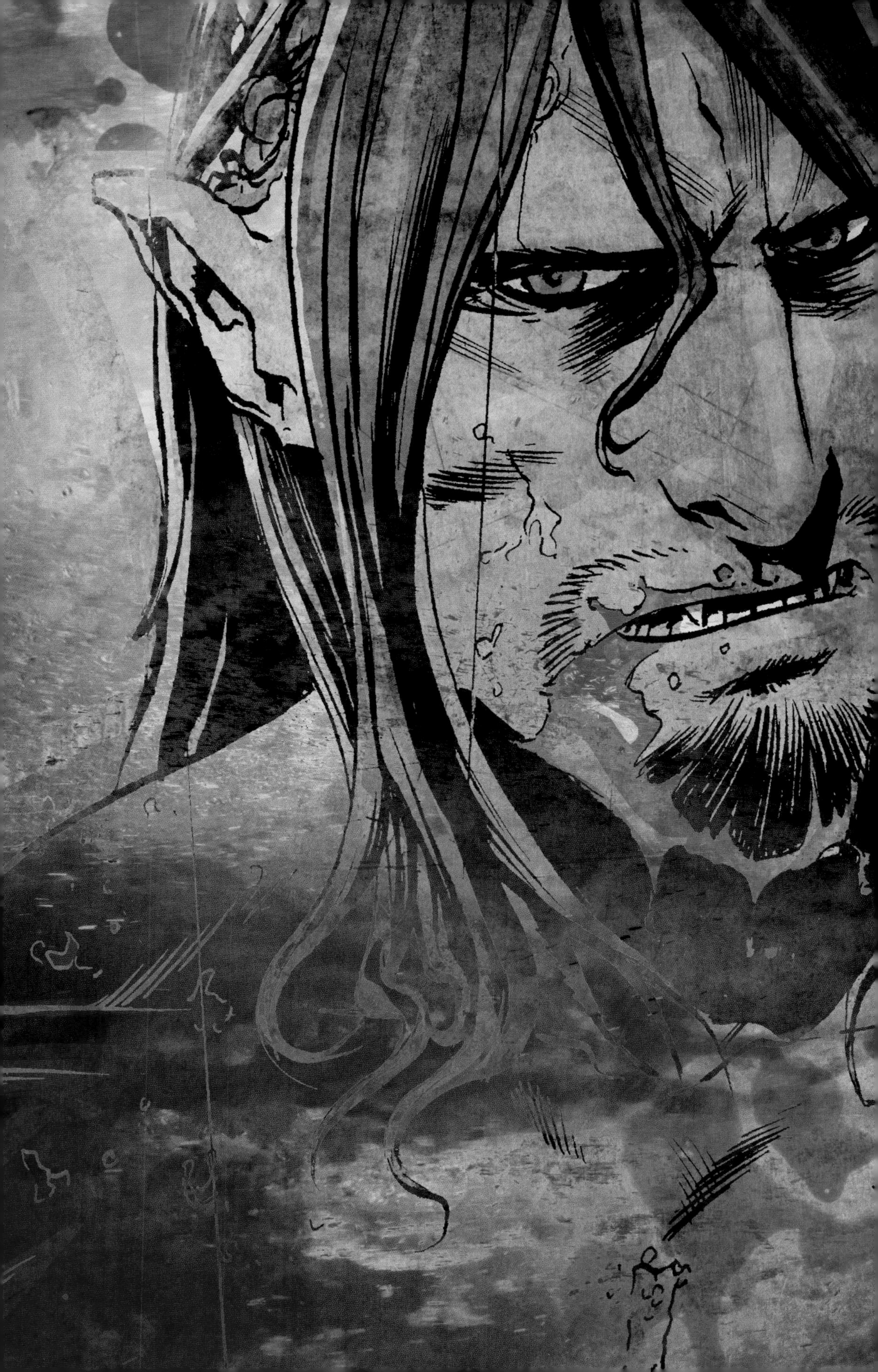

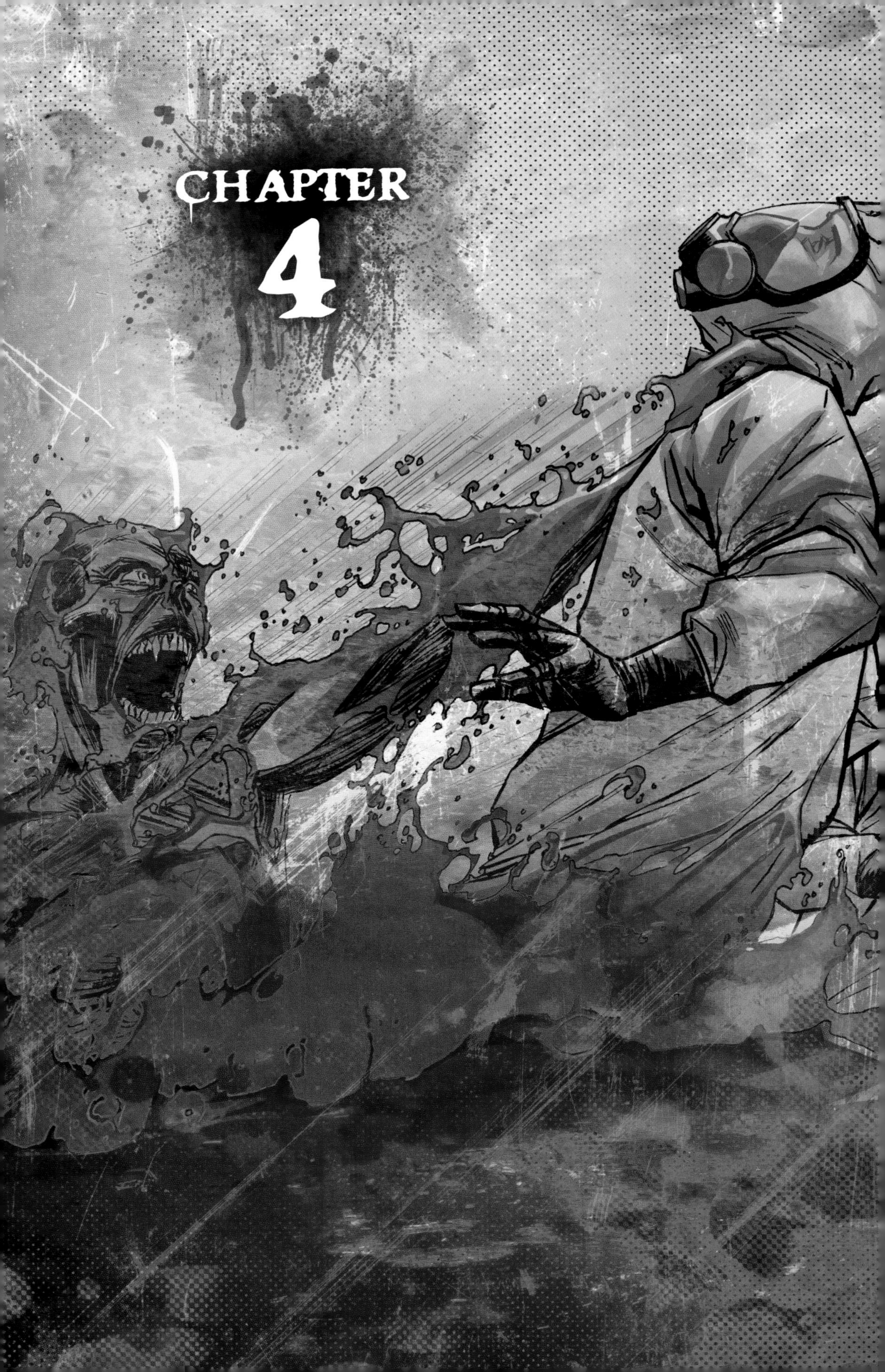
CHAPTER
4

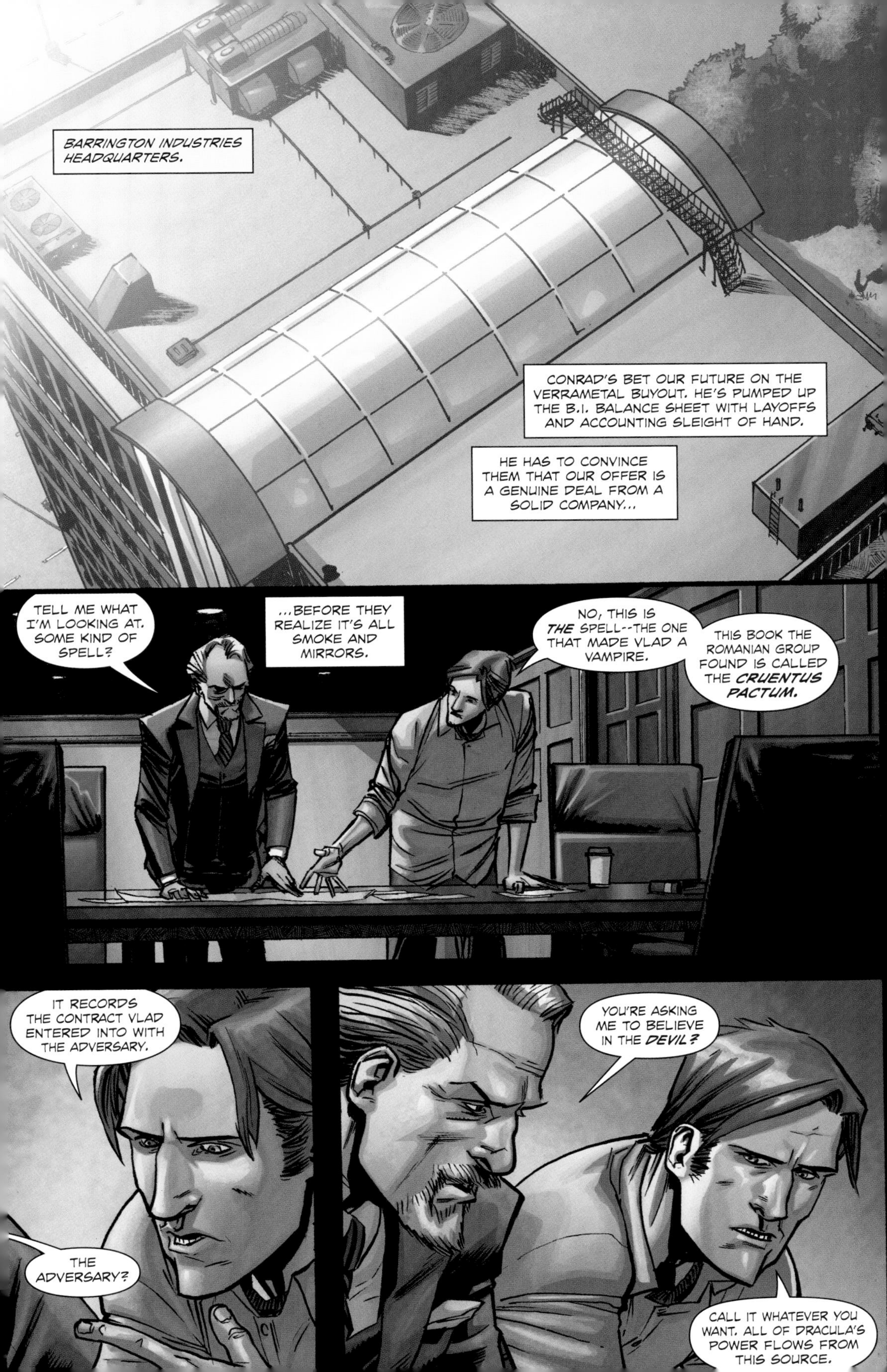
BARRINGTON INDUSTRIES HEADQUARTERS.
CONRAD'S BET OUR FUTURE ON THE VERRAMETAL BUYOUT. HE'S PUMPED UP THE B.I. BALANCE SHEET WITH LAYOFFS AND ACCOUNTING SLEIGHT OF HAND.
HE HAS TO CONVINCE THEM THAT OUR OFFER IS A GENUINE DEAL FROM A SOLID COMPANY...
TELL ME WHAT I'M LOOKING AT. SOME KIND OF SPELL?
...BEFORE THEY REALIZE IT'S ALL SMOKE AND MIRRORS.
NO, THIS IS *THE* SPELL--THE ONE THAT MADE VLAD A VAMPIRE.
THIS BOOK THE ROMANIAN GROUP FOUND IS CALLED THE ***CRUENTUS PACTUM.***
IT RECORDS THE CONTRACT VLAD ENTERED INTO WITH THE ADVERSARY.
THE ADVERSARY?
YOU'RE ASKING ME TO BELIEVE IN THE ***DEVIL?***
CALL IT WHATEVER YOU WANT. ALL OF DRACULA'S POWER FLOWS FROM THIS SOURCE.

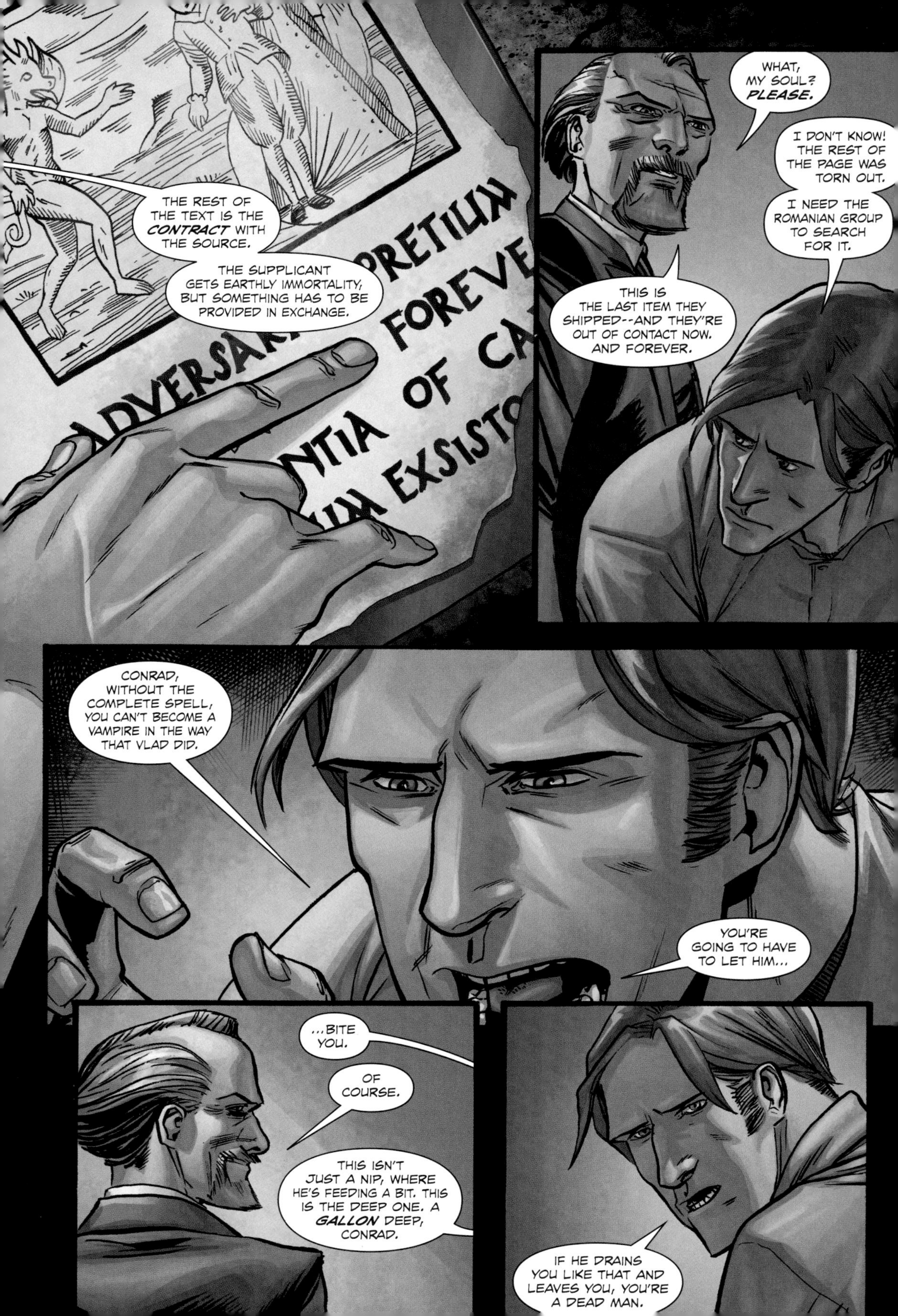
ADVERSAR... PRETIUM
FOREVE...
...NTIA OF CA...
...UM EXSISTO...
THE REST OF THE TEXT IS THE *CONTRACT* WITH THE SOURCE.
THE SUPPLICANT GETS EARTHLY IMMORTALITY, BUT SOMETHING HAS TO BE PROVIDED IN EXCHANGE.
WHAT, MY SOUL? ***PLEASE.***
I DON'T KNOW! THE REST OF THE PAGE WAS TORN OUT.
I NEED THE ROMANIAN GROUP TO SEARCH FOR IT.
THIS IS THE LAST ITEM THEY SHIPPED--AND THEY'RE OUT OF CONTACT NOW. AND FOREVER.
CONRAD, WITHOUT THE COMPLETE SPELL, YOU CAN'T BECOME A VAMPIRE IN THE WAY THAT VLAD DID.
YOU'RE GOING TO HAVE TO LET HIM...
...BITE YOU.
OF COURSE.
THIS ISN'T JUST A NIP, WHERE HE'S FEEDING A BIT. THIS IS THE DEEP ONE. A ***GALLON*** DEEP, CONRAD.
IF HE DRAINS YOU LIKE THAT AND LEAVES YOU, YOU'RE A DEAD MAN.

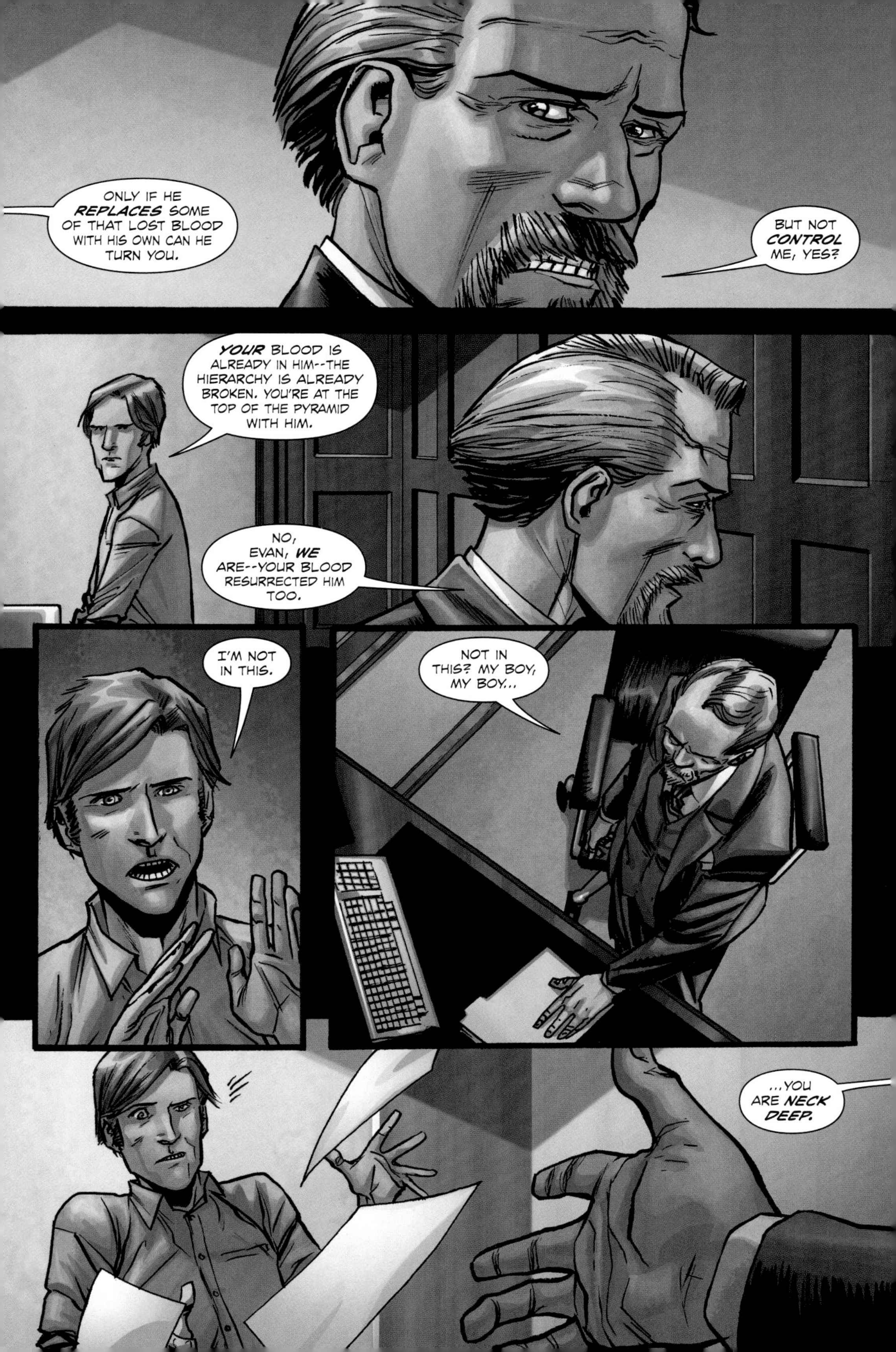
ONLY IF HE *REPLACES* SOME OF THAT LOST BLOOD WITH HIS OWN CAN HE TURN YOU.
BUT NOT *CONTROL* ME, YES?
YOUR BLOOD IS ALREADY IN HIM--THE HIERARCHY IS ALREADY BROKEN. YOU'RE AT THE TOP OF THE PYRAMID WITH HIM.
NO, EVAN, *WE* ARE--YOUR BLOOD RESURRECTED HIM TOO.
I'M NOT IN THIS.
NOT IN THIS? MY BOY, MY BOY...
...YOU ARE *NECK DEEP.*

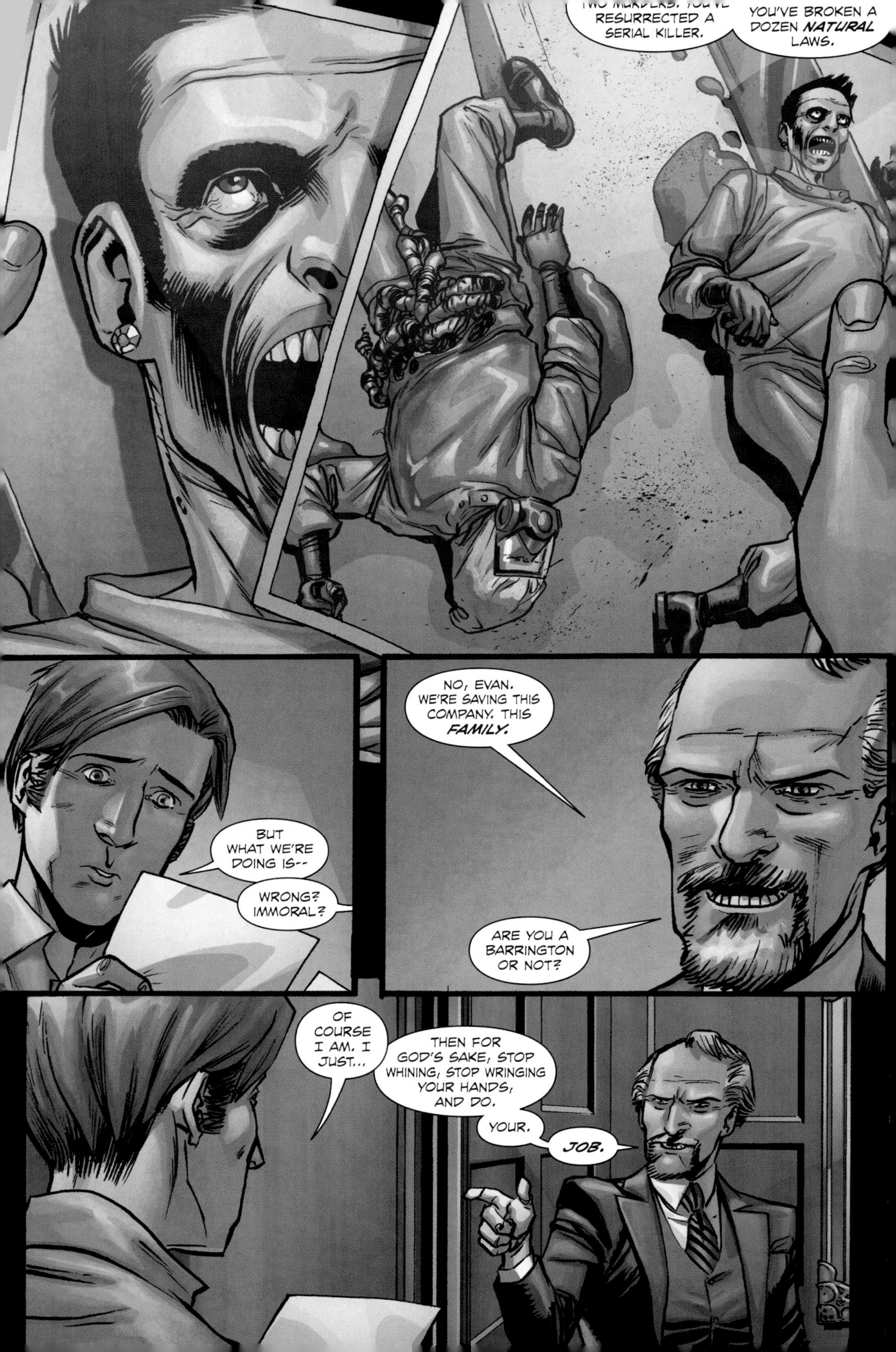
RESURRECTED A SERIAL KILLER.
YOU'VE BROKEN A DOZEN *NATURAL* LAWS.
BUT WHAT WE'RE DOING IS--
WRONG? IMMORAL?
NO, EVAN. WE'RE SAVING THIS COMPANY. THIS *FAMILY.*
ARE YOU A BARRINGTON OR NOT?
OF COURSE I AM. I JUST...
THEN FOR GOD'S SAKE, STOP WHINING, STOP WRINGING YOUR HANDS, AND DO.
YOUR.
JOB.

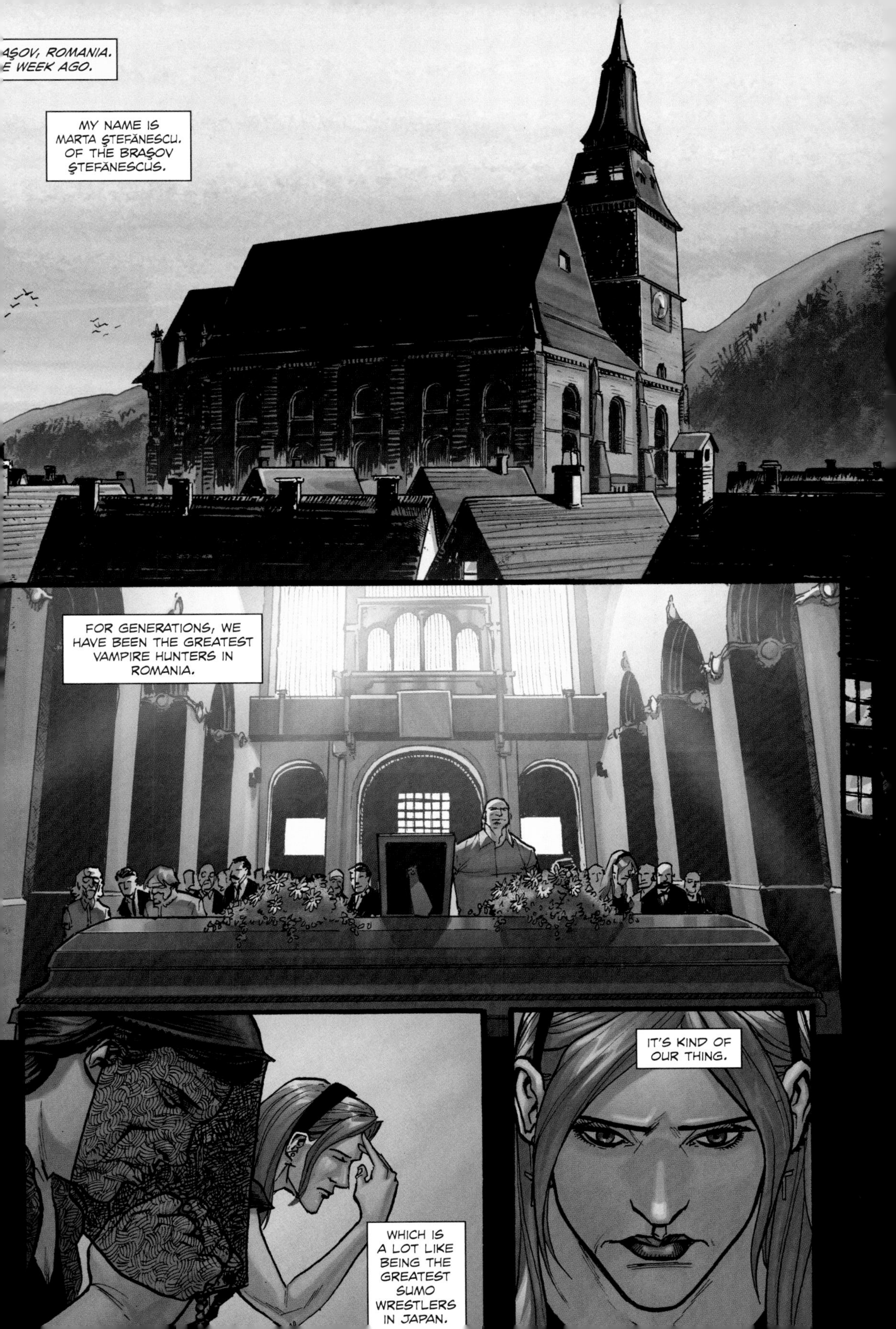
AŞOV, ROMANIA.
E WEEK AGO.
MY NAME IS MARTA ŞTEFĂNESCU. OF THE BRAŞOV ŞTEFĂNESCUS.
FOR GENERATIONS, WE HAVE BEEN THE GREATEST VAMPIRE HUNTERS IN ROMANIA.
WHICH IS A LOT LIKE BEING THE GREATEST SUMO WRESTLERS IN JAPAN.
IT'S KIND OF OUR THING.

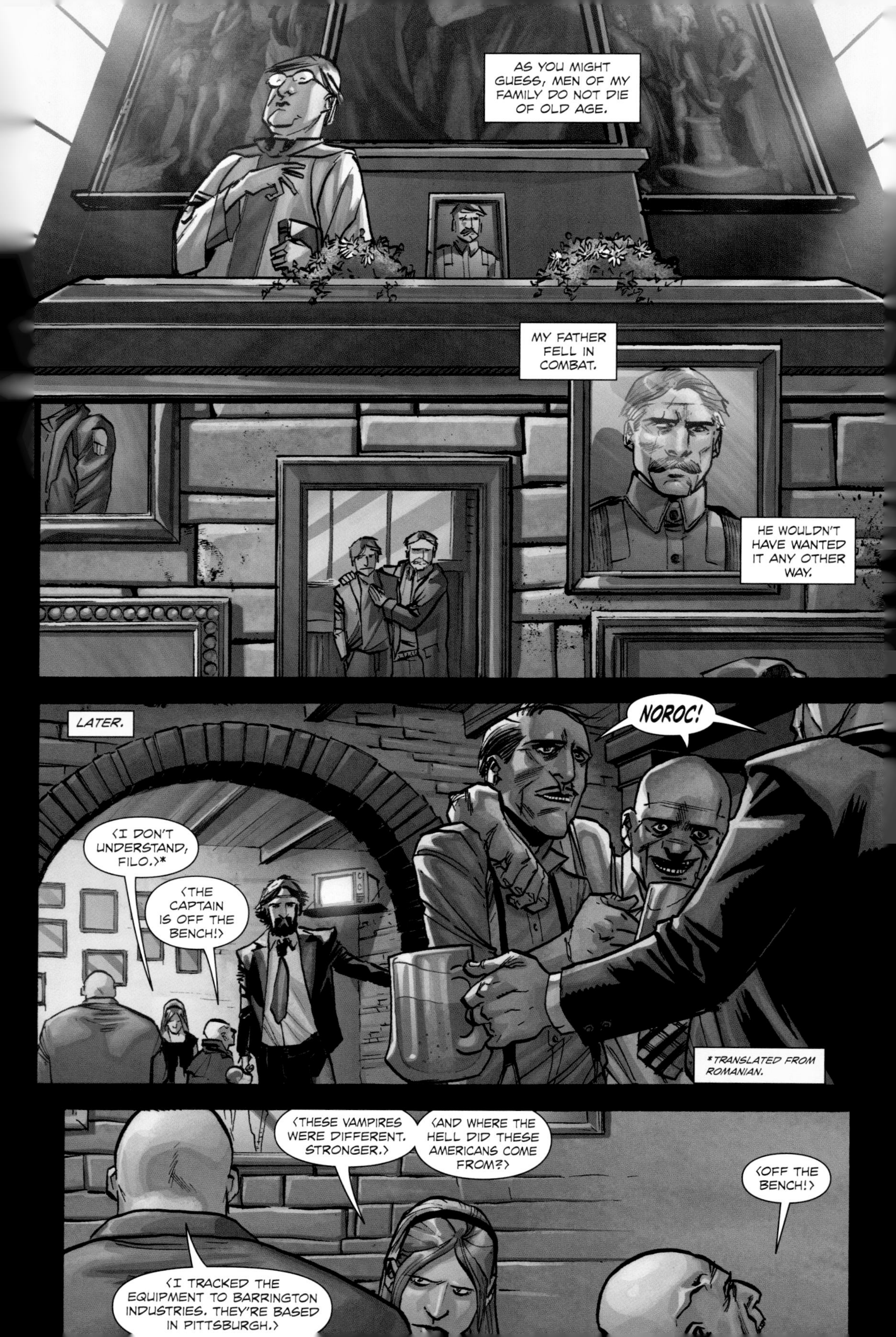
AS YOU MIGHT GUESS, MEN OF MY FAMILY DO NOT DIE OF OLD AGE.
MY FATHER FELL IN COMBAT.
HE WOULDN'T HAVE WANTED IT ANY OTHER WAY.
LATER.
NOROC!
<I DON'T UNDERSTAND, FILO.>*
<THE CAPTAIN IS OFF THE BENCH!>
*TRANSLATED FROM ROMANIAN.
<THESE VAMPIRES WERE DIFFERENT. STRONGER.>
<AND WHERE THE HELL DID THESE AMERICANS COME FROM?>
<OFF THE BENCH!>
<I TRACKED THE EQUIPMENT TO BARRINGTON INDUSTRIES. THEY'RE BASED IN PITTSBURGH.>

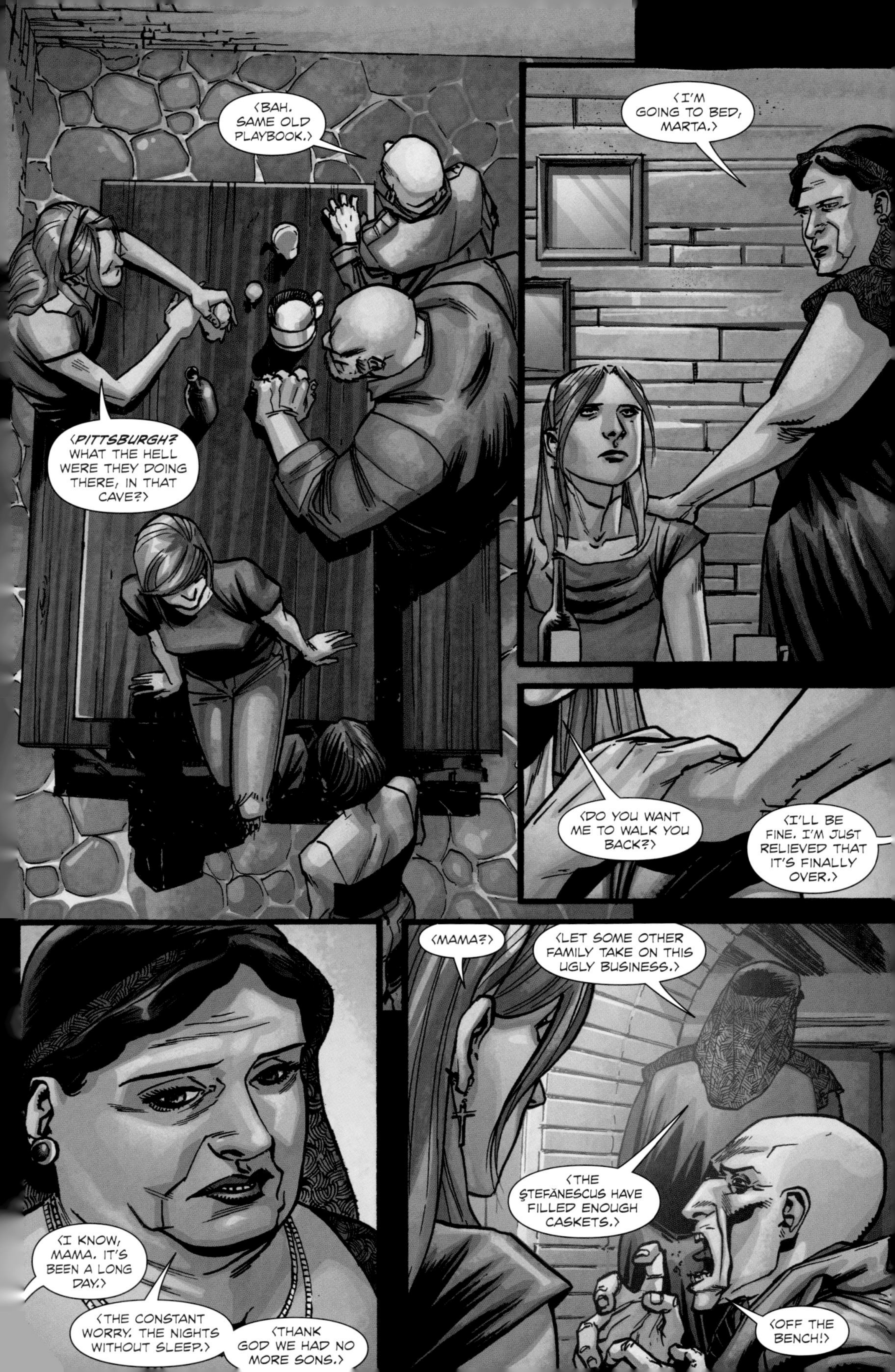
‹BAH. SAME OLD PLAYBOOK.›
‹PITTSBURGH? WHAT THE HELL WERE THEY DOING THERE, IN THAT CAVE?›
‹I'M GOING TO BED, MARTA.›
‹DO YOU WANT ME TO WALK YOU BACK?›
‹I'LL BE FINE. I'M JUST RELIEVED THAT IT'S FINALLY OVER.›
‹I KNOW, MAMA. IT'S BEEN A LONG DAY.›
‹THE CONSTANT WORRY. THE NIGHTS WITHOUT SLEEP.›
‹THANK GOD WE HAD NO MORE SONS.›
‹MAMA?›
‹LET SOME OTHER FAMILY TAKE ON THIS UGLY BUSINESS.›
‹THE ŞTEFĂNESCUS HAVE FILLED ENOUGH CASKETS.›
‹OFF THE BENCH!›

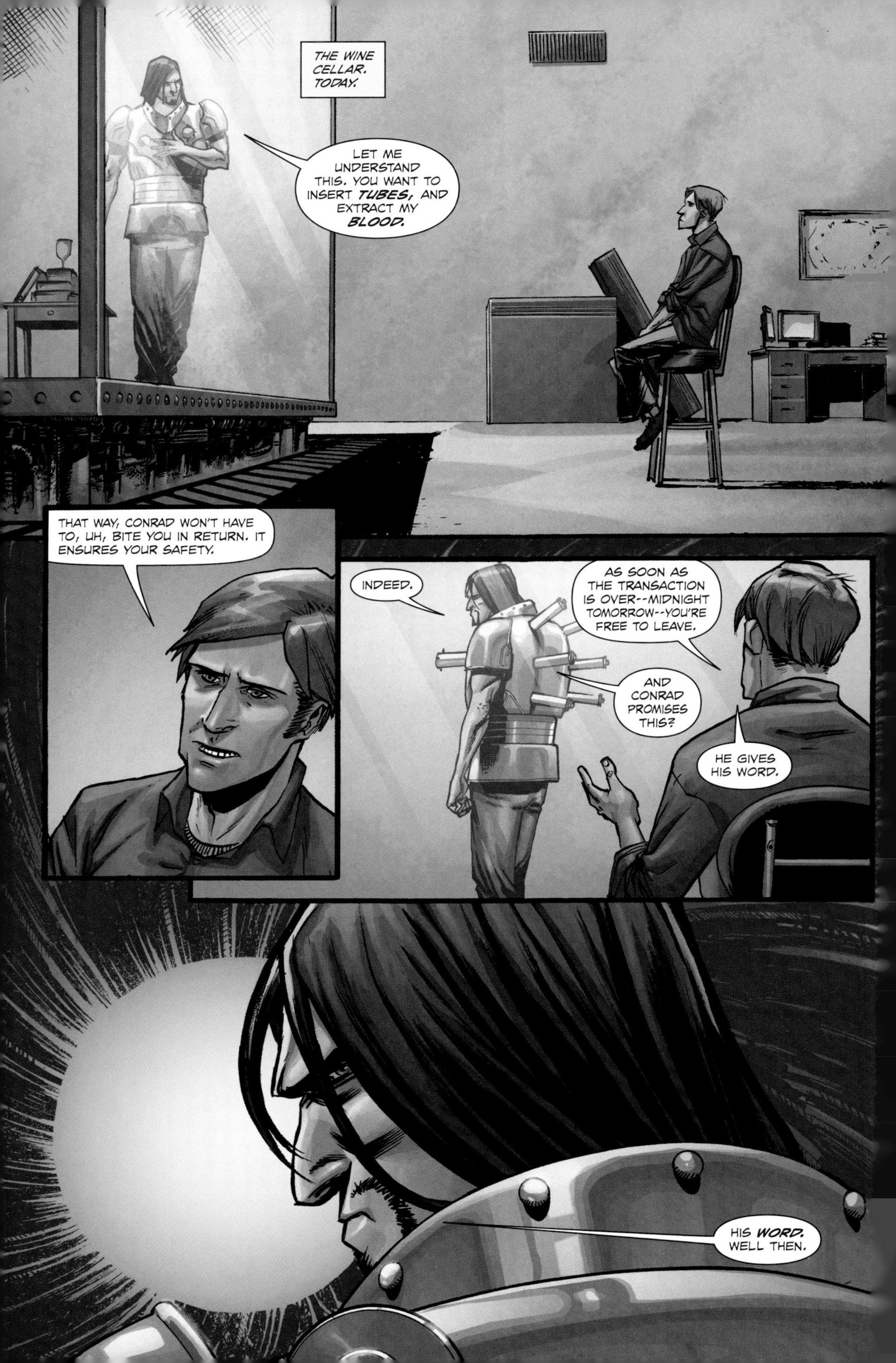
THE WINE CELLAR. TODAY.
LET ME UNDERSTAND THIS. YOU WANT TO INSERT TUBES, AND EXTRACT MY BLOOD.
THAT WAY, CONRAD WON'T HAVE TO, UH, BITE YOU IN RETURN. IT ENSURES YOUR SAFETY.
INDEED.
AS SOON AS THE TRANSACTION IS OVER--MIDNIGHT TOMORROW--YOU'RE FREE TO LEAVE.
AND CONRAD PROMISES THIS?
HE GIVES HIS WORD.
HIS WORD. WELL THEN.

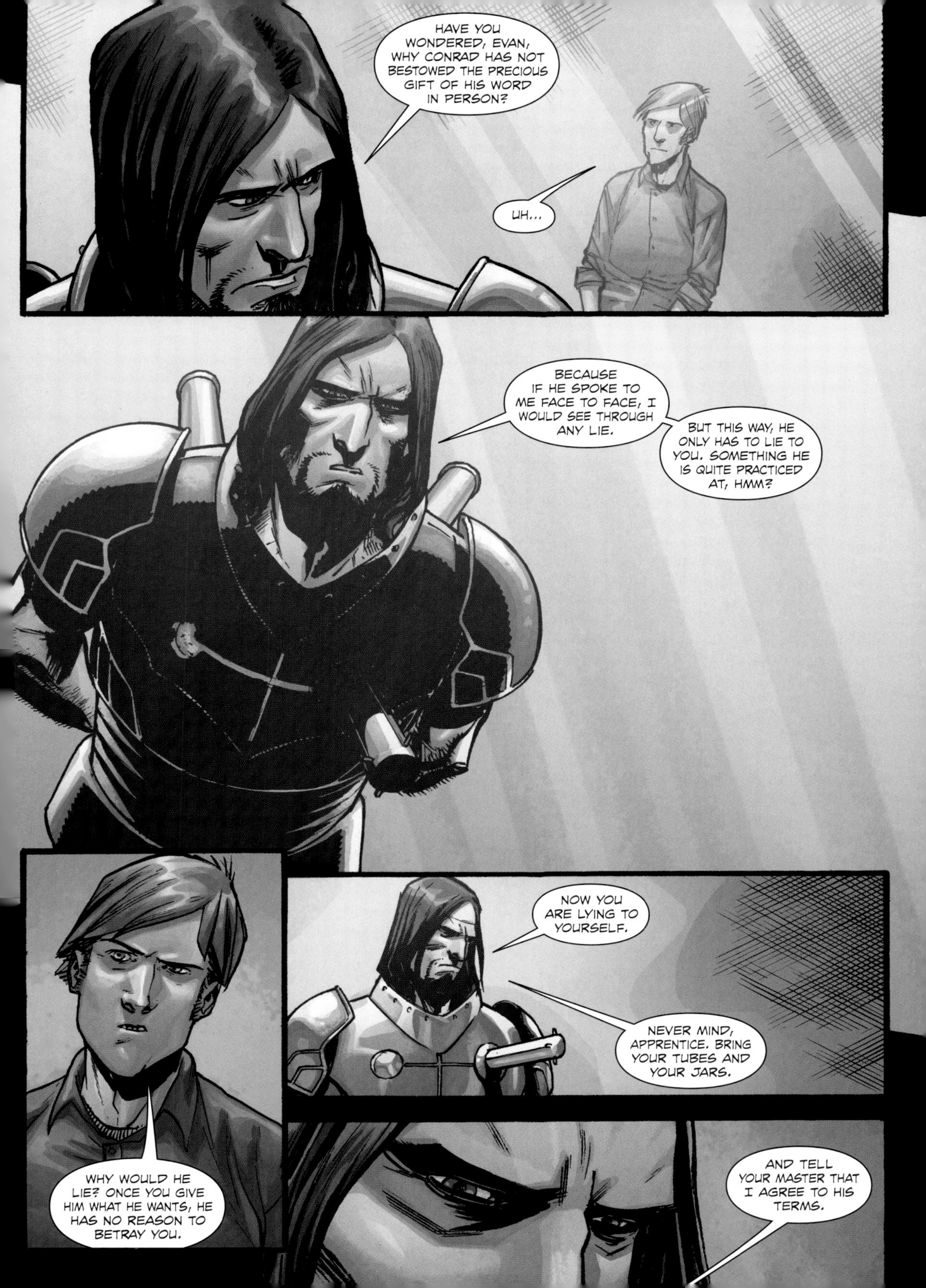
HAVE YOU WONDERED, EVAN, WHY CONRAD HAS NOT BESTOWED THE PRECIOUS GIFT OF HIS WORD IN PERSON?
UH...
BECAUSE IF HE SPOKE TO ME FACE TO FACE, I WOULD SEE THROUGH ANY LIE.
BUT THIS WAY, HE ONLY HAS TO LIE TO YOU. SOMETHING HE IS QUITE PRACTICED AT, HMM?
WHY WOULD HE LIE? ONCE YOU GIVE HIM WHAT HE WANTS, HE HAS NO REASON TO BETRAY YOU.
NOW YOU ARE LYING TO YOURSELF.
NEVER MIND, APPRENTICE. BRING YOUR TUBES AND YOUR JARS.
AND TELL YOUR MASTER THAT I AGREE TO HIS TERMS.

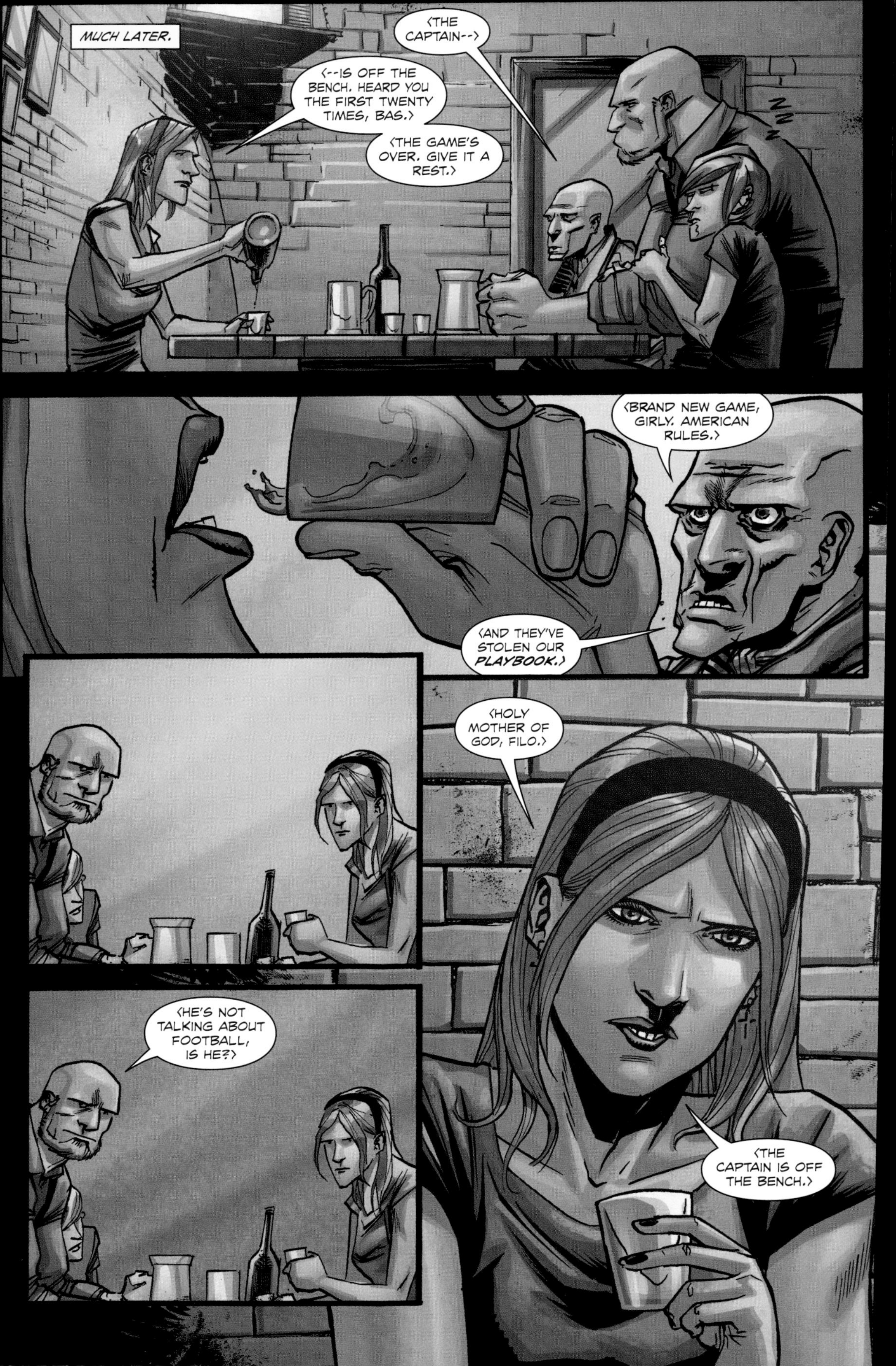
MUCH LATER.
<THE CAPTAIN-->
<--IS OFF THE BENCH. HEARD YOU THE FIRST TWENTY TIMES, BAS.>
<THE GAME'S OVER. GIVE IT A REST.>
<BRAND NEW GAME, GIRLY. AMERICAN RULES.>
<AND THEY'VE STOLEN OUR *PLAYBOOK.*>
<HOLY MOTHER OF GOD, FILO.>
<HE'S NOT TALKING ABOUT FOOTBALL, IS HE?>
<THE CAPTAIN IS OFF THE BENCH.>

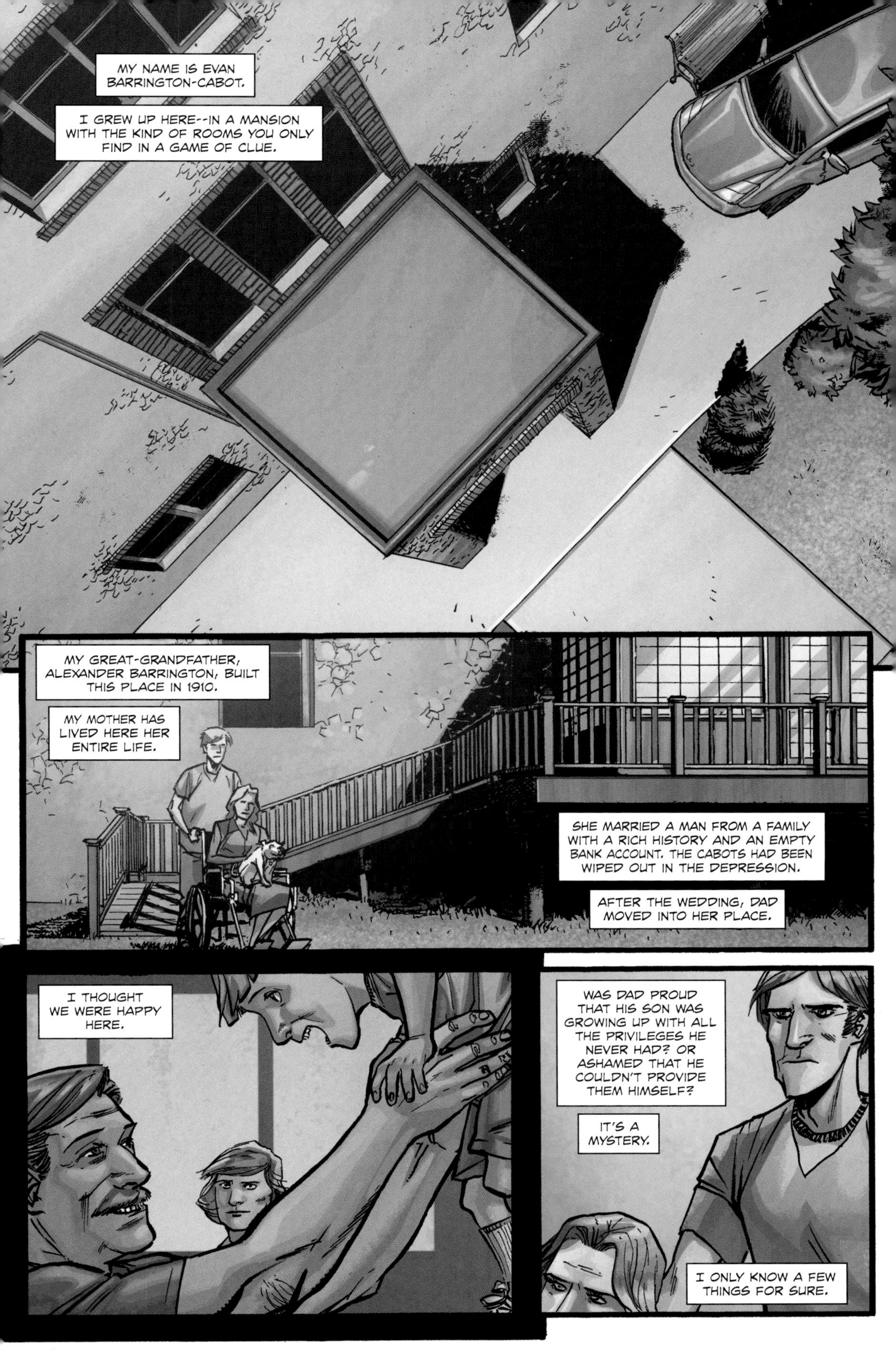
MY NAME IS EVAN BARRINGTON-CABOT.
I GREW UP HERE--IN A MANSION WITH THE KIND OF ROOMS YOU ONLY FIND IN A GAME OF CLUE.
MY GREAT-GRANDFATHER, ALEXANDER BARRINGTON, BUILT THIS PLACE IN 1910.
MY MOTHER HAS LIVED HERE HER ENTIRE LIFE.
SHE MARRIED A MAN FROM A FAMILY WITH A RICH HISTORY AND AN EMPTY BANK ACCOUNT. THE CABOTS HAD BEEN WIPED OUT IN THE DEPRESSION.
AFTER THE WEDDING, DAD MOVED INTO HER PLACE.
I THOUGHT WE WERE HAPPY HERE.
WAS DAD PROUD THAT HIS SON WAS GROWING UP WITH ALL THE PRIVILEGES HE NEVER HAD? OR ASHAMED THAT HE COULDN'T PROVIDE THEM HIMSELF?
IT'S A MYSTERY.
I ONLY KNOW A FEW THINGS FOR SURE.

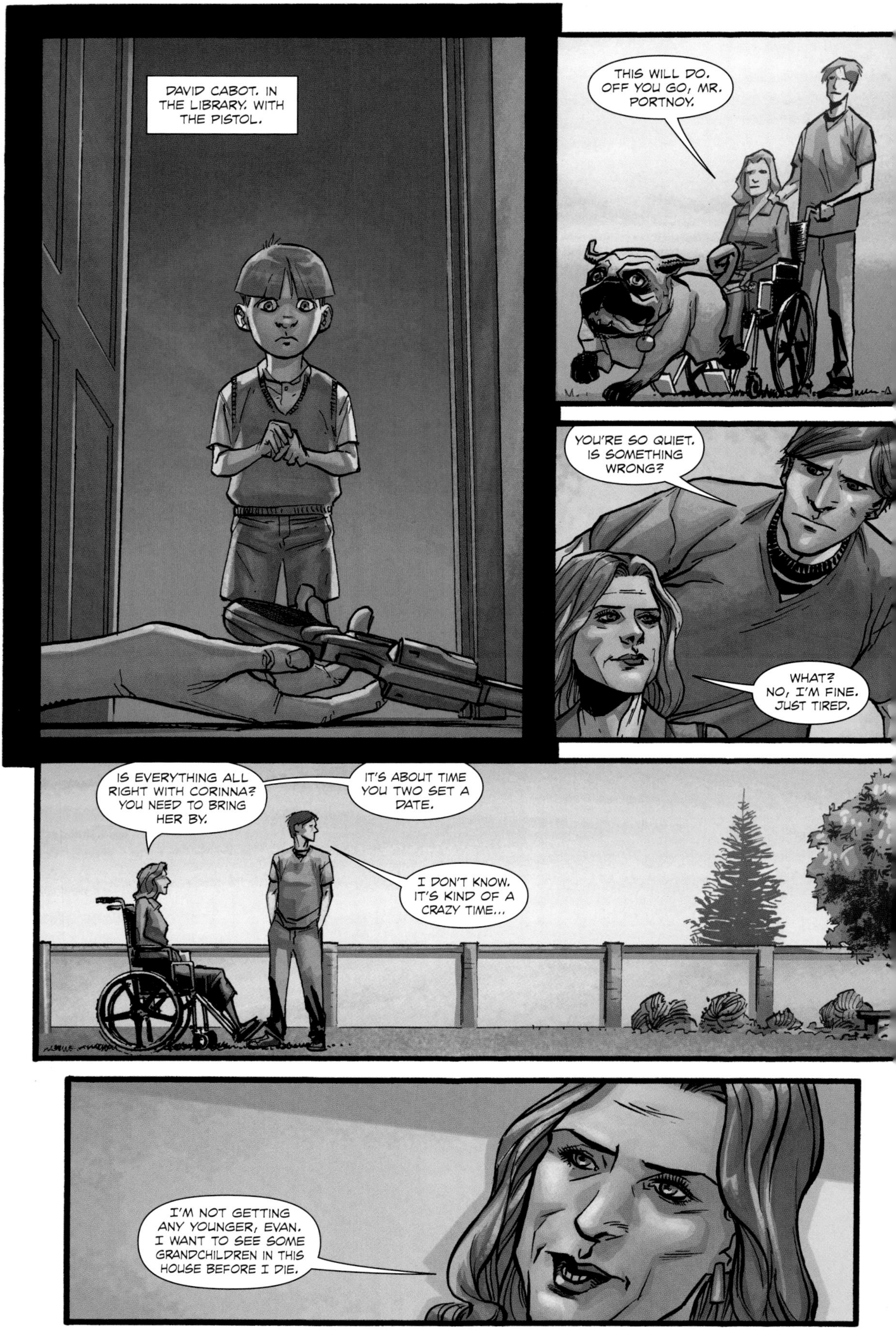
DAVID CABOT. IN THE LIBRARY. WITH THE PISTOL.
THIS WILL DO. OFF YOU GO, MR. PORTNOY.
YOU'RE SO QUIET. IS SOMETHING WRONG?
WHAT? NO, I'M FINE. JUST TIRED.
IS EVERYTHING ALL RIGHT WITH CORINNA? YOU NEED TO BRING HER BY.
IT'S ABOUT TIME YOU TWO SET A DATE.
I DON'T KNOW. IT'S KIND OF A CRAZY TIME...
I'M NOT GETTING ANY YOUNGER, EVAN. I WANT TO SEE SOME GRANDCHILDREN IN THIS HOUSE BEFORE I DIE.

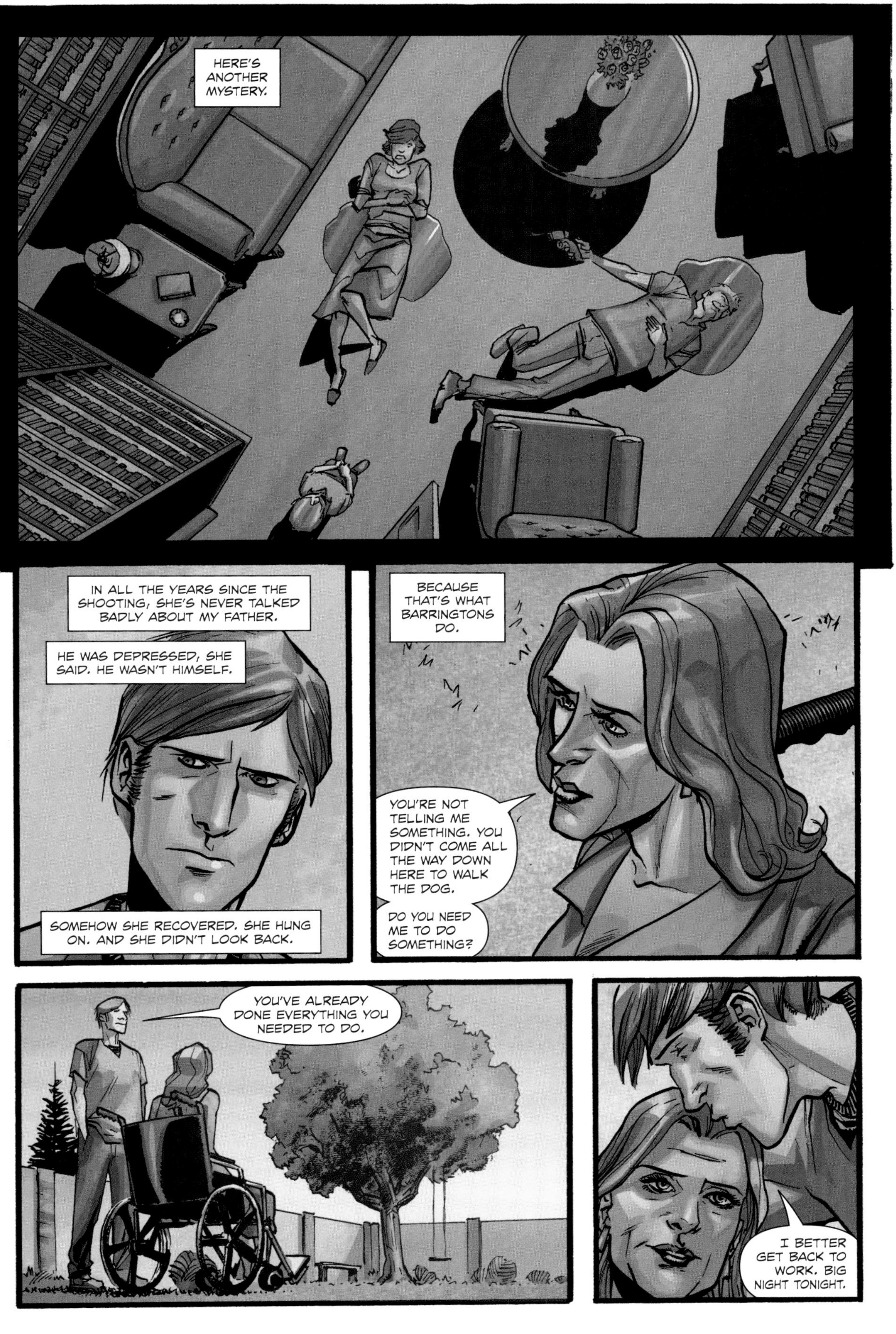
HERE'S ANOTHER MYSTERY.
IN ALL THE YEARS SINCE THE SHOOTING, SHE'S NEVER TALKED BADLY ABOUT MY FATHER.
HE WAS DEPRESSED, SHE SAID. HE WASN'T HIMSELF.
SOMEHOW SHE RECOVERED. SHE HUNG ON. AND SHE DIDN'T LOOK BACK.
BECAUSE THAT'S WHAT BARRINGTONS DO.
YOU'RE NOT TELLING ME SOMETHING. YOU DIDN'T COME ALL THE WAY DOWN HERE TO WALK THE DOG.
DO YOU NEED ME TO DO SOMETHING?
YOU'VE ALREADY DONE EVERYTHING YOU NEEDED TO DO.
I BETTER GET BACK TO WORK. BIG NIGHT TONIGHT.

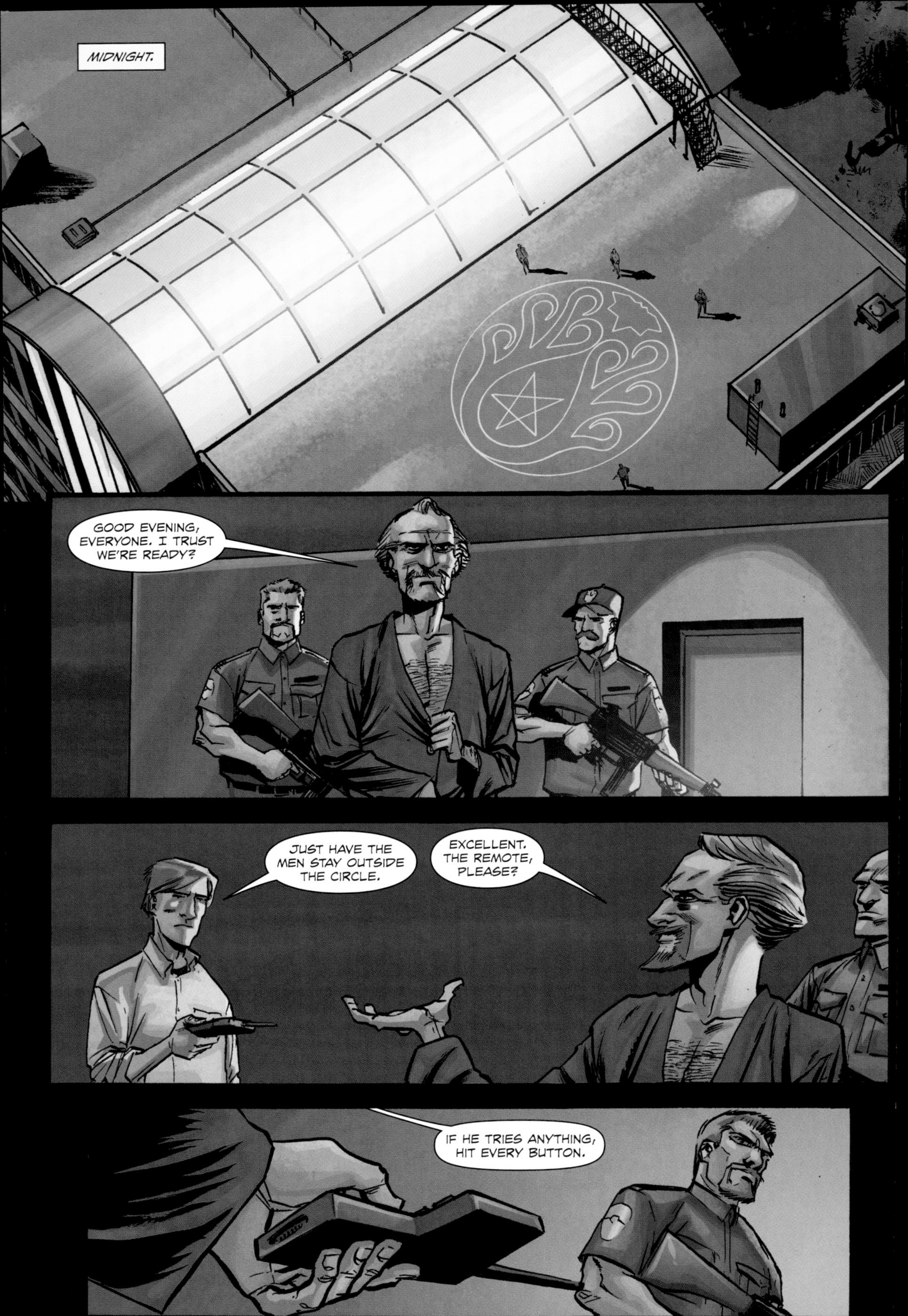
MIDNIGHT.
GOOD EVENING, EVERYONE. I TRUST WE'RE READY?
JUST HAVE THE MEN STAY OUTSIDE THE CIRCLE.
EXCELLENT. THE REMOTE, PLEASE?
IF HE TRIES ANYTHING, HIT EVERY BUTTON.

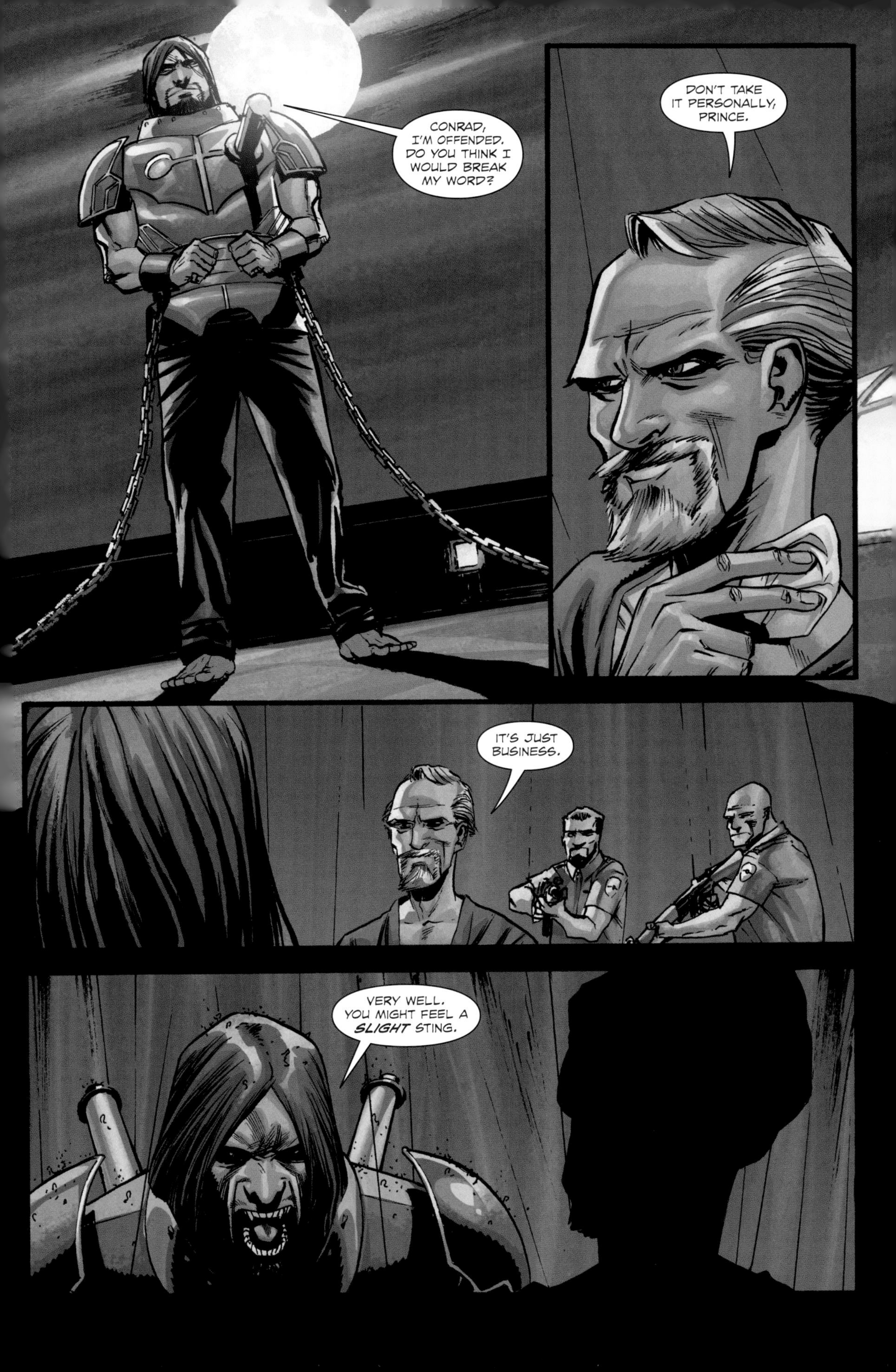
CONRAD, I'M OFFENDED. DO YOU THINK I WOULD BREAK MY WORD?
DON'T TAKE IT PERSONALLY, PRINCE.
IT'S JUST BUSINESS.
VERY WELL. YOU MIGHT FEEL A *SLIGHT* STING.

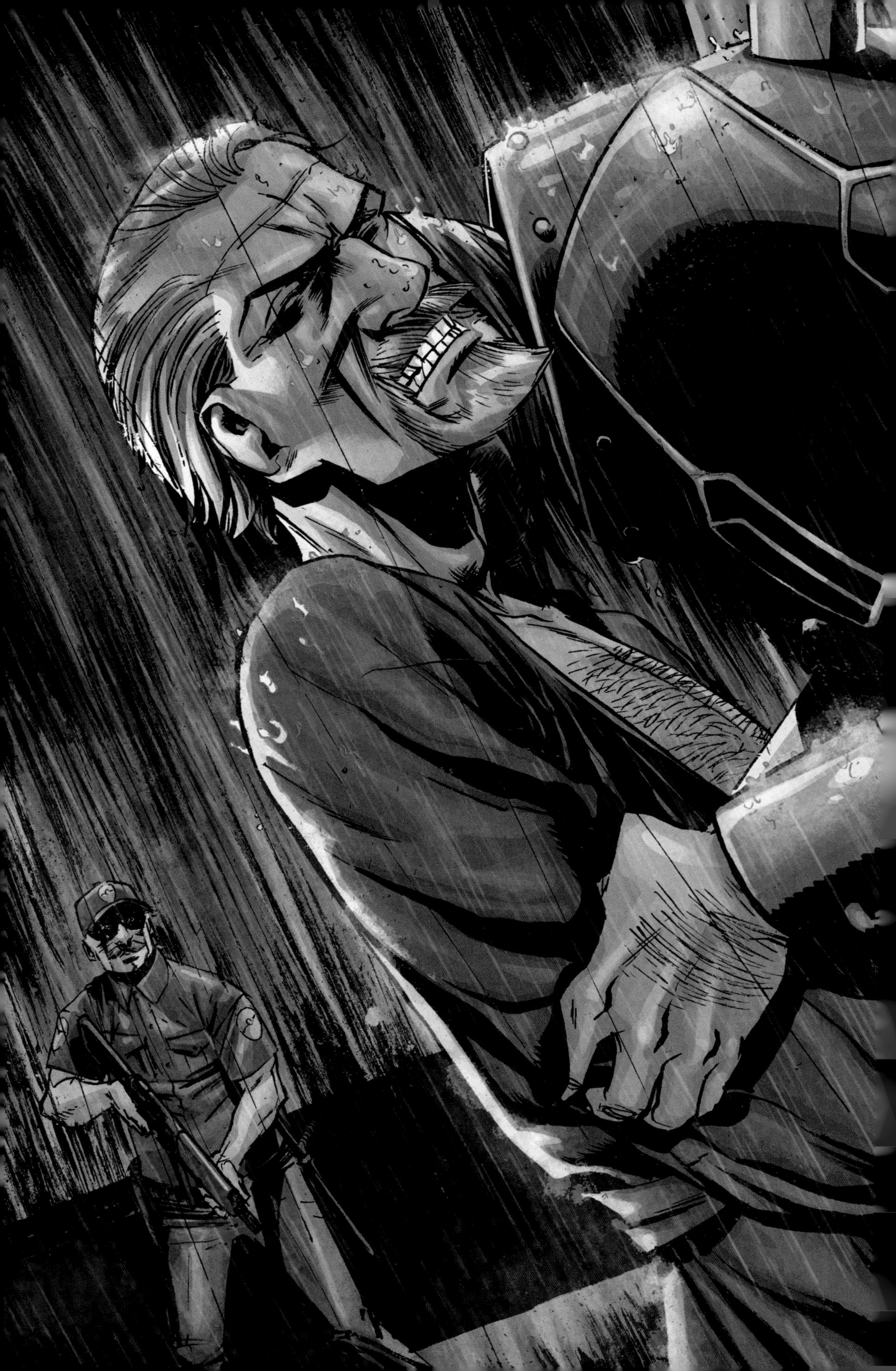

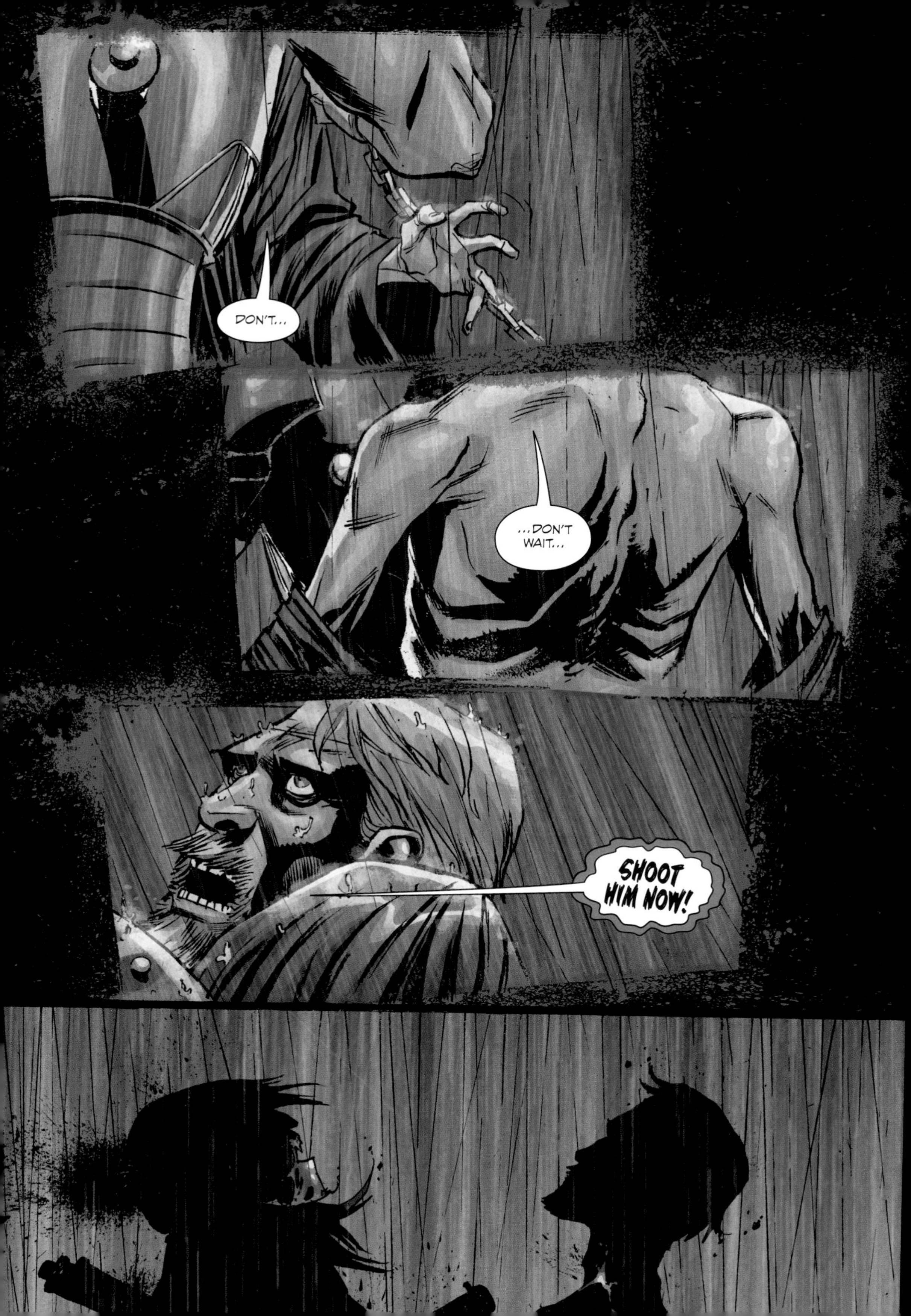
DON'T...
...DON'T WAIT...
SHOOT HIM NOW!

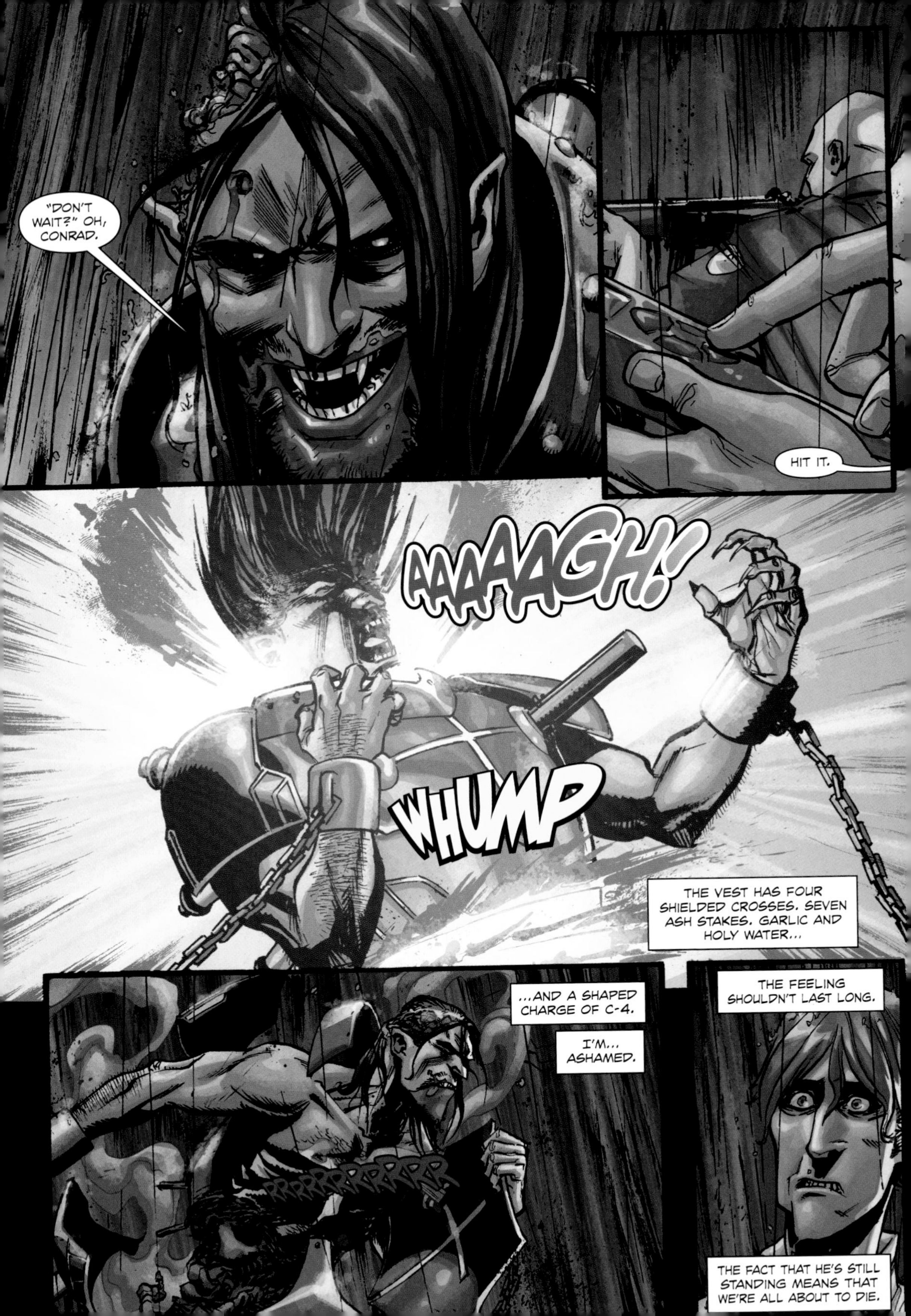

"DON'T WAIT?" OH, CONRAD.
HIT IT.
AAAAAAGH!
WHUMP
THE VEST HAS FOUR SHIELDED CROSSES. SEVEN ASH STAKES. GARLIC AND HOLY WATER...
...AND A SHAPED CHARGE OF C-4.
I'M... ASHAMED.
RRRRRRRRRRRR
THE FEELING SHOULDN'T LAST LONG.
THE FACT THAT HE'S STILL STANDING MEANS THAT WE'RE ALL ABOUT TO DIE.

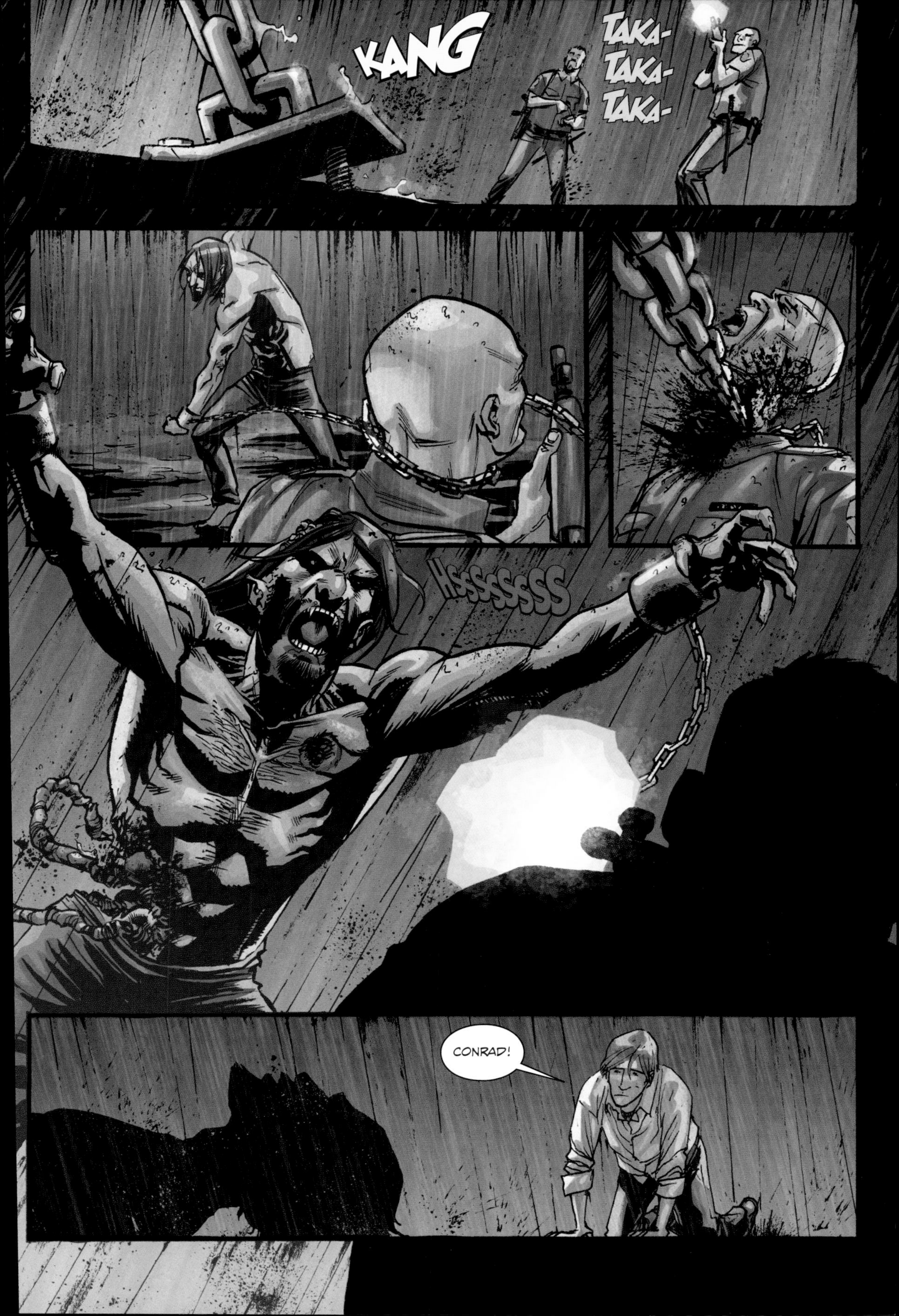
KANG
TAKA-TAKA-TAKA-
HSSSSSSS
CONRAD!

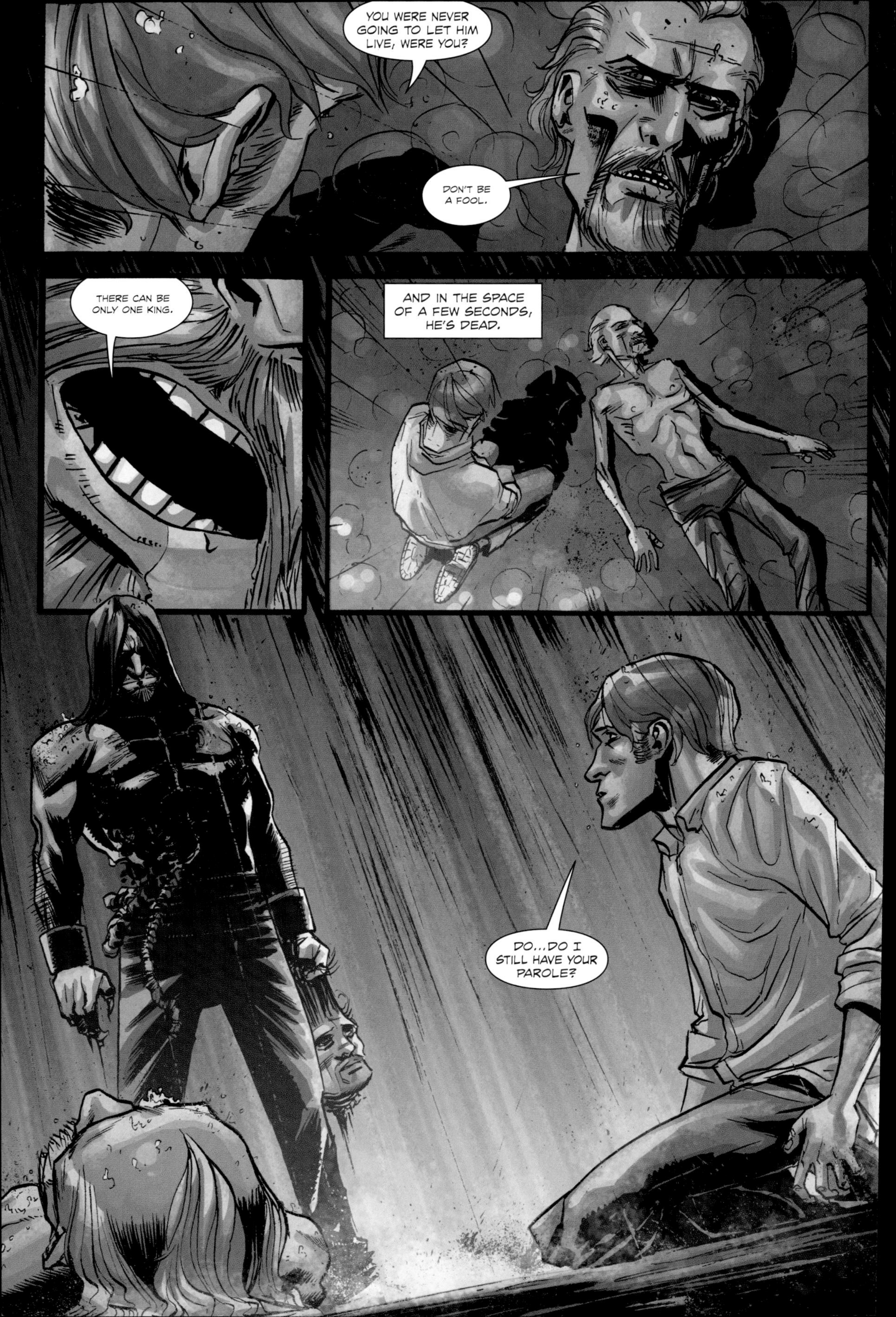
YOU WERE NEVER GOING TO LET HIM LIVE, WERE YOU?
DON'T BE A FOOL.
THERE CAN BE ONLY ONE KING.
AND IN THE SPACE OF A FEW SECONDS, HE'S DEAD.
DO...DO I STILL HAVE YOUR PAROLE?

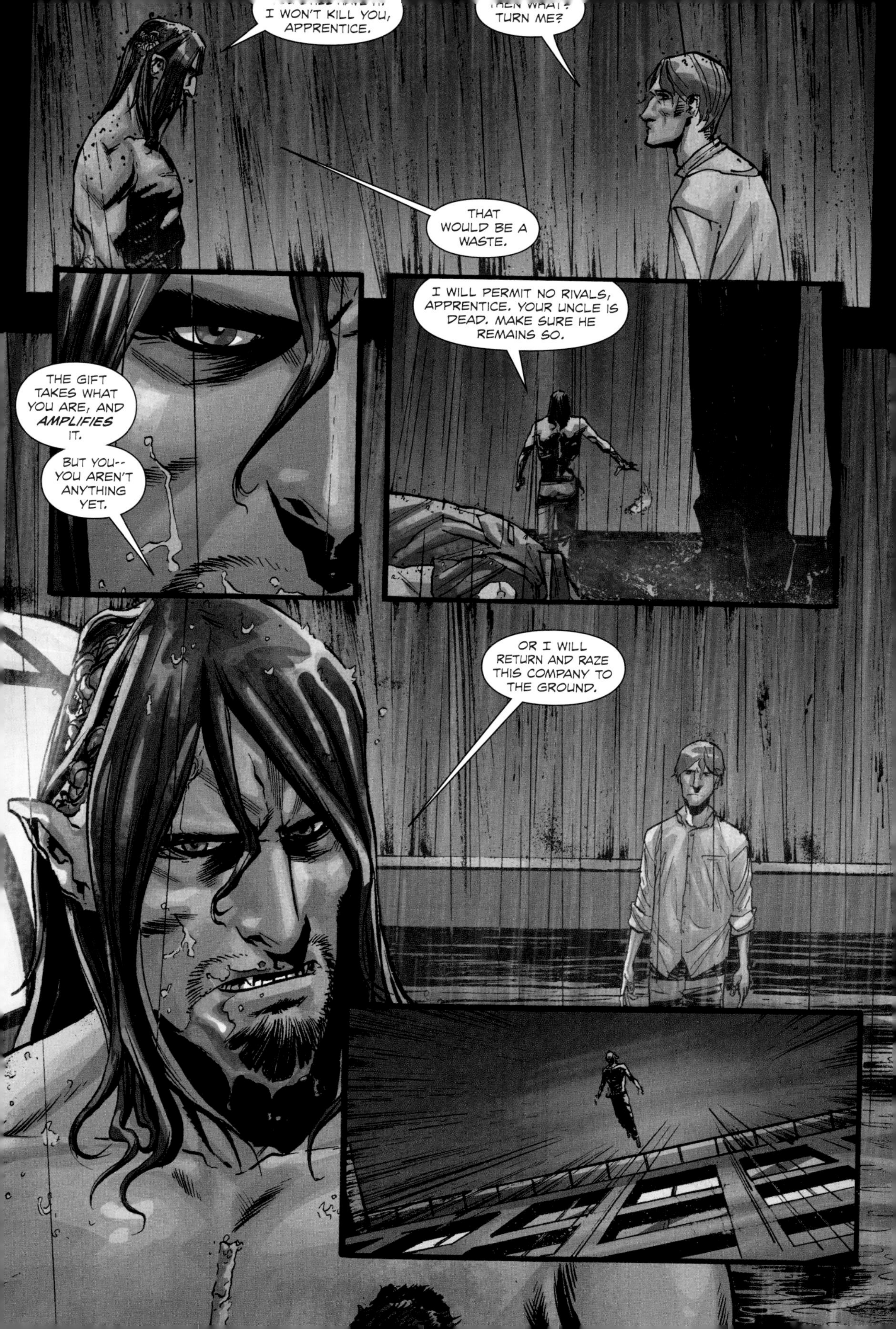
I WON'T KILL YOU, APPRENTICE.
TURN ME?
THAT WOULD BE A WASTE.
THE GIFT TAKES WHAT YOU ARE, AND *AMPLIFIES* IT.
BUT YOU-- YOU AREN'T ANYTHING YET.
I WILL PERMIT NO RIVALS, APPRENTICE. YOUR UNCLE IS DEAD. MAKE SURE HE REMAINS SO.
OR I WILL RETURN AND RAZE THIS COMPANY TO THE GROUND.

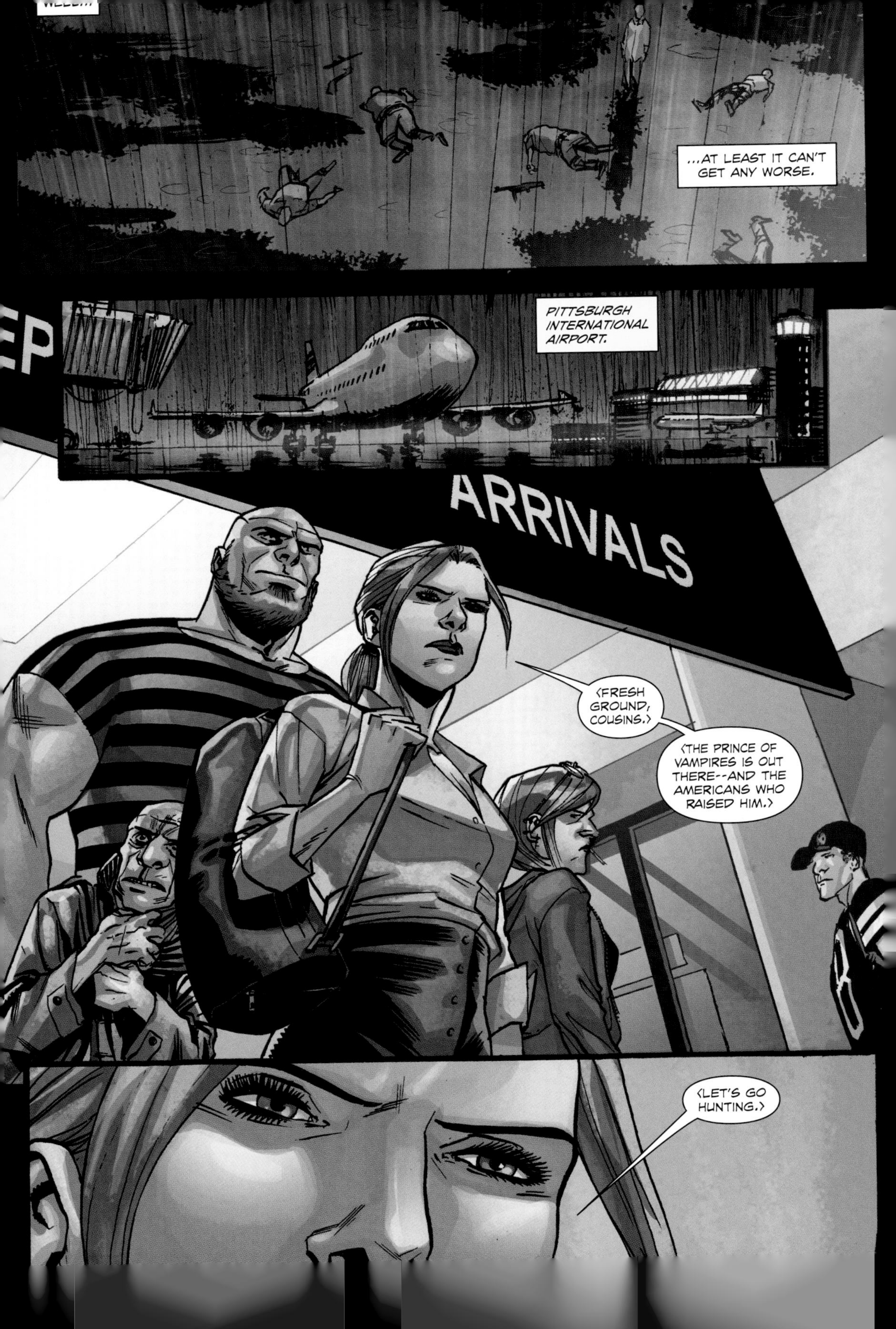
...AT LEAST IT CAN'T GET ANY WORSE.
PITTSBURGH INTERNATIONAL AIRPORT.
ARRIVALS
‹FRESH GROUND, COUSINS.›
‹THE PRINCE OF VAMPIRES IS OUT THERE--AND THE AMERICANS WHO RAISED HIM.›
‹LET'S GO HUNTING.›

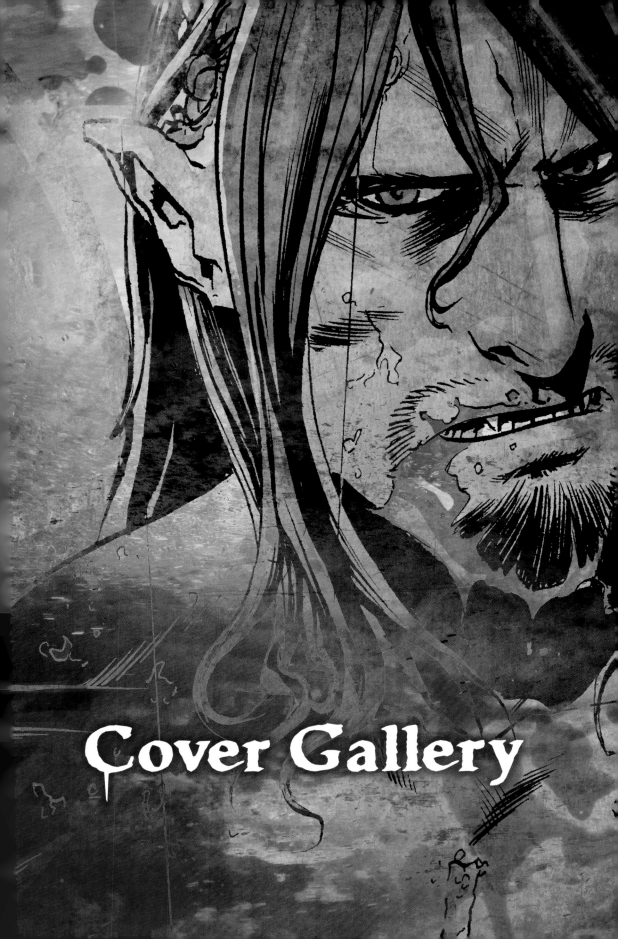

Cover Gallery

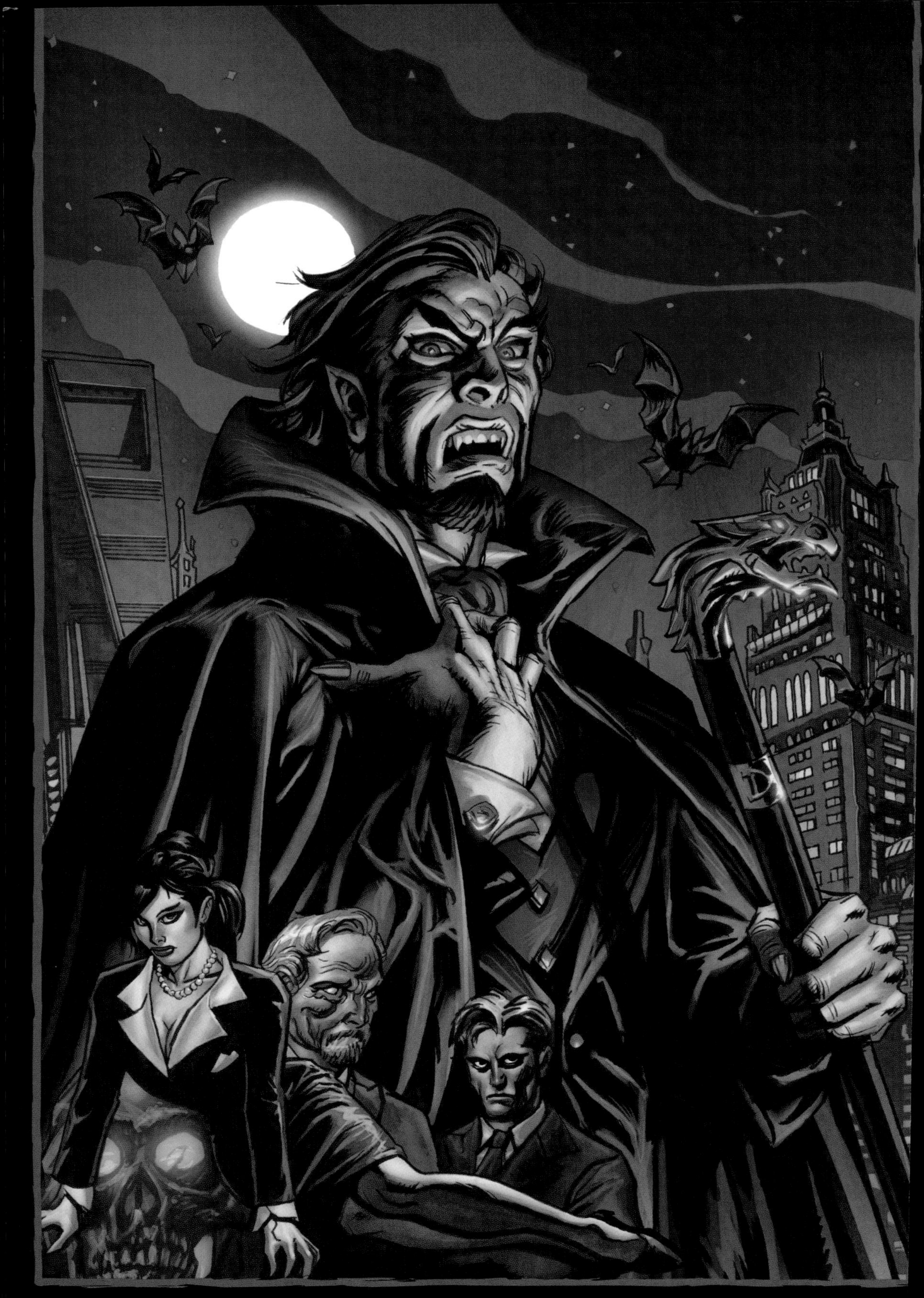

1A: Dan Brereton

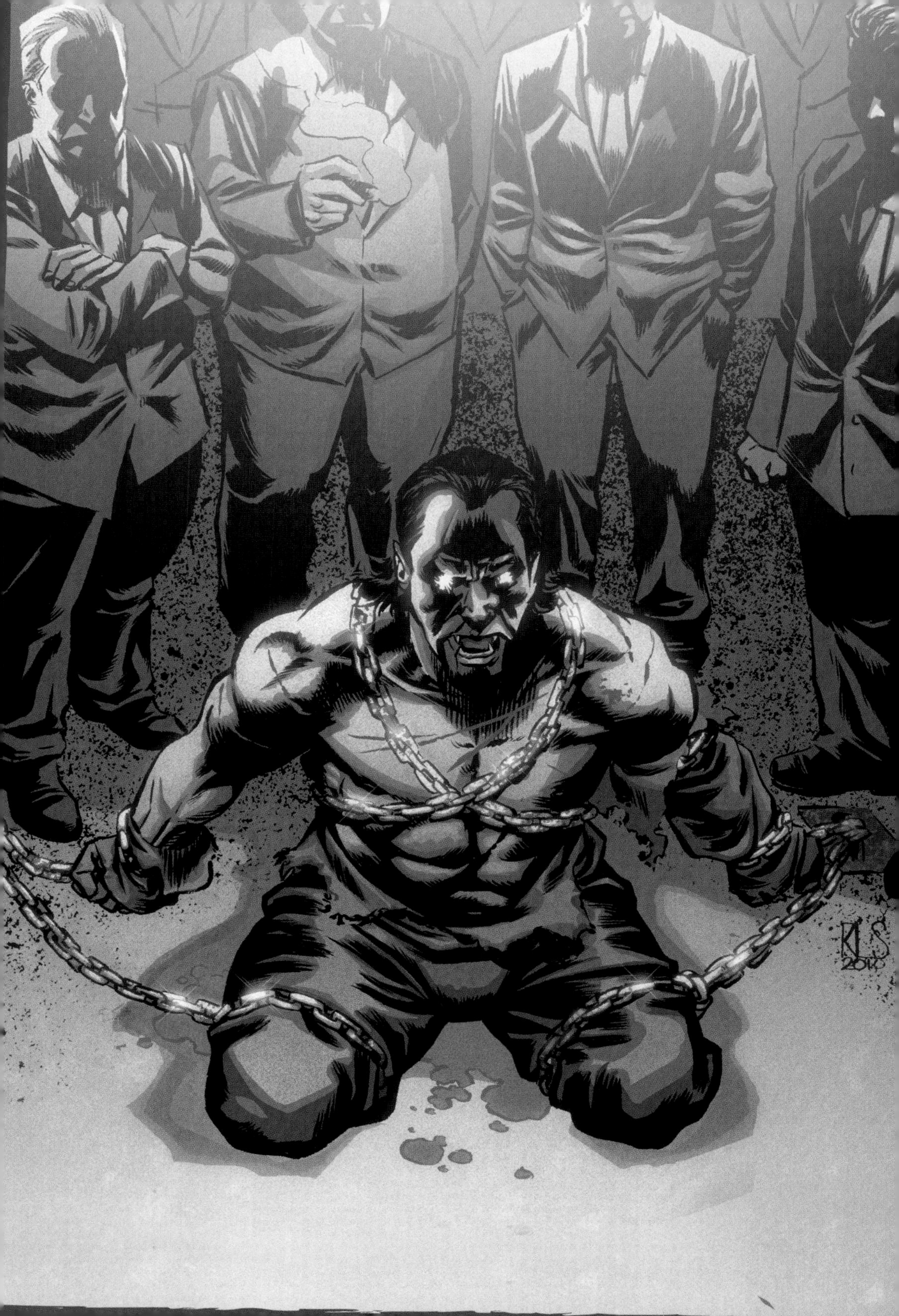

1B: R

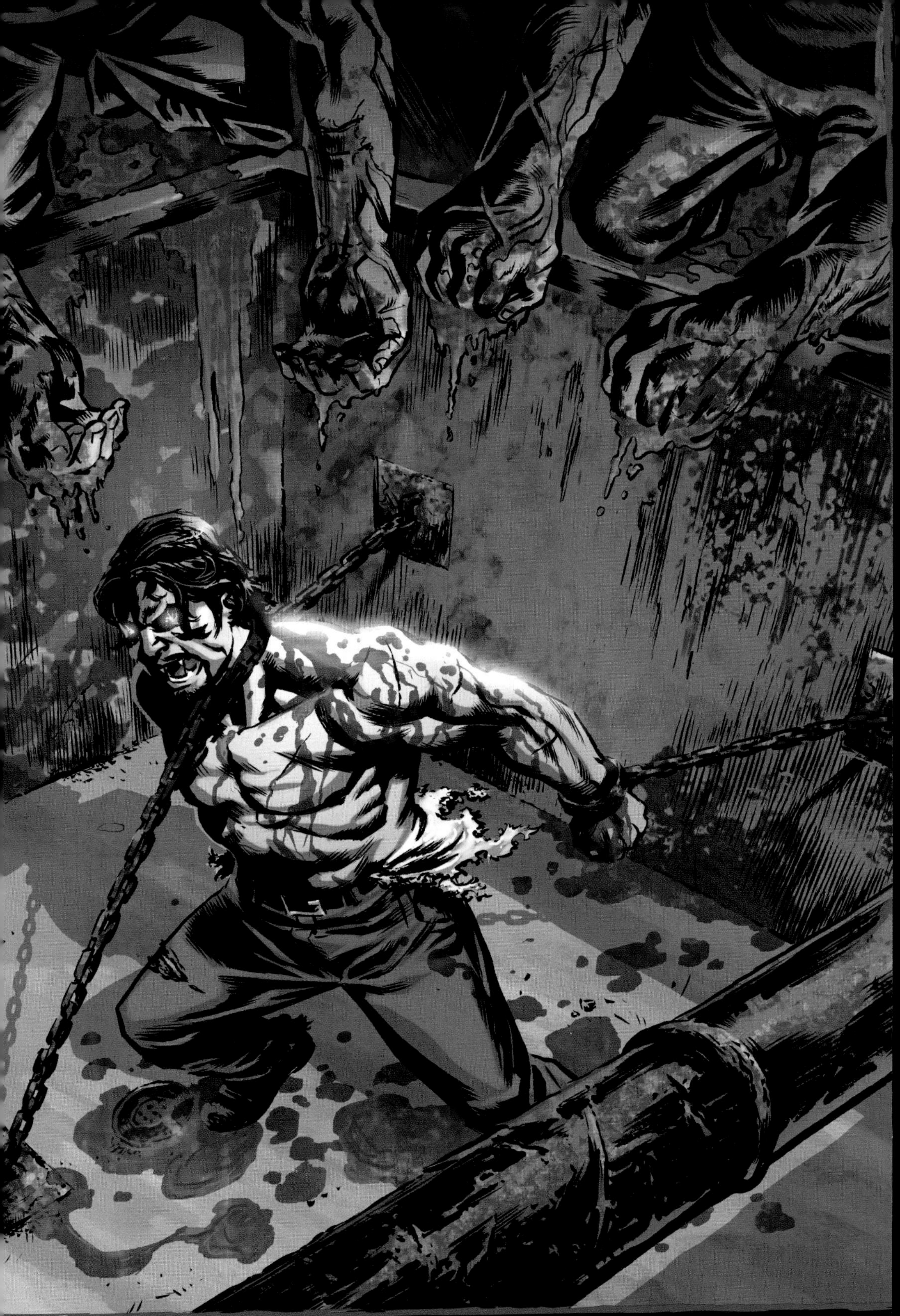

: Ron Salas

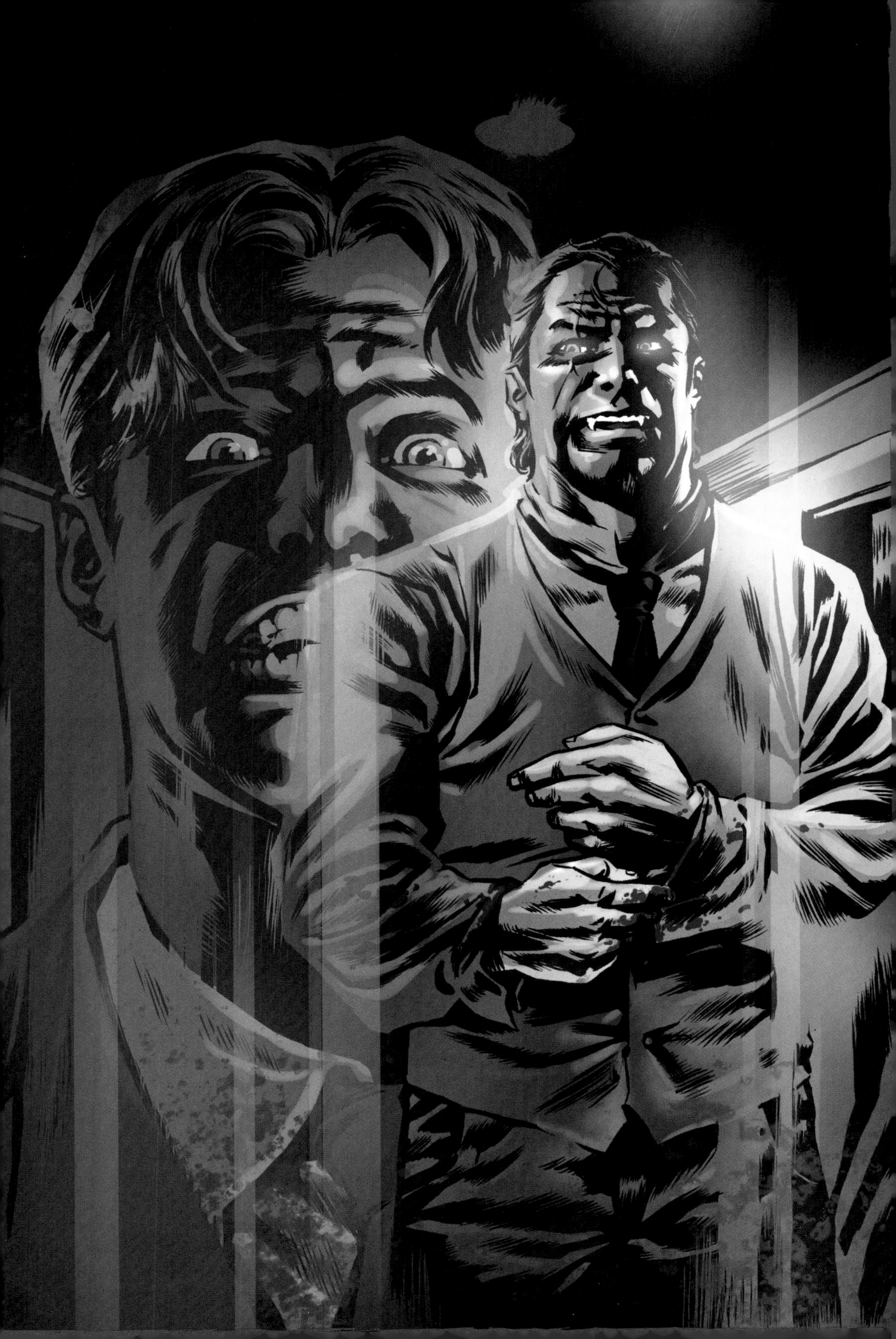

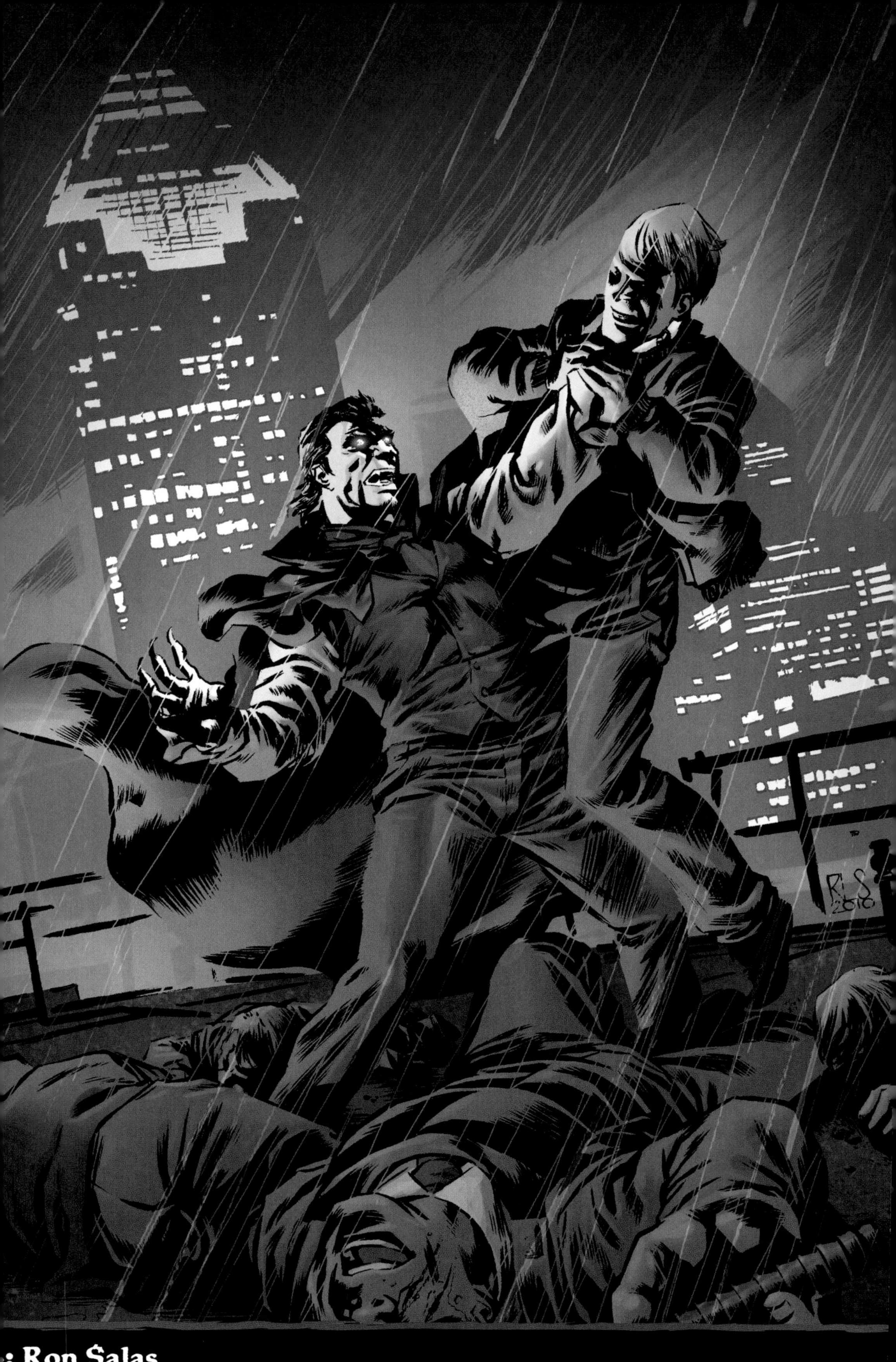
R. S.
2010

: Ron Salas
olors: Archie Van Buren

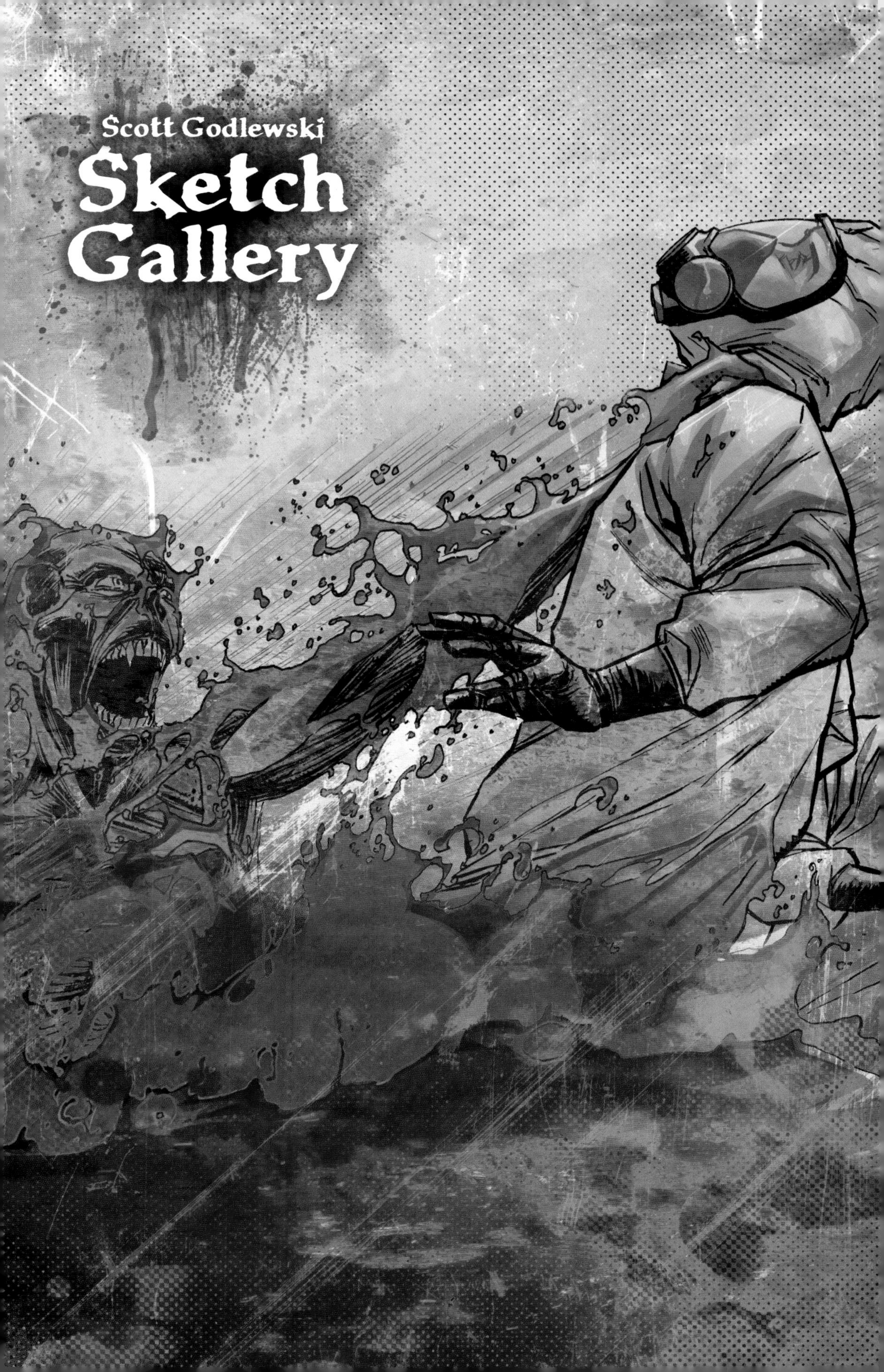
Scott Godlewski
Sketch Gallery

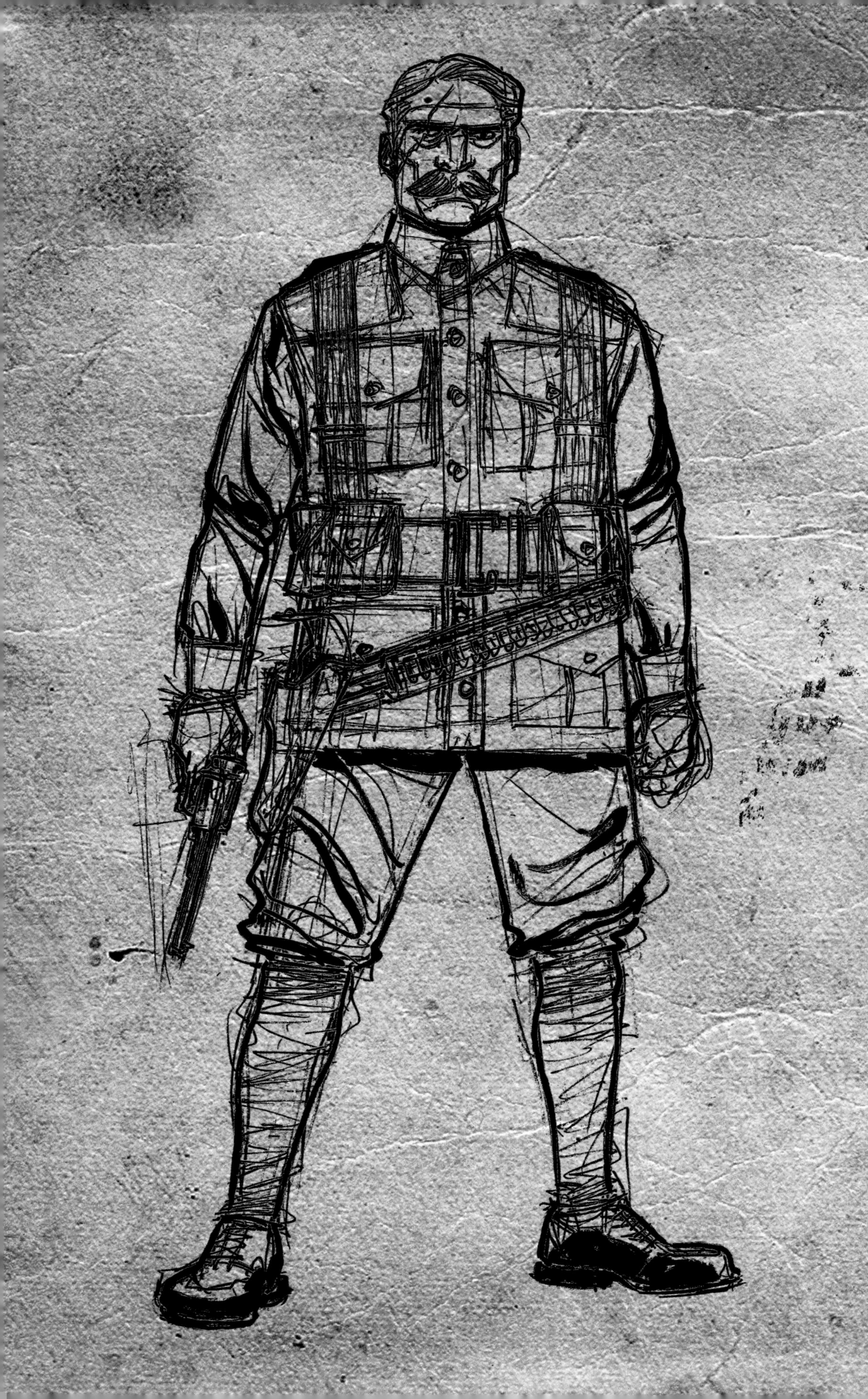

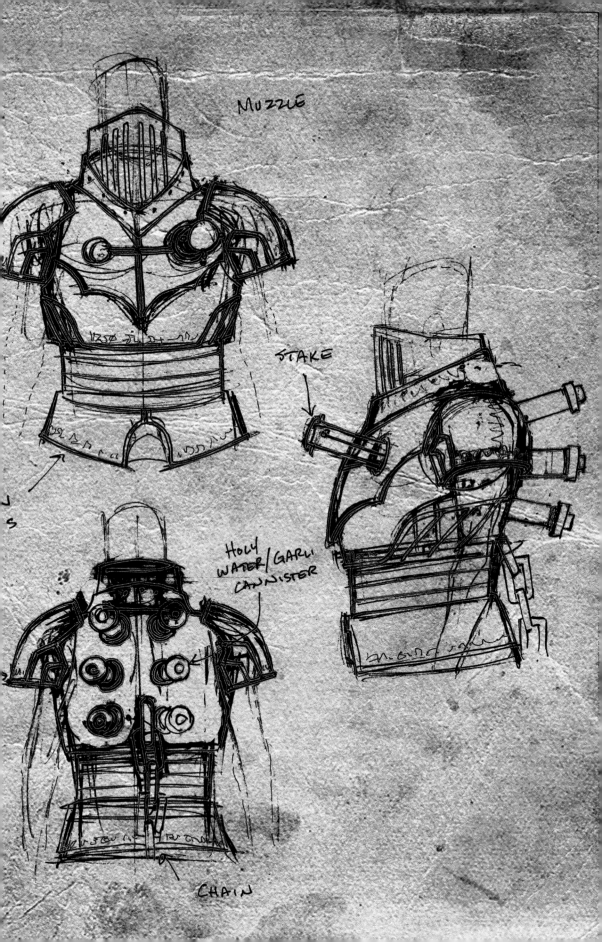

MUZZLE

STAKE

HOLY
WATER/GARLI
CANNISTER

CHAIN

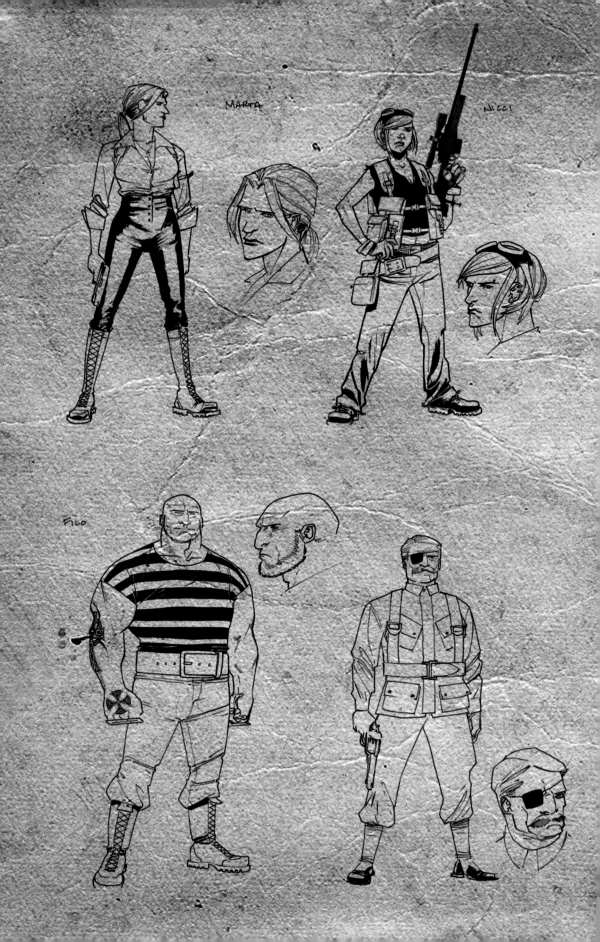

MARTA

NICCI

FILO

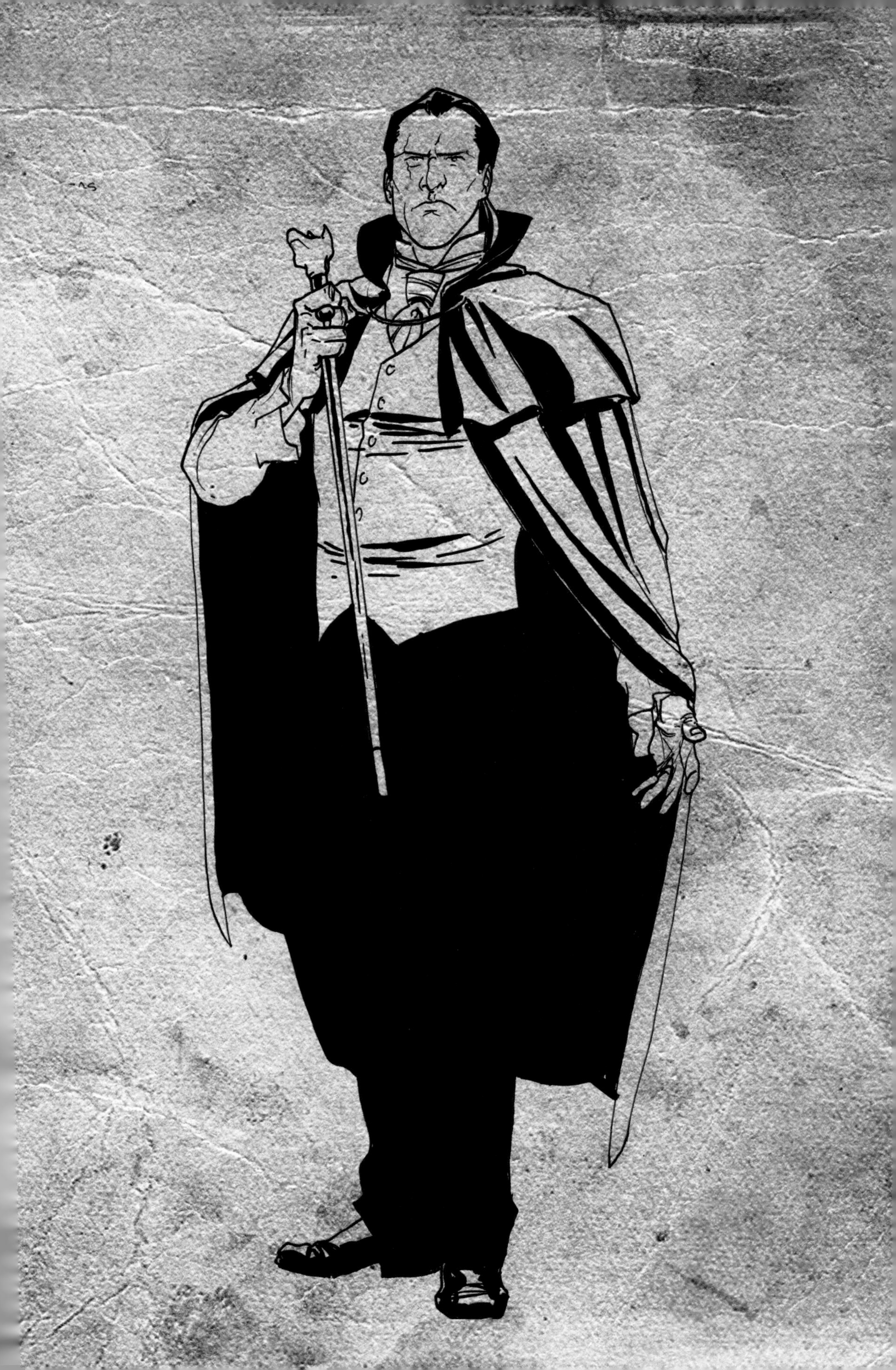

DRACULA

The Company of Monsters